LOGAN SQUARE
CHICAGO, IL

THE LULA

CAFE COOKBOOK: COLLECTED RECIPES AND STORIES

JASON HAMMEL

INTRODUCTION
7

ON HOSPITALITY
16

A GUIDE
18

RECIPES
24

ART AT LULA
256

OUR COLLABORATORS
258

INDEX
260

INTRODUCTION

"What you make from a tree should
be at least as miraculous
as what you cut down."

—Richard Powers, *The Overstory*

This wasn't the plan. Being a chef, that is. Owning a restaurant. Living in Chicago. But writing a book—yes, that was always the plan.

I wrote this collection of recipes and stories from Lula Cafe—the restaurant I opened in Chicago in 1999 with my wife, Amalea "Lea" Tshilds—during the years of a pandemic that shook my personal life and all that I knew about being a professional chef. It was written in the restaurant's basement, between services, in the room where we store napkins and oil. It has been a deeply nostalgic process. All at once, I'm looking back at twenty years of work, the collapse we experienced in March of 2020, and the exciting new life emerging from the hull of the restaurant we once knew. The two decades before the pandemic were deeply productive and passionate times, in which beautiful, self-germinating blossoms of luck just seemed to grow out of the earth and envelop me and Lea. We started a restaurant, fell in love, married, had children. Our restaurant became widely known in the city, then beyond. Our friends made films, records, books, their own families, their own restaurants, too. Together we created thousands of dishes with a group of young chefs and servers. It was a wildly joyful, expansive time. I was twenty-seven when we started. Life was just underway.

Somehow I owned a restaurant before I could really call myself a chef—no culinary school, no fancy kitchen résumé. I was an outsider, an amateur, someone who clearly didn't know what he was doing before he started to try.

So this book isn't about me as a chef; rather it's about the spirit of being young and just giving it a shot. I will share the moments that made these times in our lives, moments expressed through the language of food, in the hope that they will bear beautiful blossoms of luck in your lives, too.

Like our daily menus, each recipe has a date at the top. Think of them as diary entries or a captain's log. We will go on a trip led by the constellations of these dishes, looking for patterns, lessons, tips. Along the way I'll show you the sources, creative collaborators, farms, and artisans that make the food we serve at Lula what it has become —bright, seasonal, fresh, surprising, and totally unafraid to love.

Lula Cafe opened on North Kedzie Boulevard in Chicago's Logan Square on September 2, 1999. It is a neighborhood that was once predominantly Scandinavian and German, then Cuban and Mexican, and has now become a gentrified, upscale "hotspot." When I moved to Logan Square in 1996 I was fresh out of a graduate writing program in Normal, Illinois, two hours south of Chicago. I had followed the advice of a friend who told me that there was a coffee shop I'd like near the Square. I rented a studio, sight unseen, and drove in one summer day with my girlfriend and cat. After blocks of congested commercial buildings, passing under the viaduct at Western Avenue felt like a transgression, as the city widened and turned lushly residential.

Logan Square is known for its broad, tree-lined boulevards. These were imagined by urban planner John Wright in 1897 as a "ribbon of parks and pleasure" that would encompass the city. It was a bright summer day as we came upon the greystone mansions sitting at prime spots along the boulevard. I imagined our apartment on some vaulted upper floor of one of these estates. But the map led us down a side street. Here were modest family homes, decorated and tended to with care. A group of children raced bikes back and forth down the center of the street. We pulled over by a vacant lot, near a house that was boarded up after a fire. Our building was a yellow-brick six-flat on the corner, where radios on the windowsill played music out into the street. A curmudgeon of a landlord handed us the keys and led us through the back alley by the garbage cans, where a wooden fire escape swayed like an old tree as we carried our things up to the third floor and settled in.

After we emptied the van, we went in search of Logan Beach, the cafe my friend had recommended. It was a short walk down Logan to Kedzie Boulevard. We scoped it out first. Every inch of the exterior was covered in posters: for gallery openings, language lessons, missing dogs, socialist meetups, lost connections, punk shows at a local bowling alley. We passed back and forth a few times. You could smell cigarettes and espresso on the street outside.

Eventually we went in and sat by the bookcase in the front window, near an old grand piano, at a table raised up on a stage. From our vantage point we could see a chalkboard menu on the wall behind a charmingly cluttered counter.

Lea's Amazing Soup, it read.

"Look," I said. "The chef spells her name like you. No 'h.'"

My girlfriend, Lea, smiled. "There's not that many of us."

"Let's try the soup," I said. "Whatever it is, it's amazing."

I wish I could stamp that date. I wish I'd marked the day. Because in that moment, exhausted from our move, there I sat in the window of Logan Beach Cafe, on my first day in the big new city, across from a Lea with whom I'd lose touch, about to meet the Lea I would one day marry, minutes away from tasting a soup that would change my life. I sat unaware in the very space that would become our restaurant, Lula Cafe. At table 51—the round marble two-top in the window where we now seat people when they want to propose.

The setting sun slid low and flat across the open square. Intense, long slashes of light. The soup was sweet and sour cabbage, fragrant with coconut and ginger. The sun made the oil on the surface reflect like a prism. We looked around the room, at the mismatched tables, the sofa in the corner, the books. I did not feel the universe shift. But it did.

I always wanted to be a writer. I studied fiction in college with a mind-bending oracle of a teacher named Eurydice. It felt like the right time to tell a story—at the end of a century, cusp of the unknown. Hundreds of would-be students applied for the few spots that opened in my school's Advanced Writing program each year, just to be in the room with the mystical professor. After twice failing entry, I finally wrote a story haunting and strange enough to capture her imagination. In it, an injured swan lands on a pond at a farm where a woman has gone to mourn a lost child. I wrote it in a desperate, last-ditch effort to join the ranks of these young writers, these obsessed cool kids. Looking back, I shudder—how insufferable we were, how we played the part. There was a self-styled Cormac McCarthy-type from the Upper East Side who wore stiff cowboy boots to class, like with actual spurs. All that mattered was that you showed a potential for creative madness, that you were consumed by forces uncontrolled.

Despite allegiances to the avant-garde, I was still told to "write what you know." So I began to write stories about my Italian family. Despite my blue eyes, sandy hair, and the German last name, I am mostly of southern Italian heritage. Specifically of the east coast Italian-American kind. Listen to me argue with the produce guy, it'll come out. Or one look at my father in the '80s, as he pulled up in his T-top Datsun 280z wearing a track suit and dragging on a cigarette, and you'd know. This is the culture that raised me early on. My great grandparents came from Naples at the turn of the century. My grandfather's name was Luigi

Andreoli. Somewhere along the line he scrubbed the name of its final vowel, leaving the old world behind, both to fit in and to sever himself from the very roots I wanted to dig. Luigi became Lou. Andreoli became "DeAndrus." On my father's side, my grandmother married a German man, became a school teacher, and cooked meals of canned corn and breaded pork cutlets. And my mother, who studied French like it was an act of defiance, named me 1972's 7th most popular boy's name in America, then remarried when I was young—not to an Italian. Things got lost.

For most of my twenties, I held on to the idea that it was the dilution of my Italian heritage that gave me an interesting angle as a writer. I wanted to write about the erosion, the shadows, the fading echoes of this heritage. I latched onto the remnants of the old world still infusing our lives. I wrote about the *malocchio* charms against the evil eye that my grandmother used to cure our headaches, a spell taught only at midnight on Christmas Eve, in which olive oil was dropped into water and the dispersing pattern read like tea leaves. I wrote about the words of Neapolitan dialect ("stubborn," "anchovy," "stupid," "dishtowel") still used in my family. And I wrote about food.

It was a short story about pasta that sparked my interest in the connections between food and memory. I wrote about two women making tagliolini, threading myths and stories into the act of making dough—sheeting it, forming it with their rough hands, the shapes of lives in conflict. Like a method actor, I thrust myself into making the dishes mentioned in my stories. I bought a copy of Marcella Hazan's *Essentials of Classic Italian Cooking* and made tortellini, spaghetti alla puttanesca, and strozzapreti. I learned terms like *soffritto* and *insaporire*, along with the alluring poetry and fables of Italian cuisine. A pasta maker looks through a keyhole at a young woman and creates a shape inspired by her navel. The sailors of Napoli are drawn to a dank clash of tomato, anchovy, and caper, flavors meant to "fortify" them. Ingenious cooks (the original pasta grannies!) create a dough shape so dense it clogs the throats of visiting priests, who then have no room left to eat the expensive meats and fish. I fell captive to the power of these words, which to me were their own kind of magic.

I realized that food had always been central to my life. And not because I was served glorious culinary meals in my childhood. We didn't eat out. We didn't live in an area of natural bounty. We didn't hunt, fish, or garden. There was no Bourdainian oyster at my awakening. I grew up in a suburb outside New Haven, Connecticut, where my grandparents had settled a generation earlier.

Our food was Italian in the way my dad's gold chains or grandmother's housecoats might be considered "Italian." It could hardly be traced to a source in the hills outside of Sessa Aurunca in Campania where my family was from. Yes, for Christmas we had struffoli, the tiny honey donuts rolled in sprinkles that are typical of Naples. But there was also canned tuna in tomato sauce, a depression-era version of a coastal seafood sauce. Italian wedding soup made with frozen boxed spinach. Lasagna in slabs thick as a triple-decker sandwich. These dishes were more '50s American housewife than *Napolitan'*. Regardless, the fact is that I grew up in a household that cared deeply about our family coming together over food. Every night my parents made us sit around the table for a home-cooked meal. On Sundays, holidays, and every birthday, we sat together to eat my grandmother's food. For us, these tables were a spiritual place, a type of altar.

I also grew up in a family that had made a living through food. After a lifetime of working dead-end jobs, my grandparents saved enough to rent a little coffee shop in the sleepy town of Cheshire, just a few miles from New Haven. It was open from 7 a.m. until 3 p.m., giving my grandmother just enough time to make the soups and sauces in her home kitchen for the next day. She was the server and my grandfather the cook. When they started, they were in their fifties, an undertaking that I cannot fathom at that age. Sadly, I have few memories of Cheshire, apart from spinning myself sick on a counter stool while my grandparents closed up shop. Instead, I think back to the basement of their house after they sold the restaurant and retired. A giant stainless-steel slicer sat on a card table for my grandmother's eggplant Parmesan, which she shaved so thin the layers seemed to melt away. Two enormous chest freezers stored every scrap and trimming. A commercial blender made thick, frosty vanilla shakes. And along the wall, rows of shelves held enough dry pasta and canned tomatoes to feed our family for many months, if hard times were to come again.

After college I went to Italy to see if there was anything real I could unearth from these obsessions. But I found myself lost, unable to write, wandering dead cities in a fog. In the end, I fell back on going to school. It was Eurydice who suggested I work with a young writer who had released a book of short stories and a novel she thought I would like. He was teaching at Illinois State University. I packed up that summer and made my way from Bologna, Italy, to Normal, Illinois—eventually to Chicago, to Lula, and to Lea. The irony of my path being directed in part by a woman named for an ancient goddess won't be lost on you when you read about the impact of Lea's Greek family on Lula. Or that this oracle had led me to the Midwest, to the prairie, and to the novelist David Foster Wallace.

Eventually, my girlfriend got a job as a server at Logan Beach and I hung out there every morning, trying to write. Mostly I was making friends. It was the most inspiring crowd of doers and makers I'd ever been around. There were photographers, filmmakers, actors, painters, poets, community activists, doctors, welders, and even a long-haul trucker who cooked for extra cash at "the Beach" when he was in town.

Everyone was in a band. Independent music of all kinds flowed through Logan Square and Wicker Park, where the Chicago indie music scene grew in the upturned dirt left behind by the success of big acts like The Smashing Pumpkins and Liz Phair. I started going out to shows at Lounge Ax, HotHouse, and the Fireside Bowl. At times, being in the city felt like the main reason to be alive. I saw Neutral Milk Hotel, Palace Brothers, Stereolab, Low, Blonde Redhead, along with local acts like Tortoise, the Mekons, and The Eternals. I danced Sunday nights at the Deadly Dragon Sound System. Logan Beach was where we gathered to regroup the mornings after, to share a cup of coffee in each other's company.

The cafe was opened in 1993 by Virginia Lewey, a lawyer who left the corporate world to create this alternative universe. She named it "Logan Beach" after the group of Cuban men whose weekend morning ritual was to set up lounge chairs along the boulevard and sunbathe, Paulie Walnuts-style. She rented a run-down shop and filled it with décor donated by the neighborhood—a charming set of vintage tables (no two the same size), candelabras, antique mirrors, the baby grand piano that jazz musicians played on Friday nights. The original menu was full of sandwiches, salads, soups. But then the artist and musician Amalea Tshilds started as a cook, bringing to the food a spirit as independent, creative, and engaging as the crowd.

Neither Lea nor I remember the day we met, but I started going to the Indonesian dinners she cooked on Friday nights. These nights were a Logan Square tradition, started by a friend of the Beach who taught Lea traditional Indonesian recipes and brought her to a grocery on Argyle Street for supplies. By the time I discovered them, Lea was the head chef, serving a full meal of tempeh, gado gado, fried tofu omelets, cassava, shrimp crackers, and turmeric rice. After she served the room, Lea would join her Appalachian string band, The Paulina Hollers, and play through the night, as a crowd of neighborhood regulars shared her food and a lot of liquor store wine.

Nights at the Beach were all about friendship and camaraderie. Fridays matched an Indonesian feast with an old-time bluegrass; Saturdays you could order a portobello quesadilla while a quintet of horns and drums blasted discordant jazz. I knew everybody in the room. Staff drank with guests as the Beach filled with laughter and music and smoke. This was the '90s cafe scene I knew and loved; the connection between food and art I'd been looking for this whole time.

Logan Beach was the soul of the restaurant we would go on to create. It was the foundation for Lula.

But then the cafe changed hands. Virginia left Chicago to care for ailing parents. Lea went to work at a jazz bar

where she could be closer to the music scene. Friday nights ended. The walls were painted a mossy, saddened green. My girlfriend moved to Saint Louis and I stayed behind. Or was left behind. I can hardly say what happened anymore. There was a sadness then, a sense that the community I had found was beginning to fray.

One night I went to the rock club Lounge Ax (RIP) to hear the Dirty Three, and I saw Amalea after the show. She had been bartending nights at the HotHouse. I told her how I'd quit my job and was trying to write more seriously, and about how the other Lea and I had broken up. I told her I missed her cooking at the Beach and that it wasn't the same since she left. I must have sounded lonely.

Which, in truth, I was. Deeply so. I found myself walking great distances in the city, between breaks in writing, to cafes and shows, sometimes very late at night. Without the old crowd at the Beach and now living with roommates I hardly knew, I passed the time by covering large swaths of ground. Distance shrank the hours. I was in no hurry to go home.

We got to talking about soup. It was past midnight, the show long over. The lights were up and the band was hanging out at the bar. Lea and I sat on the edge of the stage.

Was it flirty? Did she know? Did I feel the universe moving then, as it took one big leap in my favor?

I told her about a soup I'd made with butternut squash and dates. She told me about one she was dreaming of, with fig and roasted garlic, a brothy version into which she'd stir herby lentils and cream. She said she didn't know what to do now, the bar life just wasn't for her. And suddenly it just came to us—maybe we could make soups together, sell them to other cafes around the city that didn't have kitchens of their own.

This was 1998. Nearly every subway stop had a homespun coffee shop to catch commuter traffic. We made a quick list of cafes off the top of our heads. Avanti. The Bourgeois Pig. Soon we'd struck a deal with the new owners of the Beach, to use their kitchen in the off hours and to pay them in gallons of scratch-made soups, like miso vegetable, black bean, squash tomato, sweet and sour cabbage. Delivered in leaky gallon containers that ruined the floors of both our cars, the soups gained a following, so much so that we completely outstayed our welcome at the Beach. The deal was that we would give them soup for use of the space and whatever labor was on hand to wash dishes. But the dishwashers were there to hang out, smoke, drink coffee, not spend hours scrubbing someone else's pots and pans.

This scenario ended up being short-lived. Logan Beach struggled under the new owners. After a while, they simply realized that they couldn't make it work. A solution obvious to everyone but us was suggested to Lea and me in the kitchen one night, as we made the sweet and sour cabbage soup. One of the new owners said maybe Virginia could take it back but that we could operate it, as her partners.

The original Lula Cafe took up just one 1,200-square-foot storefront of the three it is today. The morning we took over, we found a dining room trashed from a party thrown by the lovably degenerate departing crew. "Deep breath," Lea said, as we began to scrape away at years of grime. We sanded the floors ourselves. We built a new wall separating the kitchen and dining room, but with thrifted windowpanes, to let sunlight into the kitchen.

Virginia agreed to let us take over the cafe as long as she didn't have to be involved. Lea and I had two high-interest credit cards. No investors or bank loans. Instead, we scrappily put the pieces of our cafe together ourselves. We scored secondhand chairs from a pool hall that had fallen on hard times. I learned to use a saw and built a coffee bar with my stepfather who came out to lend a hand. Eventually we made a sweet, tender dining room and an ad hoc kitchen. No one could have considered it "restaurant" standard—but we didn't know better and therefore didn't know to care.

That first kitchen was a tiny space with milk crates for storage and a refrigerator better suited for keeping beers cold in the garage. There was no exhaust over the stove. To get to the bathroom you had to pass straight through this cramped space and into a literal "water closet" so small you could sit on the toilet and wash your hands at the same time.

That summer stretched out slowly but ended fast. We struggled with what to name this new thing we were creating. Lea was in a band named after the hard-living actress Tallulah Bankhead, and by the time September came we had decided just to shorten it. It meant nothing to us. It's just that the word feels nice in your mouth, pleasant to say. Tasty, even. The tip of the tongue skipping from one L to the other, between the vowels. Lu. La. Lu-La.

We stayed up three nights in a row to make the food on the opening menu. It was just the two of us and a couple friends. Jonathan Liss curated a group show of paintings. Mike McGinley came back to work eggs. We hired a few neighborhood friends to wait tables. And on September 2, 1999, Lula Cafe opened to a line.

Now I realize how lucky we were. The restaurant was pretty much handed to us by Virginia. This gift was kindness, grace, and generosity in their purest forms. She had created an ethos for which we simply had to care. We didn't have to find investors, raise money, haggle over a lease, navigate the building permit process, hire lawyers, plead our case to local officials, or bribe health inspectors—all of which (well, not that last bit, though I once came close) I've had to do since. We inherited a decade of goodwill in the neighborhood. Friends from the

Beach days came to help without asking to be paid. And the room was filled immediately with souls as kind and generous as Virginia, people who wouldn't dare criticize us local kids.

I'm not sure any of this would be possible today. Back then, restaurants were not the sport they are now. There were no listicles, no reality TV competitions, no *Chef's Table*, no sense at all that anyone was keeping score. The lack of attention gave us time to figure out who we were, without the pressure of performing for a rating system or a critical vox populi. Since we were never really considered a restaurant, we operated out of view of the Chicago media. Our first official starred review in the *Chicago Tribune* appeared when Lula was seventeen years old.

Lea and I cooked together from 6 a.m. to midnight, six days a week. I don't remember ever feeling tired. I would pick her up in the morning, then drive to the markets like my grandfather did for the diner back in the '70s. We went to the Greek shop for the feta; to the Mexican market for tortillas, spring onions, and cheese; to Stanley's, the wholesale produce guy; to the Thai grocery on Argyle for the kecap manis; to the butcher on Lincoln for chickens. There were no big box restaurant stores. No farmers' markets. No corporate semis unloading at our back door.

The opening menu had many of the Logan Beach favorites, like the "Tineka," a veggie sandwich made with Indonesian satay. But we also served what was fashionable then, including penne arrabbiata, portobello mushrooms stuffed with blue cheese and pesto, and vegetarian maki rolls of roasted red pepper, spinach, and black sesame. An old Greek pasta dish we called "Yiayia" that Lea learned from her grandmother made an appearance on the first day. It was an eclectic mix.

We'd come back from shopping with produce packed floor-to-ceiling in my car, a case of strawberries shoved under the seat. Then Lea and I would cook specials made up on the fly, serving them only when they were ready, at quantities that make me laugh when I think of them now. Sometimes there were just three or four orders a night. Cooking in this way was my crash course in becoming a chef. I could buy a leg of lamb from the Greek grocer and set it on the cutting board next to a copy of Jacques Pépin's *La Technique*, opened to the pages where black-and-white, step-by-step photos showed me how to butterfly the meat to remove the bone. We cooked through those pages until they were stained and torn.

But it was Charlie Trotter's book *Vegetables* that changed the course for us. Arranged by month, it taught us how to cook in tandem with the seasons. It brought us a new lexicon of French terms, culinary techniques, arresting fusions of Asian and continental flavors, rarefied ingredients, mushrooms and truffles and roots in vibrant colors, composed with a visual artistry that I didn't know was possible in food. Lea and I fell under a spell.

We started making our own combinations based on recipes in the book. We did the carrot cardamom cakes and served them for brunch with a savory raspberry jam. We took the crispy polenta and added mushrooms glazed with balsamic and pomegranates. We made infused oils, poached citrus, confit tomato, and watermelon *concassé*. And from one telling photo of the famous chef hand-selecting vegetables from a stall at the old Blue Island market, we were able to find Cornille & Sons, his produce supplier. After some begging, they let me into those turn-of-the-century cold storage rooms, and soon I was hand-selecting the same baby Hakurei turnips, purple Peruvian potatoes, red-veined sorrel, and candy-stripe beets that were being served across the city to Trotter's much more well-heeled clientele.

This was how I learned to cook. First from these books, as well as those by Alice Waters, Thomas Keller, and older classics from Elizabeth David and Richard Olney, and then from being with Lea, she of the preternaturally sensitive palate. "How about this? What does it need?" Her not liking what I made was devastatingly hard to take. A pleased smile propelled me on.

Soon a small core list of dishes that never changed became our "cafe menu," much of which is still there today. We expanded the specials nearly every day. Hand-cut noodles with fava beans and mint. Halibut with carrots glazed in tamarind. Mascarpone-stuffed French toast with chamomile crème anglaise. It started to get very busy. We bought chef coats and checkered pants. I finally got my own knife. We hired a crew.

Long friendships were formed among that first group of cooks and servers who worked with us as the restaurant grew in ambition and scope. Classes 2000 and 2001 were made up of folks with whom I am still close today. Nobody was thinking of these jobs as a career. All of us were artists in some form and each person brought their insight to the way Lula expressed itself through food. We came together to do something creative and fun, without pressure or consequence. No one was watching. Even if there was an "industry" back then, we wouldn't have belonged. We were outsiders, part of a culture that articulated itself in periphery to the center, the straight, the downtown.

Sometimes you say to yourself, looking back, if only I knew then what I know now. We certainly did not make strong business decisions. But the things we did not know then didn't hold us back. Instead, it was the not knowing that kept us from creating our own barriers against risk and failure. Without risk, there is no change. To me this is what being twenty-seven is all about. The willingness to take risks, to fail and try again, and to learn in the process. This remains at the core of our mission today: to embrace change and assume the best in all.

It would be several months before the cigar shop closed and we took over the space next door, built a bar and a real kitchen, before we discovered the Green City Farmers' Market, before the press connected the word "farm" to "table," and then connected those words to us, and before Chicago chefs started coming in on days off. We were suddenly much older. In the next chapter, adult life washed over us all. A core group of us became extremely close. Lula became Us. Then the Us multiplied. Lu had a baby. Anders and Cheryl became engaged. Soon we were a family of twenty, then thirty. The We grew.

Other relationships hardly made sense to me anymore. Lea finished my sentences, and I hers. I broke up with the woman I was seeing. Lea left her boyfriend from that night at Lounge Ax. For several months we skirted against the tension, but then, at the staff Christmas party in 2002, Lea and I danced to "Harvest Moon" late at night after everyone had gone home and decided that what we had been feeling all along—as she held up a spoon for me to taste, as I walked her home at 2 a.m., as we fought playfully over who would get the blackberries for that night's special—wasn't something to ignore.

That same year we started Monday Night Farm Dinner, modeled after the fixed-price menus at Chez Panisse in Berkeley, California. There would be three new dishes each week for $24. It launched the same summer I became a regular at the Green City Farmers' Market and befriended several seasonally minded chefs, particularly Paul Kahan of Blackbird. Both he and his crew introduced me to a network of small purveyors and artisans, who brought us everything from lamb to aged goat cheese to fresh white currants still clinging to the vine. I loved the fact that our humble cafe in Logan Square, with its pool-hall furniture and thrifted plates, would be buying from the same purveyors as these fancy establishments. To my knowledge, back then, we were the only all-day cafe in Chicago buying directly from farms. We would look in the back of the truck from Swan Creek or Gunthorp and see all the names on the boxes, like a Michelin guide: Trotter's. Spring. Blackbird. And then a proud stack labeled LULA.

The importance of sourcing was central to a major *New York Times* piece that ran on the front page of the prestigious Dining section in August 2001, describing the "New American Cooking" in the burgeoning Chicago restaurant scene of the time.

A new generation of young chefs in Chicago, working far from the constant jangle on the two coasts, is melding well-grounded Midwestern values with highflying global ingredients to produce consistently smart food that is both daring and coherent. Chicago is emerging as a cradle of the first truly adult American cooking.

The Midwestern values to which the author referred were both a straightforward "ingredients tasting of themselves" approach and the dedication to local farms. Of course, the winter in Chicago forces a chef to look to California and Mexico, but from June to October we have a bounty of exceptional produce from local farms.

It wasn't until we started receiving calls that day asking for reservations—no one had ever really called us before—that we understood that this article in *The Times* was, in part, about us. We were shocked. Especially to be lumped in with the "adults." We jumped in the car, found the nearest newspaper box, and read:

The meal that really brought home the notion of Chicago as the first true melting pot that really cooks, though, was brunch at Lula, a tiny, quirky, be-prepared-to-wait cafe in the Logan Square neighborhood, just beyond Bucktown and Wicker Park.

At Lula, Amalea Tshilds and Jason Hammel have moved beyond that. Their cheesy, eggy spinach strata was like a marriage of quiche and bread pudding made in Italy. And their tamales were actually grilled polenta topped with eggs and chevre, black beans, corn and a poblano sauce.

This was not Ellis Island but the mainland, not fusion but food that blurred boundaries.

All autumn, into winter, we struggled to keep up with the influx of new diners, most of them from fancier neighborhoods we tried to avoid. Some had a hard time with the "quirky" part. No one was "prepared to wait." And more than a few got frightened by the tough streets west of the highway. But it turned out that the combination of national press and our new Farm Dinner was good for the creative process. Having a set schedule forced us to churn out idea after idea, now in larger quantities, with collaborative partners in the form of sous and pastry chefs. And it gave us the opportunity to tell our farmers we would buy "whatever you have."

For the next eighteen years, we created three new dishes a week, never repeating a single one. Thousands of dishes, thousands of ingredients. We believed in fifty-two seasons, not four. The season of the romano bean. The season of the early plum. Nimrod grapes from Klug Farm that I'd peel and eat with one hand in the car. I couldn't wait, they were so sweet and elegant. Elderflowers from Peter Klein at Seedling Farm. Beth Eccles at Green Acres Farm, who knew to save bitter, crunchy treviso for me behind the stand.

We hardly paused to rest. I showed up at 6 a.m. before the markets opened. I loved the thrill of being the first, filling the back of my new pickup truck while the sun was rising over Lake Michigan. I thrived on the deadline that the Farm Dinner placed on our kitchen. There was the season of the honeynut squash and of the gooseberry. Lea and I went headfirst into a void and held on tight.

I think there is a democratizing aspect to Lula that has made it last. It isn't the cooking. It's the way you feel a deep and interstitial network of personal stories as you walk in. A forest of Chicago lives. And then the way you feel like your story belongs here, too.

The depth of these community connections is hard to measure. There are many guests I'd love to mention, many regulars, neighbors, friends, like the carpenter who once helped us turn an old shop counter into our first bar, or the photographer from the Trotter cookbooks, the very ones I loved as a young chef, who lives down the street and took our family portraits when Lea and I first had kids. All the artist friends of the early years—Andrew Bird who played violin at our wedding, musicians from Tortoise, Wilco, Drag City, and Shellac, Ira Glass who wired up our servers for one of his radio shows, Sheeba of Sparrow, Christen from Busy Beaver Buttons, all the Wandawega folk. They still come in for the Pasta Yiayia, salads, burritos, the same orders as way back when. But I think the beauty of the narrative nest you feel really comes from the staff. Young people new to the city continue to find their place at Lula in the same way I found my community at Logan Beach. They come to us with that same radical openness, searching in the mist for a future they have yet to see. They cast themselves in their own Bohemian play of nights out, art exhibitions, films, shows, assignations of the young. Living on the same precipice that led me to open Lula in 1999. Just giving it a shot. No sense that they might fall.

Though sometimes we were blindsided by events we could never foresee. In 2005, Cheryl Weaver—host, bartender, artist, who designed and printed the invitations to our wedding, and who was engaged to our cook and curator Anders Nilsen—was diagnosed with lymphoma and died tragically just a few months later. Her death shattered all our faith about what could happen to this beautiful life we shared. We gathered for her memorial at Promontory Point, where Anders scattered her ashes in the lake. As he reached out to do this impossible thing, Anders almost slipped on the wet stones closest to the water. I remember gasping audibly. His slip woke me from a daze of grief. We were all still there, alive in a broken morning. We walked back to a nearby hall and cooked the chickpea and fennel tagine. We communed. We grieved together. And when Lea and I got back home we learned that one of our servers had gone into labor and given birth to a boy named Asher.

Recently I've become fascinated with the way forests are being re-imagined as a shared community of resources, not a collection of individual trees. I like to think about us that way. My belief is that even if you don't know Cheryl and Anders, you feel their story when you walk through our front door today. Much the way you feel the weight of the past along an old forest trail. I do. I see Cheryl there. I see Amy pregnant with Asher. I see Kendal meeting her husband at the coffee bar. I see the weddings, the first exhibitions, the record releases, the new jobs, the births, moments in the lives of hundreds of our staff and guests. All these beautiful lives crossed in Logan Square. Just look up and down the street. There are restaurants lovingly run by Lula alums. There are brewers and distillers who were bartenders and food runners a few years ago. Countless makers and doers. Actors, botanists, poets, therapists, herbalists, acupuncturists, art dealers, potters, even a kickboxing pro. We remain connected to everyone whose love story has grown up alongside ours. Even those who moved away still give me the sense that they are here on Kedzie Boulevard.

What happened on March 15, 2020, when the pandemic caused the city to shut down and I sent the staff home, was that the Lula I knew did fall.

Along with everyone else, I went home during the first shelter-in-place order. Days went by, then weeks. I sent messages to our staff, urging unity, expressing regret, offering what I could to help. One morning, I found myself alone in the restaurant, dust rising as I walked the space. The door was locked, the lights off, but the voices of a hundred spirits clamored around me. I stood and tried to catch my breath. I felt my heart pound frighteningly hard.

I remember that I shook off that feeling and went downstairs, lifted a fifty-pound bag of flour from the storage shelves in the basement, and carried it out to my truck. I was going to make pizza for my family. The exertion left me panicked, sweating, losing the bag in my hands. It fell and split open on the ground. I sat down on the curb and held a finger to my neck to check my pulse. I breathed in through my nose and out through my mouth, the mask billowing and collapsing with each breath. *Stop it,* I told myself. *You're fine.* I had lifted bags like this my whole adult life and never felt tired. I certainly had never felt afraid.

Once I calmed, it was guilt that I felt. Enough of this solipsistic drama. Everywhere people were losing all they knew, their families, their lives, their livelihoods. We would make it. But what I didn't realize when the shelter-in-place first happened was that this long chapter of Lula was coming to a close.

We took it one day at a time. We gave out groceries and meals, tried to connect online, waved longingly through the windows from behind our masks. A core group of my team returned to help make Farm Dinners as takeout meals. What we imagined as a temporary project turned into eighteen months of profoundly disorienting work. Despite proclamations to the contrary, despite the good cheer passed through the gap in our takeout window, our community was broken; everyone was not okay.

When I first came to Illinois in the summer of 1995, I drove across the prairie through storms, on my way to study with David Foster Wallace, after a year in Italy and a lifetime on the east coast. I felt the vast, changeless sky guiding me west. I felt ready to tell my story, for some creative destiny to emerge. Once I arrived, I found that my confidence was hollow. Dave made sure I knew. To him, I was a pretentious kid from an even more pretentious school, who thought he was smarter than he was. He threatened to write my sentences on the board to show people how bad they were. Which, he said, would seem mean but was "actually nice." All his comments on my work were about tone and syntax, technical critiques, grammar, which was a sign that he couldn't bring himself to care about the stories I'd written. All I wanted to say was, "yes, thank you, all this is good—but what about my characters, my ideas, my vision?" Over and over again, in so many sorry ways, I begged him to answer the one question I needed to know: "Am I good at this?"

I didn't finish my thesis for several years. But the summer before Lula opened, I finally turned it in. The last time we saw each other was at my thesis defense, back in Normal. Afterwards, at a small Italian restaurant, I noticed something had changed. He seemed to like what I had written. But we didn't talk about that. Instead we talked about food.

What are you getting? he asked.

Ravioli, I said. The meat one.

Aren't you a vegetarian?

A vegetarian? Hardly.

Really?

You thought I was a vegetarian, I said.

Yeah, I did think that.

Because I brought a veggie skewer to that barbecue at your house.

You're sensitive, he said. I assumed that meant vegetarian.

We talked for a while over lunch and then I had to go. It was a long drive back to Chicago and I had to get back to the work we were doing that summer, sanding the floors, painting the old Logan Beach. As I stood up to leave, I told him about the restaurant I was opening with a friend.

He looked at me for a while and then, with a tone in his voice I'll never forget, and not just because it was the last thing I ever heard him say, he asked,

But, Jason, how will you write?

It's taken me years to get to this point, to set into words this work we did together at Lula. To write these recipes, I had to go back and ask myself: what happened on that day? August 16, 2019. April 5, 2005. I searched through archives of recipes and photos. I called former chefs and relived hard moments, because it was never just me or Lea at the stove. There were many other chefs, sous chefs, pastry chefs, cooks. And all the servers and managers and assistants and hosts who believed in us. It was them that made each day come alive.

As I worked on this book, we reopened Lula in a changed world. Haltingly, we created new dishes and reconnected with the people we'd missed. Some of the old crew came back and some chose to leave. Today the restaurant is busy and thriving, full of twenty-seven-year-olds charting their own brave paths. I don't think of it, though, as a new chapter to a continuing tale. It is a different growth, from a seed cast in the wind. I see Lula now breaking through the ground, reaching up toward light and water, toward the gentle touch of its new caretakers. I see the two of us, me and Lea, sitting together on the old tree, looking over at what's happening next to us.

On days off I cooked my way through these recipes. Whenever we finished a dish, I would take it into the empty dining room, set it on a table closest to the light, in the window on the stage, and take a photograph. These were just for me—to remember what we had done and to stamp a new date in time. We'd cook late into the evenings as the setting sun slid low and flat across the open square. Intense long slashes of light. Sometimes the light would strike in beautiful ways. The table was black marble, chipped and faded with time. This was table 51. Where last night a couple made a promise. Where tomorrow a friend will come to eat his favorite meal. Where long ago I learned your name.

March 2023
Logan Square

ON HOSPITALITY

As I mentioned in my introduction, back in my old life as a creative writing student, a certain mentor once told me that I made too many syntactical and grammatical errors in my writing "to be trusted."

He was right. In the same way that a reader has to trust an author to believe their fiction, so must our guests trust our service to believe in our food.

Let's say someone orders a bowl of soup. Normally it's a four-minute "pick" (toast bread, heat soup, mount with butter, garnish, etc). If there are a lot of orders on the board, the cook might take eight, ten minutes—a long time indeed just for soup! But now let's say that the server sets down a soup spoon right at minute number five, just to the right of the customer, and it is the correct-sized spoon, clean and polished with a nice deep bowl, clearly for no other purpose than to eat soup with. It is placed with confidence and poise and with a nice firm-yet-subtle anticipatory tap on the table. The customer thinks, "Oh yeah, this place has its shit together, my soup is being made, and everything is fine in the world." The wait goes by pleasantly. When the soup arrives, it is hot, beautiful, and deeply satisfying. Best soup ever.

But let's feel ten minutes without the spoon (or even seeing your server) until after the soup is set down and left to get cold, and the customer needs to raise her hand and ask for the spoon. That is when the soup starts to taste weird and maybe over-seasoned, and not at all as good as the customer remembers from last time—actually not at all as good as the canned soup she has in her pantry back home.

The point is this: good service is the grammar for good experiences. Which is where the Danny Meyer (of *Setting the Table*) dialectic of service and hospitality comes in. Danny said that service is how you get what you want; hospitality is how you feel when you get the thing you want. But I submit that there's way more going on here than can be expressed by this simple equation.

People come to Lula with expectations, needs, desires, and, frankly, impatience and distrust—so how do we manage all this? How do we know if we're meeting their needs? How do we measure the result? From a tip or a smile? Emotional labor takes experience and practice and conditioning. I used to think it was simply enough to be a happy person yourself to give happy service. Clearly, it may be helpful to be generally giddy, optimistic, or lively in temperament to give good hospitality, but some of the best and most hospitable servers I know are true misanthropes at heart. Today I recognize that there's a

much higher degree of "fake it till you make it" or "acting" that goes into these exchanges. Empathetic hospitality is not something essential or natural, and this expectation has come to be understood by us as a substantially false and oppressive concept. Saying that the ability to provide hospitality is some kind of natural skill or talent, or a "quotient" you can assess, as though your ability to produce an emotion in a stranger is simply a reflection of how you feel inside, is not a just and fair expectation for a workplace. Even the best actors get more than one take. A server has to produce their best work at a moment's notice, and without knowing the lines in advance. This is the emotional labor of being a server in a restaurant, and managing that labor, I believe, is the hardest challenge we have on the service team.

It is our business to "take care" of people. It is our vocation to create joy. And that means we have to listen, acknowledge, anticipate, and provide for our guests' needs. Taking care of people is only possible if you've been taken care of yourself, if you have capacity and resources at your disposal. This is the number one duty of the management team. We put ourselves in a position to listen as closely and compassionately as we can to what someone is looking for, to communicate what it is we are able to provide, and then to generously tend to the space in which this exchange takes place and thrives.

Most guests seem genuinely hopeful as they walk in the door—they want to be happier having come to visit us. They want to find something they cannot give themselves. While they expect to be pleased, they may also not have the means to communicate how, or even know what it is they want. We hope to navigate these relationships with the expectation that all of us are coming in with best intentions, and in so doing to engender experiences of mutuality, community, presence, and respect. Then yes, maybe we can say we are sharing food with love.

When people arrive at Lula and simply feel something profoundly welcoming, what they feel is years of hard work. The hard work of generative compassion and empathy. They feel it among the staff first and foremost. It is the cumulative work of warm hellos, eye-to-eye contact, caring, listening, connecting, and respecting others' needs, work that we share together as a team, and the product of which we then share out into the world, as care, kindness, love.

A GUIDE

HOW TO USE THIS BOOK

When I started out, cookbooks were the only way inside the kitchens I admired. As a self-taught chef, I depended on cookbooks of all kinds—classic doorstop tomes, monographs of Michelin-starred chefs, trendy guidebooks, church zines, even *The Joy of Cooking*—to make up for my lack of experience. Certain books were literal bibles for me, as modes of reflection, learning, accountability, maybe even prayer.

Professional line cooks usually keep a notebook in their back pockets to jot down the techniques of their mentors. But I was never anyone's mentee. I borrowed ideas, tricks, and plating styles from books. Not whole dishes, of course, but techniques, ephemera, ways of seeing. I'd take a magnifying glass to the action shots in Charlie Trotter's *Vegetables* to figure out how they set their stations, what knives they used—like, down to the actual brand. I made the agnolotti dough from *The French Laundry Cookbook*, shaped it differently, married it with Elizabeth David's Bolognese, but changed that too, from wild boar to mushroom and walnut.

That said, I've never cooked an entire recipe from any one of the many cookbooks I own. But I expect you may. Perhaps you came to this book after eating the Pasta Yiayia at Lula. Maybe you saw one of our dishes online and hope to make it for your friends. Or you want to impress for Sunday brunch. Regardless, I will share how we cook at the restaurant so that you have the option of making a whole dish or just one of its component parts.

BUILDING BLOCKS

All the dishes in this book were served at Lula in daily quantities ("pars") of fifty or more. Obviously, making hundreds of items a day requires a team of cooks, not just one chef. (I smile on the inside when a guest asks if I "made their meal tonight." Yeah, me and this army.)

At the restaurant there are chefs, sous chefs, line cooks, prep cooks, all working in tandem to get through a single busy shift. Multiple parties order the same thing, at the same time, and then expect it fifteen minutes later. We have to be ready. That chicken might have a sauce made of slowly cooked onion and butter, an oil made from herbs, a roasted piece of cauliflower. If we started all that from scratch, you wouldn't eat until the next evening. A lot of

the actual cooking is done far ahead of time, sometimes days in advance. We build dishes in component parts, setting them aside to be combined and "finished" later on the line.

Our recipes are organized into these components. A first section of ingredients will list all the things you need from start to finish, breaking them down into the various steps needed to make the final dish. Sometimes these "building blocks" are used in more than one recipe, and these are the pantry staples that we've included at the back of the book. And sometimes you'll find you have a bit more sauce or vinaigrette than you might need; I hope you'll learn to use these elements in your own creative ways.

Then I will guide you on how to make the components themselves. Each is listed in the recommended order of completion. And finally, the serving and plating details are there for you to follow—the same way we do it on the line on a busy Saturday night.

Component cooking isn't just for pros. Getting certain steps done ahead of time can be a big help when making a dinner party for friends, freeing you up to chat with your guests or have a glass of wine, and complete the plates later. For those of you used to one-pot cooking, stews and soups and the like, this book will take you on a deep dive into a different mindset.

If you don't want to go the whole way, just steal an idea or two. Fill your fridge with vinaigrettes, aioli, and soffritti. Improvise. Go with the flow and follow your own path.

ON MEASUREMENTS AND TIME

Our recipes at the restaurant are meticulously "grammed out," meaning measured by weight, not volume. I've included both types of measurement here for those of you without a scale, and so they are accessible regardless of where you live around the world.

Similarly, please note that suggestions around time (i.e. cook for 2 minutes) are merely that— suggestions. Give yourself over to the relative nature of time and instead of relying on specific measurements, simply taste and adjust. There are so many variables, including the strength of your stove, atmospheric pressure, even the minute differences in ingredients day to day. Use a timer so you don't forget to check, rather than to tell you when something is done.

So how do you know if something is done? You touch it. You taste it. You feel it with your hand.

Because let's be real and admit that recipes are themselves a very feeble translation of what happens when we cook. Don't think of them as musical notation; they aren't as intuitive or as exact. Nature simply doesn't make the same thing more than once. One leek can taste different from the next. A tomato can be juicier or more acidic than one growing on the same vine. Humid days make soft pasta. Old garlic has such a different attitude than young garlic.

I submit humbly to you here that a recipe should make something different every time. It should give you a place to create your own experiences around food. It's not a blueprint. It's there to guide and teach.

I learned this the hard way when my grandparents died. While we have my grandmother's little box of recipe index cards, when I make those dishes, nothing tastes quite the same as it did when I was a kid.

I think it's place and time. It's the past. We're missing the literal day.

This is the point I'm making by stamping the date on top of each dish. There was a certain time and place when we created this plate. And now that time is gone. So don't try to "recreate" the thing we achieved. Just use the recipes to expose the beauty of the day you're in.

A DREAM

At Lula we have a stack of fifty "tasting spoons," cheap metal teaspoons that we use to try dishes as we season them on the line. A good night will see these spoons washed three or four times. Yes, that's hundreds of mini bites.

Over the years I've had a recurring dream in which I'm invited to a dinner in a stone castle, a long, gaudy table lit with candelabras and dressed in elaborate white linen stretching out many yards in front of me. There is just one empty chair. I sit. Waiters in black tie enter with cloche-covered silver plates, setting them on the table and lifting the cloches in a synchronized, dramatic gesture. "Your dinner, sir." I look at the plates in front of me and there, like scientific specimens, are all the bites I've tasted throughout my day. A single slice of hanger steak. A spoonful of cauliflower purée. A pickled ramp. A morsel of oats. A candied pecan. A roasted beet. A tablespoon of brine. Is this really a royal supper?

I've never made it to dessert in the dream. I usually wake up terribly thirsty and maybe a little unnerved at how much food was laid out before me.

But it's not a work-anxiety dream. It's more like a statement of purpose. A duty. Taste your food. It seems silly to say it, but so many cooks forget to try what they make. Use your senses. Touch, prod, sip, lick, crunch down on everything. Try the vinaigrette before you dress the salad. Taste the lettuce before you add the vinaigrette. Check the brine, the pasta water, the first slice of the steak. Do it so much that it fills your dreams.

SOFFRITTO: THE ROOT OF THE TREE

Many of the savory dishes at Lula involve some kind of "soffritto" or savory base. This is a cooking term that has traveled extensively around the world and become elemental in many culture's cuisines. A combination of the words "under" (sotto) and "fried" (fritto), it refers to the aromatic base of a recipe, the first step. I like to translate soffritto as "the flavor under everything." It is the bedrock, the foundation, and root of the tree.

Similar to the French mirepoix of onion, carrot, and celery, an Italian soffritto is made of onions cooked slowly in olive oil or butter until they soften and melt into a deeply flavored, golden magic. It sounds simple but there's a lot going on here. Like salt, the savory underlayment of a properly cooked soffritto makes things taste even more of themselves. Marcella Hazan calls this the "architectural principle central to much Italian cooking," the beautiful idea that the onion is the original root of all flavor. The primordial seed.

The onions in a soffritto need to be cooked low and slow and in plenty of fat. A good pot helps tame the heat. Despite the "fritto," you don't want the onions to get crispy and brown. At home, where even my simmer burner still rips, I stack two burner grates on top of one another to put more distance between the bottom of the pot and flame. This allows me to keep the flame from sputtering out without the heat being too high. (You could also use a heat diffuser for the same effect.) It takes the onions at least 10 or 15 minutes to soften enough to lose their raw bite and break down languorously into the oil.

Once the onions melt, we add other ingredients, from garlic to saffron to plump yellow raisins. Sometimes we swap in fennel; sometimes we add dry spices, sometimes herbs. While a traditional one-pot recipe would have you make the soffritto, then add the rest of the ingredients on top, we tend to make it in advance and then add it like a separate component, using it to flavor seasonal, just-cooked vegetables, pastas, and grains.

I also commonly describe soffritto to my staff like the bass in a song. Most of the time you don't even know it's there. You're listening to the singer and the riffs and the groove. You're clapping on the 2 and the 4. But without the pulse of the bass laying down the cornerstones of the song, moving through the changes like an engine driving the train, the groove just wouldn't be the same.

ON SEASONING

Here's a truth: seasoning matters more than anything else you do in the kitchen. There's no idea creative enough, no skill expert enough, no ingredient perfect enough, to overcome a mistake in using salt and acid. To make anything good, you need to learn how to season food.

And by seasoning, I'm not referring to the spices and flavors in a dish, like jerk or Greek "seasoning," those dry rubs you might find in a grocery store spice aisle. For me, "seasoning" is the practice of balancing salt and acid to showcase the flavors in whatever dish you're making.

The balance is delicious and reflects graciously on the ingredients you've chosen. The imbalance is not. So the difference between an amazing dish and an average meh is nearly always the balance of salt and acid. You will notice that most of our recipes do not include a measurement for salt. There are just too many variables to give you an exact amount. You'll learn to season on your own. Salt is "to taste," which means you need to try your food, add some salt, try again.

(In Italian the term used for "season to taste," is *quanto basta*, or "whenever is enough." I love this term because it suggests that one can also go too far.)

One of the best ways to learn how to season is with a big batch of something liquid, such as a soup. Pour a few ounces into a cup. Taste, add some salt, add some acid (lemon juice, white vinegar, sherry vinegar, lime, your choice). Just see what it does. Throw it out and try again, in different proportions, always in a separate vessel. Rinse the vessel between versions. As you season incrementally, tasting what it does to the flavors, you will notice how it lifts some notes, represses others, changes the mouthfeel, making it softer or edgier. Go too far and taste what "too far" is like. Once you have something delicious, set it aside and try to make the entire batch taste exactly the same as the sample. Remember that the goal of seasoning is to create something that's craveable. I find that a lot of restaurant cooking pushes seasoning levels so far against the edge of what's acceptable that more than one bite kills your appetite. While that bite isn't technically "too salty" or "too acidic," it leaves no room for desire.

OUR INGREDIENTS

SALT

All recipes were made with medium-grain sea salt. Kosher salt is a commonly available substitute.

Remember that one measures salt as much by touch as by taste. The feel of a particular grain in your fingers will be something you learn and depend on for consistent seasoning. Decide what salt you like and keep that brand on hand. We use a medium grain because we like the natural salinity and a grit that both dissolves quickly and is still easily gripped between your forefinger and thumb.

OILS AND VINEGARS

I believe in using a variety of oils for different purposes, depending on how dominant you want the flavor of the oil itself. When it's just a vehicle for other flavors, I'd rather it take a backseat. Olive oils can be very intense and there are many instances in which I want more neutrality—fat without the flavor.

Most of our recipes call for "blend oil" for a soffritto and many vinaigrettes. This is our term for a 50/50 combination of extra-virgin oil and neutral vegetable oil (canola/rapeseed, grapeseed, or sunflower work well). I feel extra-virgin oil is often too strong a flavor to use as a base. I want a soffritto to support the rest of the flavors without bringing any attention to itself. Similarly, in many vinaigrettes I want some neutrality, some blank space.

When searing at a high temperature we use rice bran oil. For items that need a flavorless oil, we use grapeseed.

Vinaigrettes can be a touchy subject. I find that pure extra-virgin olive oil overwhelms the acidic bite of whatever vinegar or citrus we're using. So I use the neutral oil. Likewise, I often want a more nuanced approach to the vinegars. Sometimes I combine two or three vinegars together, creating my own mix, such as cider and honey vinegar, or sherry and red wine.

I may also dilute a vinegar by adding a little distilled white vinegar, which maintains the sharp bite without the dominant flavor. I like the way you get diverse acidic notes. A vinaigrette is meant to highlight the flavors of what it's dressing, not cover it up.

White distilled vinegar is a workhorse of our kitchens. We use it as I've described above, but also in many preparations (like soup), where a thimbleful of bright acid makes everything pop.

By the pass at Lula, we keep a finishing oil, drizzling it on everything, anointing pastas, roasted fish, and salads.

The oil comes from Lea's Greek family in Sparta, who since 1880 have been producing a luscious, deeply verdant oil from organic Athenolia olives. It is hand-harvested, cold-pressed, with just the right amount of bite. Finishing oils have their own personality; find one that suits yours. And realize that while an olive oil might feel too grassy and intense on your tongue, when drizzled over a bitter green or a buttery, anchovy-infused pot of beans . . . it might be just the edge it needs.

PASTA

While we make a number of fresh pastas in-house, both extruded and hand-shaped, dried pasta remains the number one staple in our pantry. We like Italian brands Rustichella D'Abruzzo, Martelli, Faella, and Gentile, all steeped in tradition and artisanal practices. These dried pastas use 100% hard durum semolina extruded through bronze dies, producing a slightly roughened surface that clings to condiments while cooking to a true al dente bite. My only exception to this preference is for the Yiayia. For this recipe we use Misko Brand #2, which is the brand and size most Greek-American families use for pastitsio. That said, a bucatini from any of my favorite Italian brands would make a delicious substitute.

FLOUR

The past decade has seen a rise in interest in the production of artisan flour, and you can almost certainly find a producer freshly milling heirloom or ancient grains in your local community. We use a range of flours in our recipes—like the rye from Janie's Mill, or unique options from Anson Mills—but we still need a basic go-to for baking, battering, dusting, etc. For these we use either the organic Beehive All-Purpose flour from Central Baking, or the workhouse King Arthur "Sir Galahad." These flours are standard-bearers for the basic-but-good category: no GMOs, unbleached, easy to work with, and tender when they need to be.

For fresh egg pastas we use the "00" from Caputo, and for extruded shapes we use the Semola Rimacinata from Caputo or 5 Stagioni. For chickpea flour we grind our own using freshly dried chickpeas from Rancho Gordo —the best.

ANCHOVIES

Like soffritto, the use of anchovy at the beginning of a preparation, when it melds away into undertones of savory umami depth, makes everything taste more full. Anchovy casts shadows into flavors, dramatizing them, pulling them forward, making them more complete expressions of themselves. Anchovies are like the music in a film. At home I use the sea-salt-packed artisan anchovies from Il Nettuno. I also love the colatura (Italian fish sauce, basically) from this producer, too.

Simply rinse anchovies before using, though with the Nettuno brand you'll need to split them open and remove the spine. You can also use anchovy fillets packed in oil, like those from Ortiz, if you'd like to skip these steps entirely.

YUZU KOSHO

There's something mysterious and arresting about this Japanese condiment that reminds me of the magical power of anchovies, making it a useful addition to our mostly Mediterranean pantry. Yuzu kosho is made from fresh chiles fermented in salt with yuzu, both the juice and the peel. There are green and red versions, the former a little grassier and more vegetal. It's spicy, funky, sweet, and zippy, all at once, without inhibiting the flavors present in a dish. A tiny bit goes a long way, sending flavor combinations into a kind of heightened passion.

DRIED SPICES

I can't emphasize freshness and quality more emphatically when it comes to dried spices. There are simply two different classes here: one of musty, desiccated, ancient pebbles that smell; and the other of exploding orbs of wonder and merriment, floral and complex as perfumes, nuanced and alluring, aggressive and pungent and extreme. The latter can only be obtained by finding a good source. For us, that's Diaspora Spice Co., Reluctant Trading, and Terra. The turmeric from Diaspora is truly a kaleidoscopic monster. A psychedelic. And the tellicherry pepper from Reluctant Trading makes you wonder what fraud used to sit in your mill. It's not surprising that these companies care about the way in which these special plants are harvested and how the people doing the harvesting are being cared for.

USING YOUR FANCY BLENDER

A high-speed blender is the go-to tool in restaurants for making many purées, soups, and other sauces. You want the best one you can afford, with a variable speed control and Maserati-levels of horsepower. Regardless, I have tips on how to achieve consistent and quality results whether you have one or not.

To achieve silky smooth purées, you need the right proportion of liquid to solid in the blender's canister, otherwise the blender can't do its work properly. Let's say, for example, you are making a green asparagus purée and you've just blanched an entire bunch of stalks—simply sticking them in the blender and turning it on will not give you a rich, unctuous, glossy result. The stalks will spin around, crushed to a stringy mush at the bottom, untouched on top.

- First, cut whatever you're puréeing into pieces so it can move around inside the blender.
- Second, start with the motor on low, adding liquid if necessary to get the solid pieces spinning but not so much as to make the final product watery or loose. Remember you can always add water, though you can't remove it.
- Third, get the product to spin, increasing the speed incrementally.
- Fourth, use either the plastic plunger that comes with the machine or a metal ladle to press down the solid mass as it spins. I like to use the small ladle because I can put the handle through the hole in the blender's rubber top, then press the solids down using the convex bottom of the ladle's bowl. The shape of the ladle prevents it from hitting the blade. Using an implement like this will also allow you to limit the amount of liquid in the purée. The thicker the mix, the smoother your purée, as long as the product spins. You want to see a swirling, centrifugal pattern, the entire mix moving at once. I've seen cooks make the mistake of running the blender on high while the blade spins uselessly at the bottom, everything else stuck at the top.
- Fifth, run the machine on high and let it rip. You want at least 15–20 seconds of pure RPMs to really smooth out the purée.

And please note that friction causes heat, and heat can change the flavor or color of the product—especially when making a purée or oil from blanched green vegetables or herbs. I like to cool these right away over an ice bath.

THE IMPORTANCE OF STRAINING

Many of our recipes call for purées and sauces to be passed through a fine-mesh strainer or tamis.

While some sauces can be strained without any effort, many of the purees we "pass" need to be pushed through the mesh to come out the other side. In the conical strainer, we use the bottom of a small ladle to push the product against the mesh.

Straining your food removes random fibers, skin, and other detritus you don't want in there; it also homogenizes the particles of a purée and "smooths" it out. There's an elegance to a silky purée, both in its visual aesthetic and the texture on your tongue.

OUR MENU

The recipes that follow reflect the way things work at Lula.

Lea is a Gemini. I'm a Taurus. So we have two menus, of course.

The first, called Cafe Classics, features original classics like the Pasta Yiayia. The second menu features our ever-changing list of seasonal dishes.

The Cafe Classics section of the menu (and of this book) is there to make you feel at ease, to trust us. We've been cooking these simple dishes since 1999. They are hearty, real, affordable. Flip the page and you'll see seasonal creations, often with ingredients that may be new to you. We want to extend the trust built on the cafe side of the menu so you'll take a risk and try something new. I have organized the seasonal dishes in the book by category—brunch, snacks, soups, salads, vegetables, pastas, meat and fish, and desserts. But when you eat at Lula, such categories aren't as explicit.

Every day at Lula feels like a change in time. It was the graphic designers at NiteWerk who first came up with the idea of stamping the menus with a banker date, to emphasize the frequency with which we changed dishes and to mark each moment of the season. Over the years, guests who celebrated special nights with us have collected these menus as keepsakes.

One of the things I love most about eating at Lula is that we don't ask you to choose. One person can order a sandwich while the other gets a crêpe with morels. A table can share a spaghetti and a plate of raw fish dressed in basil oil. It doesn't matter. There are no codes, no rules, no judgment.

And so, hi. Welcome in. We hope you enjoy these recipes and stories. Thinking and talking about food has found a unique and unexpected place in my life. And the more my knowledge grows, my sense of what's left to explore does too. As does my realization that I'll never master anything. It's limitless, really, what you can know about even the smallest thing, and so the goal will never be to know, never to reach the end of a sentence, a destination, to master a task. My goal, instead, is to reach a peace with my scrappy, imperfect self and share what I've found along the way.

Served all day long, these were some of
the first dishes we cooked back in September
1999 and they have never left the menu.
They are familiar dishes to make you feel
at peace. These recipes point to what
we inherited, from our families, and from
the '90s cafe culture Lea and I both loved.
They are resolutely casual, comforting, soulful,
a bit quirky maybe. And even today, they make
me feel at home in the world.

PASTA YIAYIA

09 99

I married into this dish. This is the recipe my wife most associates with her grandmother and namesake, Amalia, who came to Chicago from a village near Sparta, Greece as a child. I never got the chance to meet this wide branch of the family tree. But I can see Amalia now when I set Pasta Yiayia in front of my children. There is nothing more central to my wife's family than this maternal line—a branch of creativity, grit, beauty, and bravery—traced back to Amalia herself and now carried on by the flavors, stories, ingredients, and techniques in this recipe.

I imagine my wife as a child, as her grandmother set down a bowl of pasta dressed with feta, brown butter, garlic, and cinnamon. I can only imagine that these flavors connected her to a place in an old world she'd never know.

This simple dish was our guiding star as we learned to cook professionally, in large part because of the brown butter and cinnamon. I see these elements as guides for all the cooking we've done since—a combination of continental technique, Mediterranean lineage, and some kind of delightfully surprising, unexpected, "outside" flavor that still melds in a harmonious way, which is what I like to think I did when I joined the family. The legacy of Pasta Yiayia matters to me; it's like a surname, an heirloom, the passing of a gene.

Generations ebb and flow. History erodes. And since this recipe became a staple at Lula, I've learned that other families cook similar versions at home. But I've never tasted one with the same combination of brown butter, garlic, feta, and cinnamon; so I'll hold the idea that the Pasta Yiayia at Lula is indeed the hand of my wife's grandmother, still here, still cooking for us, still making sure we have what we need.

αιώνια η μνήμη. May her memory be eternal.

SERVES 4

Yiayia Sauce

1¼ cups (10 fl oz/300 g) milk
1 tablespoon Roasted Garlic purée (page 246) + 1 teaspoon oil from the Roasted Garlic
2 teaspoons minced garlic
½ teaspoon ground cinnamon
1 cup (5 oz/150 g) crumbled feta
⅛ teaspoon xanthan gum (optional)

To Serve

8 oz (225 g) bucatini (we use Misko No. 2)
1 cup (3½ oz/100 g) grated Parmesan
Generous ½ cup (2¾ oz/70 g) crumbled feta
Ground cinnamon, to taste
¼ cup (2¼ oz/55 g) butter
2 cloves garlic, peeled and thinly sliced
Salt

MAKE THE YIAYIA SAUCE

In a small pan, combine the milk, roasted garlic, garlic oil, minced garlic, and cinnamon. Bring to a simmer over low heat and cook for 15 minutes, stirring constantly to prevent scorching. Remove from the heat and let cool. Transfer the milk mixture to a blender, adding the feta and xanthan gum, if using. Purée until smooth. Gently warm the sauce in a large, wide pan over low heat while you prepare the pasta.

TO SERVE

Bring a large pot of water to a boil over high heat. Salt generously. Add the bucatini to the boiling water and cook until al dente, about 8 minutes. Strain and transfer the pasta to the pan with the warmed sauce, tossing until thoroughly coated.

Add half the Parmesan and feta, and toss again until just incorporated. The feta can be chunky and half melted. Transfer the pasta to warm serving bowls or a platter and top with the remaining feta and Parmesan. Sprinkle cinnamon on top and keep the serving vessel(s) in a warm place.

In a small pan set over medium heat, combine the butter and sliced garlic, swirling them around as the butter melts and begins to simmer. This will be your brown butter. Adjust the heat so the butter foams and simmers without burning. You'll see the cloudy mixture eventually separate and brown. Shake the pan in short forward–backward movements to aerate the foaming butter and circulate the slowly caramelizing milk solids. As the butter caramelizes, it should smell sweet, rich, and nutty (in French, the term is *beurre noisette*, for "hazelnut"). When both the garlic and butter are golden brown, remove the pan from the heat and drizzle the brown foaming butter all over the top of the pasta. It will sizzle evocatively. Serve.

CAESAR SALAD

09 99

We've all had Caesar salads in our lives that spoke of dystopian collapse—brown, shredded romaine, crown-cracking croutons, Parmesan dry as plaster—so I thought I'd point out a couple factors in our version. First of all, the lettuces are tender, juicy, local Little Gem romaine, mixed with escarole for a bitter note. Next, the celery, which in my opinion is the most underappreciated vegetable of all time. We lightly pickle ours for a sweet, tangy crunch. Our croutons are made from sourdough and toasted in olive oil, just long enough to make them crunchy on the outside and chewy inside. We source our salt-packed anchovies with care. We freshly grate the cheese and crack the pepper. And then we add a little house-made fennel pollen salt, some dill, and a flash of zested orange.

NB: Full disclosure here, I took the idea of cooking celery and blending it for this dressing from Jeremiah Stone and Fabián von Hauske Valtierra, the chefs of Wildair in New York City, who do such madness as grilling and juicing green cabbage for a salad dressing. That blew my mind.

SERVES 4

Caesar Dressing
3 oz/80 g celery, diced
⅓ cup + 1 tablespoon (3½ fl oz/ 100 g) blend oil
1 egg + 2 egg yolks
½ oz/15 g grated Parmesan
1 tablespoon Roasted Garlic purée (page 246)
2 teaspoons red wine vinegar
1 teaspoon Dijon mustard
¾ teaspoon minced anchovy
½ teaspoon nutritional yeast
½ teaspoon minced garlic
¼ teaspoon salt
¼ teaspoon black pepper
1 tablespoon olive oil

Marinated Celery
2 tablespoons white balsamic vinegar
1 teaspoon sugar
2 tablespoons blend oil
⅛ teaspoon salt
1 cup (3½ oz/100 g) thinly sliced celery

Fennel Pollen Salt
½ teaspoon fennel pollen
2 teaspoons Maldon sea salt
½ teaspoon coarsely ground celery seed

To Serve
2 heads Little Gem lettuce, cleaned and leaves separated
1 head escarole, cleaned and torn into irregular pieces
4 cups (4 oz/120 g) Sourdough Croutons (page 253)
2¾ oz/70 g Parmesan, shaved, plus extra to garnish
1 teaspoon lemon juice
½ cup (¼ oz/8 g) dill sprigs, stems removed
Grated zest of ¼ orange
Salt and freshly ground black pepper

MAKE THE CAESAR DRESSING
Place a small saucepan over low heat. Add the celery and oil and cook until the celery is soft and translucent. Remove from the heat. Once cool, transfer the cooked celery to a blender, along with the egg, yolks, Parmesan, roasted garlic, red wine vinegar, mustard, anchovy, nutritional yeast, minced garlic, salt, and pepper. Purée until smooth. With the machine running, add the olive oil in a thin stream and continue blending until thoroughly emulsified.

MAKE THE MARINATED CELERY
In a mixing bowl, whisk together the vinegar, sugar, oil, and salt. Toss with the celery and set aside.

MAKE THE FENNEL POLLEN SALT
Combine all the ingredients in a bowl and set aside.

TO SERVE
In a mixing bowl toss the Little Gem and escarole with the dressing, marinated celery, croutons, shaved Parmesan, and lemon juice. Taste for seasoning, but leave underseasoned as you're about to dust with fennel pollen salt. Divide among 4 plates and garnish with dill, shaved Parmesan, a little orange zest, and a sprinkle of fennel pollen salt and black pepper.

THE "TINEKA"
SANDWICH

09 99

The "Tineka" Sandwich was on the menu at Logan Beach years before I arrived. Lea learned to make it from a Dutch concert pianist, whose aunt made a version of this sandwich for him as a child. The spread is essentially a satay sauce, typically used for grilled meats or vegetables. Here it makes for a delightfully crunchy (in both the textural and cultural sense), sweet, sticky spread for a very '90s veggie club sandwich. The recipe for the satay will make more than you need for this sandwich, or even several more, but it can be refrigerated for up to a week and works beautifully as a dressing for cold noodles.

Heat a griddle or large skillet (frying pan) and add a thin layer of oil. Add the bread and toast on one side until lightly golden.

Spread the spicy peanut sauce on the untoasted sides of the bread, then add the cucumber, lettuce, tomato, red onion, and sprouts (in that order). Top with the other slice of bread. Cut in half.

MAKES 1 SANDWICH

2 tablespoons blend oil, for toasting

2 slices bread (we use a multigrain sourdough pan loaf)

1½ tablespoons Spicy Peanut Sauce (page 250)

1½ oz (40 g) cucumber, sliced into rounds

2 lettuce leaves (we like crunchy varietals like Green Oak)

4 × ¼-inch (5 mm) thick slices tomato

¼ red onion, thinly shaved

¼ cup (¼ oz/8 g) alfalfa sprouts

BEET
BRUSCHETTA
09 99

Sometimes you learn best from other people telling you what *not* to do. I remember this Italophile Lula regular, one of those farmers' market aesthetes, who insisted on correcting a server's pronunciation of "bruschetta" in a particularly loud and domineering way. And while he still has my gratitude for some other things he did for us, I have not forgiven him for pompously clacking that "C" against the roof of his mouth. As though he knew more about this dish than she did.

In college, I took a comparative literature class team-taught by two professors, one classically trained in the New Critical close reading of texts and one embedded in the world of postmodern theory. The idea was that they would share the stage by giving two very different approaches to the same group of texts—a "comp," if you will. The class devolved into a two-party polemic of culture, ideology, and identity. The followers of the New Critical teacher sat on the right in their scruffy, comfy sweaters. The theory heads to the left in their black leather. Each tuned out during opposing lectures, until the very last day of the semester, when, in a brilliant move, both professors took the stage to show solidarity by reading out loud the parable *Before the Law* by Franz Kafka.

This is a story of a man who travels to the house of the Law and meets a gatekeeper who tells him he cannot enter. The door is open, and he can see inside, but he cannot pass the threshold. The man decides not to challenge the gatekeeper and waits to be allowed entry, like for his entire life. Eventually the man dies in stasis, unable to enter, unable to leave, but before he does, he asks why no one else has attempted to enter in all his time before the Law. He is told that this entrance was built only for him. Then the door is shut, he dies, the parable is done.

Reading this story, and experiencing this moment in class, shaped me more than any other in college. I think of it often and meditate on it myself from time to time, looking at the walls, both real and imagined, that I see constructed around me. It says a lot to us in the hospitality industry, those who work with the emotions of strangers, navigating their walls, too. And it speaks to the power of empathy and to the weakness in dogma. So, damn this gatekeeper and whatever house of Law he thinks he's built by knowing how to say—yes, correctly—the word "bruschetta."

SERVES 4

Smoked Pecans

Hickory and fruitwood chips,
for smoking

1 cup (3½ oz/100 g) raw pecans

Salt

To Serve

2 tablespoons blend oil, for toasting

1 fresh baguette, sliced on an extreme bias into 4 slices ¾-inch (2 cm) thick

¼ cup (2 oz/50 g) Whipped Goat Cheese (page 253)

4 oz (120 g) Roasted Beets (page 255), diced into ½-inch (1 cm) cubes

2 cups (1 oz/25 g) baby kale

2 tablespoons Simple Vinaigrette (page 249)

2 tablespoons each chopped parsley, basil, and chives

¼ red onion, sliced paper thin

MAKE THE SMOKED PECANS

Using a combination of fruitwood and hickory, preheat an electric smoker, or similar, to 200°F/95°C. Add the pecans and smoke for 30 minutes. Roughly chop and season with salt.

Alternatively, you can create a makeshift smoker with a cast iron skillet (frying pan). Heat the skillet and wood chips over a high flame. Once smoking, add a layer of aluminum foil and nest the pecans inside. Then cover the skillet with a tight-fitting lid or second layer of foil. Reduce the heat to low and smoke for 15–20 minutes.

TO SERVE

Heat a griddle or large skillet (frying pan) and add a thin layer of oil. Add the bread and toast on both sides until lightly golden. Remove, cool slightly, then spread the whipped goat cheese on one side of the bread. Top with roasted beets (beetroot).

In a small mixing bowl, toss the kale with the vinaigrette and taste for seasoning. Add the pecans, herbs, and red onion. Top the bruschetta with small handfuls of the kale salad, making sure not to leave any herbs or nuts behind in the bowl.

SPAGHETTI WITH
SALSA ROSSA
AND PANCETTA

09 99

One (perhaps easily forgotten) part of Chicago '90s culture was a string of Italo-Mexican mashup restaurants. They were very much in vogue when I arrived in 1995. As were roasted red peppers. Roasted peppers were everywhere. We even put them in veggie sushi rolls. I know not everybody gets it, but for me these ingredients give Y2K vibes.

Lea and I wrote a sketch for this recipe on a yellow pad in the middle of a brutal heatwave. We were drinking iced coffees in a cafe near Irving and Kildare with a line of noxious summer Chicago traffic stalled outside. The lights at the corner would change red to green to red with the cars at a smoldering standstill. It was hot in that stagnant way I've only felt in Midwestern cities, as though the air were made of gelatin. Lea had the idea to blend dried chiles with sweet red peppers, cooked slowly in a soffritto. I wanted to start with pancetta, like you might with a pasta in Rome. The combination became what we called salsa rossa, which is the name of an actual Italian sauce made of red peppers and/or tomatoes, sweet and usually puréed, closer to ketchup really than to a pasta sauce, and certainly never made with dried hot chiles. But I liked how the "salsa" was like a double entendre, a malaprop. And it stuck.

Every spaghetti we make at Lula has a half-ounce of delicious pancetta drippings to begin the recipe. Our pancetta is made in-house from local Gunthorp Farms pork bellies, cured with salt, rosemary, black pepper, garlic, and sugar. We roast it in a low-temperature oven, where the large batch renders generous amounts of fat. In this home version, we render the pancetta in the same pan you'll use for the spaghetti sauce. That said, feel free to make this pasta without the pork, or using vegetable stock; it's great for vegetarians too.

MAKE THE SALSA ROSSA

Put the blend oil and onions into a small saucepan and set over medium heat. Cook, stirring occasionally, until the mixture comes to a simmer. Reduce the heat to maintain a slow simmer, using a diffuser if necessary to maintain the temperature. Cook until the onions have softened, about 30 minutes. Add the roasted and dried peppers and cook for an additional 30 minutes. Set aside.

TO SERVE

Bring a large pot of water to a boil over high heat. Salt generously. Add the pasta and cook until al dente, 1 minute less than the package instructions.

Meanwhile, set a large sauté pan over low heat and add the oil and pancetta. Gently cook until the fat is rendered and translucent and the pancetta is crisp at the edges. Add the salsa rossa, increase the heat to medium, and cook for 1 minute,

stirring and swirling the salsa in the pan. Add the stock and cook for 1–2 minutes, until the sauce is reduced by half.

Drain the pasta, reserving at least 1 cup of pasta water, and add the pasta to the sauté pan off the heat. (I use tongs to pull the spaghetti from the pot and put it directly into the sauce without a thorough draining. This way the starchy, salty water is still coating the spaghetti and provides the sauce with some hydration.)

Return the sauté pan to medium heat, add the parsley, and toss the pasta several times to coat in the sauce. Taste for seasoning, and for the doneness of the pasta. If the pasta seems dry, which is likely, add 1 or 2 splashes of reserved pasta water. Once you love it, remove the pan from the heat and add the butter (see *mantecare*, page 176). Toss the pasta several more times to emulsify the butter into the sauce. Divide among 4 plates and top with Parmesan and queso fresco.

SERVES 4

Salsa Rossa

4 tablespoons blend oil

½ cup (4 oz/120 g) diced onion

½ cup (4 oz/120 g) diced Roasted Peppers (page 255)

1 teaspoon dried, toasted, and ground ancho pepper

1 teaspoon dried, toasted, and ground guajillo pepper

To Serve

8 oz (225 g) spaghetti (we use Rustichella D'Abruzzo and Martelli)

2 tablespoons olive oil

¼ cup (2¾ oz/70 g) ½-inch (1 cm) diced pancetta

¼ cup (2¼ fl oz/65 g) Chicken Stock (page 254)

1 tablespoon + 1 teaspoon finely minced parsley

1 oz (25 g) cold butter, diced

1 oz (25 g) Parmesan, grated

¼ cup (1 oz/25 g) crumbled queso fresco

Salt

CHICKPEA AND FENNEL TAGINE

09 99

A tagine is both a North African long-simmered stew and the type of conical clay vessel used to cook it. The shape of the traditional vessel allows a braise to simmer gently, concentrating flavors without drying things out. Thick clay walls insulate the stew inside, and as steam rises up the chimney, water condenses on the sloped interior and drips back down, regulating heat and moisture. This process can also be done in a heavy braiser or ceramic pot, which is what we do at Lula.

We learned about the tagine from longtime Lula manager Natalie Sternberg, whose mother studied belly dancing in Morocco and then traveled with a Berber family to continue her practice. She performed dance with her own troupe for years. When Natalie was growing up, her parents used to host wild, drug-infused drum parties full of dance, music, and Moroccan food. Friday nights mortified her as a teen. She remembers a sleepover that ended up with her having to explain to a friend why her parents were outside howling at the moon. As a love song to her mother, who passed away tragically in 1991, Natalie resurrected these dishes at Logan Beach. And so it happened that this searching, artistic woman, whom I never met, passed a tagine to her daughter, then to me, and now to this book.

One of the best things about this stew is that you can pretty much do what you want with it—change up the ingredients, substituting vegetables, dried fruit, and herbs at will. The key to the flavor is the combination of sweet and tangy elements—our turmeric spice mix, golden raisins, and fennel—all cooking languorously with dried chickpeas and lots of onion. When you finally open the lid and breathe in, you might find that the fragrance of aromatics and spices simmered so long propels you deep into your own memories of home.

MAKE THE TAGINE

Place a large, heavy pot with a tight-fitting lid over low heat. Add the oil and onions and cook for 5–7 minutes, until the onions begin to soften (do not let them brown). Add the tagine spice mix and stir to combine. Cover and cook over low heat for 30 minutes. Add the fennel, jalapeños, garlic, and ginger. Cook for 15 minutes. (Take care not to let the soffritto burn. You don't want the mixture to become darker than the color of the spice mix itself.)

Add the white wine and simmer 3–5 minutes, until the alcohol has cooked off. (Test this with your nose; if the burning sensation is gone, you're good to go.)

Add the soaked chickpeas and vegetable stock and cover. Bring to a gentle simmer and let cook for 45–60 minutes, until the chickpeas have achieved an unctuous, creamy, nut-butter consistency. If the liquid in the pot reduces too far below the surface of the beans, add more stock or water. Add the kale, stir to combine, and let wilt. Season with salt and lemon juice.

MAKE THE ROASTED CARROTS AND FENNEL

Heat the oven to 350°F/180°C. In a large bowl, toss the carrots and fennel with olive oil, salt, and 1 tablespoon water. Spread in an even layer on a baking sheet. Roast for 12–15 minutes, until lightly caramelized.

TO SERVE

Add the roasted carrots and fennel to the tagine and cook for a few minutes, until the vegetables are heated through. Fold in the sweet potato butter, followed by the golden raisins and preserved lemon. Taste and adjust the seasoning, then transfer the tagine to a serving vessel. Spoon drizzles of green harissa over the top, followed by lots of fried chickpeas and cilantro (coriander), parsley, and mint leaves.

SERVES 8

Tagine

2 tablespoons blend oil

1 small onion (5½ oz/160 g), minced

3 tablespoons Tagine Spice Mix (page 248)

½ medium fennel bulb (2½ oz/60 g), minced

1 small jalapeño (2½ oz/60 g), seeded, stemmed and minced

3–4 cloves garlic, minced

3 tablespoons minced fresh ginger

½ cup (4 fl oz/120 ml) dry white wine

8 cups (2½ lb/1.2 kg) dried chickpeas, soaked 24 hours

2¾ cups (23 fl oz/680 g) Vegetable Stock (page 255)

3 cups (3½ oz/100 g) chopped lacinato kale

1½ teaspoons salt

1 tablespoon lemon juice

Roasted Carrots and Fennel

3 skinny-ish carrots (7 oz/200 g), peeled

1 bulb fennel (4 oz/120 g), cut into small wedges

¼ cup (2 fl oz/60 ml) olive oil

1 teaspoon salt

To Serve

4 tablespoons Sweet Potato Butter (page 249)

2 tablespoons Pickled Golden Raisins (page 247)

1 tablespoon sliced preserved lemon

2 tablespoons Green Harissa (page 251)

1 quantity Fried Chickpeas (page 247)

A few sprigs of parsley, cilantro (coriander), and mint, leaves picked

Salt

LULA HOUSE SALAD

09 99

Our lettuces and breakfast radishes are grown year-round in the greenhouses of Werp Farms in Buckley, Michigan, by Mike and Tina Werp. We use a mix of Green and Red Oak and Little Gem romaine, cut by hand the day before they are delivered. Buckley isn't the kind of place you'd expect to source year-round greens—it's closer to the Canadian border than to our kitchen door. Tina and Mike drive their lettuces almost five hours each way to deliver them every Thursday night, so we purchase what we need for the week. I've seen pictures of the greenhouses in February under snowbanks taller than me, the wood fires burning through the night. I often tell our cooks that while all ingredients deserve respect, these lettuces are among the most precious to me. Even more so than imported delicacies like truffles, morels, or salsify. Wherever you are, find someone who grows lettuces with this kind of care and then match their care with yours.

Use a soft touch when "tossing" the greens in the mixing bowl. Fold and turn the leaves gently, without tongs. In fact, I straight up beg you to dress the salad with your clean bare hands. Feel the "aliveness" of a vegetable. Greens can be crushed and wilted just by the act of being dressed. Some need more handling, but most need a light touch. It's all about how tender, wet, crunchy, or firm a particular lettuce is.

In the middle of a gray Chicago winter, with little to no sunlight for months, these beautiful greens from Werp Farms are a kind of supplement to my spirit. They do the mood-boosting work of the sun. And this is why I eat the Lula House Salad nearly every day at this time of year. Not for the roughage, but to fortify my will to live in the face of the cruel, cold world outside.

In a mixing bowl, toss the lettuce with the dressing and salt. Taste and adjust the seasoning. Divide among 4 chilled bowls and top with everything else, dividing evenly.

SERVES 4

14 oz (400 g) mixed lettuce leaves; we use Red Oak, Green Oak, and Little Gem

6 tablespoons Caper Lemon Dressing (page 250)

¼ cup (5 g) parsley leaves

½ cup (8 g) dill leaves

1¼ oz (30 g) red onion, thinly sliced and rinsed

½ cup (1¼ oz/30 g) radishes, thinly sliced

2 teaspoons white sesame seeds, toasted

2 cups (1¼ oz/30 g) pea shoots

Salt

SPICY SESAME SLAW

0999

Over the years, we've made tens of thousands of gallons of this crunchy, spicy, tangy coleslaw. I know there have been a few requests for the recipe during this time. Here, finally, is a home version that doesn't start with "slice 12 whole cabbages."

Mix all the ingredients together in a large bowl and refrigerate. It's frankly better the next morning.

SERVES 6

½ oz (15 g) fresh ginger, finely minced
½ oz (15 g) garlic, finely minced
1½ oz (40 g) sugar
1 teaspoon salt
1 tablespoon + 1½ teaspoons sesame oil
3 tablespoons red sambal
¼ cup + 2 tablespoons (3 fl oz/90 g) distilled white vinegar
¼ cup + 1 teaspoon (2¼ fl oz/65 g) blend oil
1½ oz (40 g) red onion, thinly sliced
1¼ lb (20 oz/580 g) cabbage, shredded

BAKED FRENCH FETA WITH MARINATED OLIVES

09 99

Years before we met, Lea's Greek cousins took her on a trip to a tapas-style restaurant in Athens. There she had feta baked in a wood oven and dressed with a salad of chopped jalapeño, newly pressed olive oil, and fresh herbs. When Lea and I first started cooking together, she told me that this meal, in particular this dish, was one of the first experiences that really engaged her creativity around food. It was both traditional and confrontational—like, jalapeños in Greece?

Soon it was 1999. All of a sudden we were professional cooks in a restaurant of our own. And we were heavily influenced by the times. This was the golden era for green herb oils, so when we created our own version of that baked feta, for which we blasphemously chose a briny version from France, we made a flavored oil of jalapeño and basil to drizzle on top. Make sure you wait till the last minute before broiling (grilling) the cheese, so you can make a dramatic entrance. This dish does have a *saganaki* effect in a dining room. We may not light it on fire, but everyone loves the smells and sounds of a sizzling hunk of broiled cheese wafting through the dining room. It's as close to *Opa!* as we get.

NB: We use pitted (stoned) olives because the idea is that you spread the sizzling cheese and olives on the bread, which would be difficult indeed if you were fighting against the pits.

SERVES 2

Marinated Olives

⅔ cup (5 fl oz/150 g) blend oil

4 swaths orange peel

4 swaths lemon peel

1 teaspoon Roasted Garlic purée (page 246)

½ teaspoon dried oregano

½ teaspoon Marash chile flakes

½ cup (2¾ oz/75 g) picholine olives, pitted (stoned)

½ cup (2¾ oz/75 g) Castelvetrano olives, pitted (stoned)

½ cup (2¾ oz/75 g) kalamata olives, pitted (stoned)

Jalapeño-Basil Oil

½ cup (¼ oz/10 g) packed parsley leaves

¼ cup (¼ oz/10 g) packed basil leaves

⅛ cup (4 g) packed mint leaves

½ cup (4 fl oz/120 ml) + 2 tablespoons blend oil

¼ cup (1 oz/25 g) chopped jalapeño

1 tablespoon chopped garlic

2 tablespoons chopped scallion tops

Grated zest of ¼ lemon

¼ teaspoon salt

To Serve

5 oz (150 g) feta (we use Valbreso or similar sheep's milk feta)

⅛ red onion, sliced paper thin

4 slices cucumber (use a small variety, such as Persian)

A few parsley leaves

Grilled bread

MAKE THE MARINATED OLIVES

In a medium bowl, combine the oil, citrus peels, roasted garlic, oregano, and chile. Massage the peels to release the flavors. Then add the olives and toss to coat. Let marinate in the refrigerator for at least 24 hours; it gets better with age.

MAKE THE JALAPEÑO-BASIL OIL

Bring a medium pot of water to a boil over high heat. Salt generously. Fill a small bowl with a 50/50 mix of ice and water. Blanch the herbs in the boiling water for 10 seconds, remove with a slotted spoon, and immediately plunge into the ice bath to stop the cooking. Scoop out the herbs with a slotted spoon and remove excess water by wrapping them in cheesecloth and wringing them out. Chop, then set aside.

Set a stainless-steel mixing bowl over the ice bath. In a small saucepan, heat 2 tablespoons of the oil over medium heat. Add the jalapeño and garlic. Cook until fragrant and the garlic turns lightly golden. Scrape the contents of the pan into the mixing bowl over the ice bath (the chill prevents the garlic from over-browning).

When cool, transfer to a blender with the herbs, scallion tops, lemon zest, and salt. Purée until smooth and bright green. Refrigerate until cold.

TO SERVE

Preheat the broiler (grill) to a medium heat. Place the feta in a shallow ovenproof vessel and broil until the cheese is browned and lightly charred.

Meanwhile, in a small bowl, mix the marinated olives with the red onion, cucumber slices, and parsley leaves. Remove the hot feta from the oven and drizzle the jalapeño-basil oil directly on top of the cheese. Spoon the olive-herb mixture over the top, and serve with grilled bread.

Served every day of the week until the kitchen closes to prepare for dinner, our seasonal brunch specials bring the more refined techniques and specialized ingredients that we use at dinner, but in a casual setting.

BRUNCH

BUTTERMILK PANCAKES

09 99

I love that our pancake recipe is first in a line of the more elaborate, seasonal dishes that we serve for brunch. This is a "basic" buttermilk pancake recipe—think blue jeans, white tee. But I like to think you can wear a blazer with your blue jeans and white tee shirt, dress it up, accessorize, or just slay it plain and simple. At Lula, brunch is our place where the plain is elegant and the simple sophisticated. It doesn't matter if you mix and match.

My grandparents owned a tiny, four-booth diner in the '80s. Lea's grandparents, too. And when I was a kid my dad ate nearly every meal at the Acropolis Diner outside New Haven, Connecticut. They always called him by his name and knew his order. In return he'd throw a couple of twenties down on the table, sticky with syrup and creamer, the tip way bigger than the bill. Since Lula started serving breakfast and brunch, we've taken steps to honor certain elements of those experiences (greeting regulars by name, for example) and leave some behind, especially with respect to service. For too long the brunch shift got the short end of the respect stick in our industry. Here we do our best to give the service team the same resources, training, and sense of purpose as the dinner crew. We wipe the table before handing over a check. We never start a conversation with "Who wants coffee?" We fold your napkin if you leave the table. A plate of pancakes might look simple, but doing the simple things right takes far more intention than it seems.

The fewer the ingredients, the more important the provenance. And this pancake recipe has credibility. We get our buttermilk from Old Heritage Creamery here in Illinois, the syrup is from Milligan's in nearby Ohio. Our preferred flour for great flavor with a classic vibe is the all-purpose (plain) "Beehive" flour from Central Milling.

There are a few things to remember about technique: Don't overmix the batter, use fresh, cold butter on your griddle, and practice dolloping the batter with a quick, confident turn of your wrist. You want a round pancake, not some kind of amoeba.

MAKES 8-10 PANCAKES

1¾ cups (8 oz/225 g) all-purpose (plain) flour
3 tablespoons superfine (caster) sugar
2 tablespoons baking powder
½ teaspoon salt
1 cup (8 fl oz/250 ml) milk
2 eggs
¼ cup (2 oz/60 g) butter, melted, plus cold butter for cooking
2 tablespoons buttermilk
2 tablespoons sour cream
Powdered (icing) sugar, to garnish
Real maple syrup, to serve
Whipped cultured butter, to serve

In a large mixing bowl, whisk the dry ingredients together. In a separate bowl, whisk together the milk, eggs, melted butter, buttermilk, and sour cream until smooth. Pour the wet mixture over the dry, then gently fold the mixture together with a spatula, taking care not to overwork the batter and develop too much gluten. Continue folding until only small lumps of flour remain.

Heat a griddle or large skillet over medium heat until hot (sprinkle a little water on the surface; it should sizzle for a second and then evaporate). Add 1 tablespoon cold butter and allow to melt. Drop 4-ounce (120-gram) dollops of batter directly into the pan, evenly spaced apart. Allow to cook for 1–2 minutes, until the underside is golden and the top is covered in tiny, mostly popped bubbles. Flip the pancake and cook 2–3 more minutes.

Transfer to a plate and keep warm. Repeat with the remaining batter.

To serve, dust each pancake with powdered (icing) sugar and serve with a side of maple syrup and cultured butter.

WHITE GRAPEFRUIT WITH CANDIED SEEDS

02 09

When I was young, my sisters and I were actually encouraged by adults to sprinkle white sugar on fresh fruit such as strawberries and melon. Oh, the '70s. I loved the way the undissolved crystals felt on my tongue, the crunch in my teeth as I chewed. Which is why my favorite breakfast at the Acropolis Diner was a half grapefruit, no matter how sad and dried out it looked in the case behind the counter.

These are the memories conjured by our white grapefruit with candied seeds. A cross between a pomelo (tart, delicious, but maddeningly hard to eat) and a white grapefruit, the Oro Blanco grapefruit is less bitter than others, yet it's not too sweet either. Its flesh is a prism, the kind of thing that almost makes rainbows when the light hits it just right. I love the way the candied seeds glitter across the surface, glistening with fresh juice. You'll want to pick the whole thing up when you're done, give it a little squeeze, so that the leftover peel makes an oval bowl, and slurp those last sips up.

MAKE THE CANDIED SEEDS

Preheat the oven to 300°F/150°C. Line a baking sheet with parchment paper and spray with oil.

In a small saucepan, heat the glucose, honey, canola (rapeseed) oil, and maple syrup over medium heat to 250°F/120°C, stirring constantly with a heat-resistant spatula. Add the baking soda (bicarbonate of soda). The mixture will react with the volcanic fury of a kid's science project. Do not fear. Add all of the seeds and peppercorns and stir to combine.

Scrape the mixture onto the parchment-lined baking sheet and spread evenly. Bake for 7–10 minutes, until the spices are fragrant and toasty but not brown. The seeds should be in brittle clumps when cool. If the seeds are still chewy or sticky when cool, reduce the temperature of the oven to 250°F/120°C and continue to toast until the mixture has dried. Leave to cool, then crush or break apart.

MAKE THE GRAPEFRUIT

Cut the grapefruit in half laterally, then trim the rounded top off each half to make a level base (otherwise they tend to tip and spill juice). Using the tip of a small paring knife, make incisions on all sides of each segment to separate them from the white membrane surrounding them. Make sure the knife separates the fruit from the bottom as well. Then, with the knife at a 30-degree angle, cut the circumference of the fruit away from the interior edge of the peel, so each individual fruit segment can be lifted out effortlessly with a regular spoon.

TO SERVE

Sprinkle the seeds on the segmented grapefruit halves, like sprinkles on ice cream. Scatter the mint leaves on top, drizzle the olive oil over the fruit, and finish with the grated lime zest.

SERVES 2

Candied Seeds

Vegetable oil spray
Generous ½ cup (4½ fl oz/130 g) glucose syrup
⅓ cup (2½ fl oz/80 g) honey
2 tablespoons canola (rapeseed) oil
1 tablespoon maple syrup
1 teaspoon baking soda (bicarbonate of soda)
3 tablespoons fennel seeds
¼ cup (¼ oz/10 g) white sesame seeds
3 tablespoons pink peppercorns, crushed
2 tablespoons white poppy seeds
1 tablespoon coriander seeds, crushed
1 tablespoon Sichuan peppercorns, crushed

Grapefruit

1 white grapefruit (we use the Oro Blanco variety)

To Serve

A few mint leaves
2 teaspoons olive oil
Grated zest of 1 lime

SWEET CORN **GRITS** WITH CHERRY TOMATOES AND A **60-MINUTE EGG**

08 17

This is a blurry mix of *cucina povera*, U.S. Lowcountry, continental Spanish, and Mexican ingredients that just seem to belong together in the same bowl. I love the way juices from the ripe tomatoes—here we used black cherry tomatoes from Green Acres Farm—bleed out into the warm grits, sweet as jam, with an acidic zing and bite. A warm bowl of hearty grits can fuel you for a long day. We nestle a slow-poached egg in the hot cornmeal, and though any style of egg would work, I do love the way the custardy yolk makes the grits even more creamy, rich, and unctuous. When trying out this recipe at home, a regular poached or boiled egg will work just as well.

In our quest to use fine dining techniques at brunch, we were early adopters of the "sous vide" egg, which is what you get when you drop a whole egg in a water bath at 140°F/60°C for 60 minutes. I can't tell you how many times guests have half-joked, "What, if I want this dish, do I have to come back in an hour?" No, when we cook eggs in this style, they are shocked in an ice bath, then reheated upon ordering. A slow-cooked egg produces a custardy yolk but also a rather undeveloped white. So I've decided that 60-minute eggs work best when set into a surrounding environment that will firm up their whites, like a hot liquid (ramen, for example, from whence the onsen egg came) or something like these corn grits. I'm just not into a half-cooked egg on toast.

SERVES 4

Roasted Cherry Tomatoes
Scant 2 cups (10 oz/275 g) cherry tomatoes
1 tablespoon olive oil

Corn Butter
6½ oz (190 g) butter
¼ cup (2¼ oz/60 g) finely diced onion
2 cups (11 oz/300 g) corn kernels
¼ teaspoon salt

Corn Stock
1 cup (5 oz/150 g) corn kernels

Sweet Corn Vinaigrette
⅓ cup (2½ fl oz/75 ml) olive oil
1 cup (5 oz/150 g) corn kernels
2 tablespoons minced shallots
2 tablespoons lemon juice
1 tablespoon chopped oregano
Grated zest of ½ lemon
¼ teaspoon Aleppo pepper
¼ teaspoon salt
Black pepper

Grits
1 cup (3½ oz/100 g) white corn grits
½ teaspoon salt
⅔ cup (2¾ oz/70 g) grated Parmesan

MAKE THE ROASTED CHERRY TOMATOES

Preheat the oven to 250°F/120°C. Line a baking sheet with parchment paper.

In a mixing bowl, toss the tomatoes with the olive oil. Spread in an even layer on the parchment-lined baking sheet. Roast for about 2 hours, until shriveled and golden. Let cool.

MAKE THE CORN BUTTER

Melt 1 oz (25 g) of the butter in a small saucepan over low heat. Add the onion and cook for 5–7 minutes, until soft and translucent. Add the corn and salt and cook for 2 minutes, until tender. Remove from the heat and let cool.

In the bowl of a food processor, combine the remaining butter with the cooked corn mixture. Purée until smooth. Pass through a fine-mesh strainer or tamis and set aside.

MAKE THE CORN STOCK

In a high-speed blender, combine the corn kernels and 1½ cups (12 fl oz/350 ml) water. Purée until smooth. Pass through a fine-mesh strainer or tamis and set aside.

MAKE THE SWEET CORN VINAIGRETTE

Heat 1 tablespoon of the oil in a medium sauté pan over medium heat. Add the corn and cook for 2 minutes until just tender. Transfer to a mixing bowl and let cool. Whisk in the remaining olive oil and the rest of the ingredients. Add the cooled roasted cherry tomatoes.

MAKE THE GRITS

In a medium, heavy pot, bring 3 cups (25 fl oz/750 ml) of water to a boil. Whisk in the grits and the salt. Reduce the heat to low and bring the grits to a steady, low simmer, whisking constantly. Stream in 1½ cups (12 fl oz/350 ml) of the corn stock. Don't stop whisking. Cook until tender with no rawness. Depending on the type of grits, this could take anywhere from 8–30 minutes. When tender, add the Parmesan and ½ cup (3½ oz/100 g) corn butter, whisking to incorporate. Taste and adjust the seasoning.

TO SERVE

Ladle the finished grits into 4 bowls. Crack a cooked egg into a slotted spoon, using the holes in the spoon to encourage any loose egg white to fall off. Drop 1 egg into the center of each bowl of grits. Add a little of the corn vinaigrette mixture to each bowl, along with a few raw cherry tomatoes. Garnish with oregano, arugula (rocket), cotija, and a generous drizzle of pimentón-tomato oil.

To Serve

4 eggs (we serve 60-minute eggs—see recipe introduction—but you can serve any eggs of your choosing, cooked with a soft yolk)

12 cherry tomatoes, halved

Oregano leaves, to garnish

Arugula (rocket) leaves, to garnish

¼ cup (1 oz/25 g) crumbled cotija cheese

¼ cup (2 fl oz/60 ml) Pimenton-Tomato Oil (page 246)

Image on page 52

POTATO **CRÊPE WITH** SPRING LEEKS AND MOREL MUSHROOMS

A lacy, shatteringly thin marriage of latke and crêpe that you can fill with whatever you'd like. This version comes from an early spring menu, but we've also done versions in later months with cauliflower, cherry tomato, even truffle. I'll admit it takes some touch (and practice) to get the crêpe thin enough to just hold the potato together without being gluey or dense. Our trick is to tilt and rotate the pan while adding the batter, so it runs in streams and rivulets, finding its way into the filigree of crispy shoestring potato.

SERVES 4

Potato Crêpe Batter

2 lb (900 g) russet potatoes, peeled
1 egg
½ cup (4 fl oz/120 g) whole milk
2 teaspoons melted butter
1 teaspoon brandy
⅓ cup (1½ oz/40 g) all-purpose (plain) flour
¼ cup (1½ oz/40 g) potato starch
¼ teaspoon baking soda (bicarbonate of soda)
¼ teaspoon salt

Braised Leeks

1 tablespoon butter
3¾ oz (110 g) baby leeks, whites only, cut in half lengthwise then sliced
2 tablespoons white wine
1 teaspoon whole grain mustard
1 teaspoon apple cider vinegar
Salt

Roasted Apples and Mushrooms

1 cup (3½ oz/100 g) peeled and medium-diced apples
4 cups (8 oz/225 g) morel mushrooms, cleaned
1 teaspoon thyme leaves
½ teaspoon blend oil
1 tablespoon chopped golden raisins
Salt

MAKE THE POTATO CRÊPE BATTER

Place the potatoes in a medium pot and cover with cold water. Bring to a boil over medium heat. As soon as the water reaches a boil, remove the pot from the heat and let the potatoes rest in the hot water for 5 minutes. Drain the potatoes and allow to cool.

Prepare a large bowl of cold water. Once the potatoes are cool, shred on a medium box grater or in a food processor (which is what we do) directly into the cold water. Rinse the shredded potatoes. You will need about 3½ oz (100 g) shredded potatoes per crêpe.

In a medium bowl, whisk together the egg, milk, butter, and brandy. In a separate large mixing bowl, sift together the dry ingredients. Pour the egg mixture into the dry ingredients. Whisk gently to combine (do not beat). Refrigerate for 1 hour.

Keep the crêpe batter and the potatoes separate until ready to serve.

MAKE THE BRAISED LEEKS

Melt the butter in a small saucepan over low heat. Add the leeks and cook for 6 minutes, until soft and translucent, taking care to keep them from browning or caramelizing. Add the white wine, mustard, and apple cider vinegar and cook until the liquid has evaporated. Season with salt and set aside.

MAKE THE ROASTED APPLES AND MUSHROOMS

Preheat the oven to 350°F/180°C. Line a baking sheet with parchment paper.

In a small bowl, toss together the apples, mushrooms, thyme, oil, and a little salt. Spread on the baking sheet and roast for 12 minutes. Let cool. Add the golden raisins. Season with salt and set aside.

TO SERVE

Whisk the crêpe batter, then transfer to a squeeze bottle. Drain the potatoes and squeeze dry.

Heat an 8-inch (20 cm) cast iron skillet (or similar) over medium-high heat. Add one-quarter of the butter and one-quarter of the shredded potato. Season generously with salt. Using a fork, spread the potatoes over the surface of the pan, creating a lacy, weblike pattern. Cook for 4–6 minutes without touching, so the potatoes fuse together. If they seem to be browning too quickly, decrease the heat and rotate the pan.

Once the potatoes are cooked through and crisp at the edges, lift the pan and tilt 60 degrees. Using the squeeze bottle, squirt the batter into the pan in a zig zag pattern, starting at the top edge and going down, finally circling the outer circumference of the potatoes, all while rotating the pan and adjusting the angle of the tilt. (This keeps the crêpe batter from sitting in one place and pooling, which would make it thick and gummy. You want as thin and even a layer of batter as possible.) Return to the flame and cook, without disturbing, for 1 minute, until the underside is crispy and golden brown.

While the crêpe is cooking, reheat the apple-mushroom mixture on a small tray in the oven, if needed. Once hot, place one-quarter of the vegetable mix on half the cooked crêpe and top with a quarter of the Comté. Using a flexible fish spatula or offset spatula, fold the crêpe in half and place on a large plate. Repeat the process 3 times.

Cook 4 sunny-side-up eggs and place 1 alongside each crêpe.

In a small mixing bowl, combine the spring greens, radishes, and vinaigrette. Season with salt and pepper and place a handful alongside the finished crêpes. Season the egg with black pepper and Maldon sea salt.

To Serve

3¼ oz (90g) butter, cubed
2 oz (50 g) Comté, shredded
4 eggs
8 cups (3½ oz/100 g) mixed spring greens (arugula/rocket, mustard, pea shoots, etc.)
1½ oz (40 g) radishes, shaved
2 tablespoons Simple Vinaigrette (page 249)
Maldon sea salt
Salt and freshly ground black pepper

Image on page 53

SPELT CRÊPE WITH APPLE MOSTARDA AND GRUYÈRE

10 20

Spelt flour is a genetic precursor to wheat—same family, different species—with a distinctively nutty, sweet flavor. Although it can be substituted in many recipes on a 1:1 basis, we caution that the gluten in spelt flour behaves less reliably. To keep the structure of the crêpe, we substituted a small percentage of the all-purpose (plain) flour in our usual recipe with spelt flour, then changed from butter to extra-virgin olive oil to get a silky texture and luxurious mouthfeel.

Some notes on making crêpes. Your goal here is to pour the thinnest layer of batter in the pan as possible without gaps or tears, going edge to edge, with enough heat that you get a golden color on either side. Remember that you, not the stove, are in control of the heat! You may need to cook off a crêpe or two before you get the temperature dialed in just right. You want to cook the crêpes quickly, without burning. The batter itself is cold, so every time you make a crêpe, the temperature of the pan will drop. So keep the heat up medium-high. Know that you can control the heat not just with the knob on the stove, but also by changing the distance between the bottom of the pan and the flame. Lift the pan up if it gets too hot. As you get to know the viscosity of the batter and dial in your technique, the process gets easier, I promise.

MAKE THE SPELT CRÊPES

In a medium mixing bowl, whisk together the egg, milk, and olive oil. In a small mixing bowl, combine the all-purpose (plain) and spelt flours with the sugar and salt. Whisk the dry ingredients into the wet until smooth. Transfer to a blender and purée, then set aside and chill for 1 hour.

Heat a nonstick 10-inch (25 cm) skillet (frying pan) over medium heat. Coat with vegetable spray (yes, even with a nonstick pan). Lift the pan off the heat, then pour in 2 oz (50 g) of crêpe batter, rotating the pan like a gyroscope so the batter spreads evenly across the entire surface. Return the pan to the heat and cook for 2–3 minutes, until the edges are set and the underside is beginning to color. With an offset spatula or just with your fingers (tough-hand chef move, but it's the easiest), pick up the crêpe and flip it onto its other side. Cook for 2–3 minutes, until golden, and set aside. Repeat with the remaining batter to make 4 crêpes.

MAKE THE SWISS CHARD

Heat the oil in a medium saucepan. Add the onions and sauté for 5–7 minutes, or until translucent. Add the Swiss chard and sauté for about 3 minutes, just long enough to wilt the greens. Season with salt.

MAKE THE APPLE MOSTARDA

In a medium saucepan, combine all the ingredients (except the lemon juice and pepper) and add ½ cup (4 oz/120 g) water. Cover and cook over low heat for 20 minutes, until the apples have completely softened. Purée with an immersion blender. Add the lemon juice and a few cracks of black pepper.

TO SERVE

Preheat the oven to 350°F/180°C. Lay the crêpes flat on a clean work surface. Spread the center of each with ½ tablespoon of mostarda. Top with the Gruyère and Swiss chard, dividing equally. To fold the crêpe, think of it like a clock. The first fold will start by pinching the crêpe at five o'clock, then fold that edge into the center. Next, pinch the crêpe at 7 o'clock and fold that edge over the other. You should have a stuffed triangle of sorts. Place this on a baking sheet and reheat in the oven for 2–3 minutes, until warmed through.

SERVES 4

Spelt Crêpes

1 egg
6 tablespoons whole milk
2 teaspoons extra-virgin olive oil
¼ cup (1¼ oz/35 g) all-purpose (plain) flour
½ oz (15 g) spelt flour
½ teaspoon superfine (caster) sugar
⅛ teaspoon salt
Vegetable oil spray

Swiss Chard

2 tablespoons olive oil
1½ oz (40 g) onion, chopped
1 bunch Swiss chard (11 oz/300 g)
Salt

Apple Mostarda

2 cups (8 oz/225 g) finely diced apple
1 oz (25 g) fennel, minced
1 teaspoon grated fresh ginger
1 teaspoon sugar
1 tablespoon + 1 teaspoon whole grain mustard
2 teaspoons white wine vinegar
½ teaspoon lemon juice
Black pepper

To Serve

1¼ oz (35 g) Gruyère, shredded

BROWN BUTTER TURMERIC GRANOLA

05 20

Full of texture, five different cereals, grains, and seeds, fresh local pecans from Three Sisters Garden, chewy morsels of dates and golden raisins, and a totally addictive combination of brown butter and spices, this granola has become my go-to snack. So much so that the sous chefs hide it from me; my daily snacks were throwing off the pars.

We serve it with house-made yogurt, seasonal fruit, a drizzle of olive oil, and leaves of herbs and flowers. But you do you. Add a dice of juicy fresh fruit like apples or berries, or maybe pomegranates, mandarin slices, grapes tossed with lemon—whatever you crave, whatever looks good at the market, whatever keeps you going through the day.

SERVES 4

Candied Pecans
2 cups (7¾ oz/220 g) pecans
1 tablespoon honey
¼ cup (2 oz/50 g) sugar
¼ teaspoon salt

Turmeric Granola
¼ cup (2 oz/50 g) millet
¼ cup + 1 tablespoon (2¼ oz/60 g) quinoa
1¾ cup (5½ oz/160 g) rolled oats
¾ cup (3½ oz/100 g) sunflower seeds
2 tablespoons sesame seeds
3¼ oz (90 g) butter
½ teaspoon ground turmeric
½ teaspoon ground coriander
¼ teaspoon ground fenugreek
¼ teaspoon ground black pepper
⅓ cup (2½ fl oz/75 g) honey
¼ cup + 2 tablespoons (2¾ oz/70 g) brown sugar
½ teaspoon salt
½ cup (2½ oz/60 g) golden raisins, chopped
¼ cup + 1 tablespoon (2 oz/50 g) dates, chopped

MAKE THE CANDIED PECANS
Preheat the oven to 350°F/180°C. Line a baking sheet with parchment paper.

Place the pecans on the baking sheet and toast for 7 minutes. Remove from the oven but leave the oven on.

Combine the honey, sugar, 2 tablespoons water, and salt in a small saucepan. Bring to a boil over medium heat. Add the toasted pecans and stir with a heatproof spatula, coating the nuts in the syrup. Reduce the heat to low and cook, stirring constantly, until there is no liquid left at the bottom of the pan. Transfer the nuts back to the parchment-lined baking sheet and bake for 15 minutes, until the pecans are nicely caramelized and no longer sticky.

MAKE THE TURMERIC GRANOLA
With the oven still at 350°F/180°C, line another baking sheet with parchment paper.

Bring 1 quart (1 liter) of water to a boil in a saucepan set over high heat. Remove from the heat and add the millet and quinoa. Soak for 30 minutes, then drain.

In a large mixing bowl, combine the oats, sunflower seeds, and sesame seeds.

Melt the butter in a medium saucepan over medium heat and cook until the solids are golden brown and lightly caramelized with a nutty fragrance. Add the turmeric, coriander, fenugreek, and black pepper, then immediately remove from the heat. Add this butter-spice mixture to the oat mixture and stir to combine.

In a separate large saucepan, combine the honey, brown sugar, and salt. Cook over low heat until melted and smooth, then pour in the oat mixture and the soaked grains. Stir thoroughly to combine.

Spread the mixture out on the parchment-lined baking sheet and bake for 45 minutes, rotating the pan and stirring the mixture every 10 minutes.

Remove from the heat and stir in the candied pecans, raisins, and dates. Allow to cool and store in an airtight container.

CARDAMOM **SWIRL** FRENCH TOAST

01 22

For a long time, we served two different French toasts: a regular and a "special." The special one was sourdough topped with seasonal fruit, while the regular one was the same bread, bought from a local bakery, served with syrup and butter. But then we started making the bread ourselves and got wild with the types of creations used for French toast—brioche, cornbread, chocolate challah, Meyer lemon loaf—as well as the accompanying sauces and toppings. Because these were so popular, we stopped offering the regular version altogether.

There were a few kids disappointed by the switch. Some adults, too. But once they tried the house-made specialty breads like this gorgeous cardamom swirl made by baker Kevin Quinn, the pain of losing the "regular French" was gone. It's something about the way the cardamom in this recipe works its allure. Paired with candied pistachio, citrus, and white chocolate, the fragrant spice in this bread makes a breakfast staple into a composed dessert. Full of nuance and surprising turns of phrase. You won't miss the maple syrup at all.

SERVES 4

Custard

2 eggs
½ cup + 2 tablespoons (4½ oz/125 g) superfine (caster) sugar
2 cups (16 fl oz/475 g) whole milk
Scant ½ cup (3¾ fl oz/115 g) heavy (double) cream
½ teaspoon vanilla extract
¼ teaspoon salt

Satsuma Marmalade

3¾ oz (110 g) minced citrus peels
3 tablespoons granulated sugar
½ cup (4 fl oz/120 g) grapefruit juice
½ cup (4 fl oz/120 g) orange juice
1 teaspoon apple pectin

White Chocolate Crème Anglaise

½ cup + 2 tablespoons (4¾ fl oz/145 g) whole milk
½ cup + 1 tablespoon (4½ fl oz/135 g) heavy (double) cream
2¾ oz (70 g) white chocolate, chopped
¼ teaspoon vanilla extract
2 egg yolks
2 tablespoons superfine (caster) sugar

Whipped Yogurt

Scant ½ cup (3¾ fl oz/115 g) heavy (double) cream
2 tablespoons powdered (icing) sugar
⅓ cup + 2 teaspoons (2¾ fl oz/85 g) Greek yogurt

MAKE THE CUSTARD

In a medium mixing bowl, whisk together the eggs and sugar, then whisk in the milk, cream, vanilla, and salt. Refrigerate until ready to use.

MAKE THE SATSUMA MARMALADE

Bring a small pot of water to a boil over high heat. Blanch the citrus peels in the boiling water for 10 seconds, then strain. Discard the hot water and bring a fresh pot of water to a boil. Blanch the cooked peels once more.

In a small saucepan, combine 1 tablespoon of the sugar and the citrus juices. Bring to a boil over high heat.

Meanwhile, in a small bowl, whisk together the apple pectin and 2 tablespoons of sugar. Add the pectin mix to the juice mix, whisking constantly to avoid clumping. Cook over low heat for 15–20 minutes, until the mixture has thickened. Allow to cool, then transfer to an airtight container and refrigerate.

MAKE THE WHITE CHOCOLATE CRÈME ANGLAISE

In a medium saucepan, combine the milk, cream, white chocolate, and vanilla. Bring to a bare simmer over low heat. In a medium bowl, whisk together the egg yolks and sugar. Pour one-third of the milk mixture into the egg mixture while whisking vigorously, tempering the eggs so they don't scramble. Return this mixture to the saucepan and whisk to combine. Continue cooking over low heat, stirring constantly and making sure to stir along the bottom, until the mixture reaches 180°F/82°C. Remove from the heat and stir for 90 more seconds. Transfer to an airtight container, allow to cool, then cover and refrigerate.

MAKE THE WHIPPED YOGURT

In the bowl of a stand mixer fitted with the whisk attachment, whisk the cream and powdered (icing) sugar on high speed until stiff peaks form. Reduce speed to low and slowly whisk in the yogurt until combined.

MAKE THE CANDIED PISTACHIOS

Preheat the oven to 350°F/180°C. Line a baking sheet with parchment paper.

In a small saucepan, combine the vinegar, sugar, and 2 tablespoons water. Bring to a boil over medium-high heat. Add the pistachios and cook for 5 minutes. Drain any excess liquid and transfer the nuts to the parchment-lined baking sheet. Sprinkle with a pinch of salt. Bake for 10–12 minutes, until toasted. Let cool, then chop coarsely.

TO SERVE

Preheat a griddle or large sauté pan over medium heat.

Dip a slice of brioche into the custard for 15–20 seconds, until it is thoroughly soaked but not sodden. Cook on the griddle for about 1–2 minutes, until golden brown. Turn over and repeat on the other side. Transfer to a platter and keep warm. Repeat with the remaining slices.

Divide the crème anglaise among the plates. Add the toast, followed by a heaping tablespoon of satsuma marmalade, then the candied pistachios, whipped yogurt, and a sprinkle of powdered (icing) sugar.

Candied Pistachios

2 tablespoons apple cider vinegar
6 tablespoons granulated sugar
½ cup (2½ oz/65 g) shelled pistachios
Salt

To Serve

8 × ¾-inch (1.5 cm) thick slices Brioche with cardamom filling (page 253)
Powdered (icing) sugar

Image on page 62

OMELET WITH FRENCH BEANS AND HAZELNUT TOAST

09 16

If your introduction to the omelet came at an American diner, as mine did, in the form of an enormous "Montana," which your father ordered and which arrived on an oval plate with hashbrowns and eight damp slices of white toast, you might need an open mind to appreciate this recipe. Our omelets at Lula are of a style commonly referred to as "French" and are to U.S. diner omelets as instant pudding is to pot de crème.

That said, sometimes I do love a good, plump diner omelet. So what, then, is the difference? First, a French omelet is delicate and tender, rolled, not folded, with an almost crêpe-like exterior filled with gooey, custardy, softly scrambled egg. It is never browned and never "fluffy." It is always cooked with rich butter in an amount that is measurably more than a "pat." Sometimes it is flavored simply with herbs or crème fraîche, or maybe, as with this recipe, a morsel of cheese.

Making a good French omelet is an experience of pure, transformative beauty. Very similar to the deep feelings I get when making risotto. One simple ingredient, the egg, is stirred into a complex web of texture and form, into something so unlike its original state that it's shocking every time you do it. It's an example of the power of our human hands.

It can be maddeningly hard to learn how to make these things yourself, especially if you've seen firsthand how beautiful they can be. In 2016, a bit of good luck found me at a chef's symposium where the opening ceremony featured Jacques Pépin, live on stage, making an omelet in front of an entire audience of chefs. He showed no sign of stress. This was the man whose *La Technique* was like a Cooking 101 textbook when Lea and I first started as professional chefs. I felt a kind of circle closing around me. I watched him swirl the butter in a pan. He scrambled the eggs with a fork in a flurry of tiny motions. The word I'd use for him is fluent.

As I witnessed the sublime human touch of Jacques Pépin, a man making breakfast into a poetic form, I saw how much I had to learn.

SERVES 4

Sorrel Aioli

1 egg yolk
2 teaspoons white wine vinegar
1 clove garlic
¼ teaspoon salt, plus extra for seasoning
¾ cup (6 fl oz/175 ml) blend oil
1¼ oz (30 g) sorrel leaves (stems removed), chopped

Sorrel Gremolata

¼ oz/10 g sorrel, finely chopped
¼ oz/10 g parsley, finely chopped
1 clove garlic, minced
¼ cup (2 fl oz/60 g) blend oil
⅛ teaspoon salt

Wax Beans

3¾ oz (115 g) wax beans, green (pole) beans, or haricot verts
Salt

Hazelnut Butter

¼ cup (1¼ oz/30 g) hazelnuts
3¾ oz (115 g) butter, softened
1½ teaspoons Roasted Garlic purée (page 246)
½ teaspoon grated lemon zest
¼ teaspoon white wine vinegar
¼ teaspoon salt

MAKE THE SORREL AIOLI

In a blender, combine the egg yolk, vinegar, garlic, and salt. Purée until smooth. With the blender running, slowly pour the oil in a thin, steady stream to create a thick emulsion with a mayonnaise-like texture. If the mixture becomes too thick, add a couple drops of cold water. When all the oil has been added, add the chopped sorrel and taste for seasoning.

MAKE THE SORREL GREMOLATA

In a small bowl, stir together the sorrel, parsley, and garlic with the oil and salt, then turn out onto the cutting board and chop again, oil and all. Set aside.

MAKE THE WAX BEANS

Bring a small pot of water to a boil over high heat. Salt generously. Fill a small mixing bowl with a 50/50 mix of ice and water. Cook the beans in the boiling water for 30 seconds, then immediately plunge into the ice water to stop the cooking. When cold, drain and cut into thin rounds. Place in a small mixing bowl and toss with the sorrel gremolata. Taste and adjust the seasoning.

MAKE THE HAZELNUT BUTTER

Preheat the oven to 350°F/180°C.

Place the hazelnuts on a baking sheet and toast in the oven for about 10 minutes, until slightly golden. Cool, then finely chop. In a small mixing bowl, combine the hazelnuts with the remaining ingredients.

TO SERVE

In a large mixing bowl, whisk the eggs until completely blended (no weird strands of whites and no clumps of yolk; this is going to take some muscle). Season with salt and pepper.

Make the omelets one at a time. Heat an 8-inch (20 cm) non-stick egg pan over medium heat. Add 1 tablespoon butter, which should melt and foam but not sizzle or brown. (Do not cook an omelet in scorched butter. If the pan is too hot, remove it from the heat and wait.) Add a quarter of the eggs, or about 3 fl oz (90 ml) to the frying pan. Either with a rubber spatula, silicone whisk, or the back of a fork, start whisking right away, shaking the pan as you mix. Stir the eggs constantly, pulling them from the pan's periphery to its center, until the eggs have set into a very soft scramble. You want quick, vigorous movements and a result that can only be described as "custardy" —soft, creamy, with little curds and tight ribbons of cooked egg. Remove the pan from the heat. Knock the pan on the stove to settle the egg mixture.

Place 2 tablespoons of the sorrel aioli and a quarter of the stracciatella in the center of the omelet before rolling it. Then, using a fork or rubber spatula and starting at the edge closest to you, begin to roll the omelet back onto itself. Once you've rolled half, rotate the pan and start rolling from the other side so you have 2 rolls meeting in the center, like a scroll. Turn the omelet onto a plate with the seam-side down.

Repeat with the remaining butter, eggs, aioli, and stracciatella until you have 4 omelets.

Top the omelets with the beans. Serve each with a slice of sourdough bread smeared with a heaping tablespoon of hazelnut butter.

To Serve

8 eggs
4 tablespoons butter
3¾ oz (115 g) stracciatella
4 × ¾-inch (1.5 cm) slices sourdough toast
Salt and black pepper

Image on page 63

SMOKED **TROUT** SCRAMBLE

06 02

Rushing Waters Fisheries trout farm in Palmyra, Wisconsin, is our source for truly local, high-quality farmed fish. Over ten thousand years ago, a glacier rolled through this land, leaving behind an imprint of hills and valleys, lakes and ponds. If you're not from the Midwest, the sheer flatness and limitless sky of the prairie is something you'll never get used to. One of the reasons I was so drawn to this farm when I first visited it on a sourcing trip was that the landscape didn't make me feel like I was going to fall off the earth into the sky. I felt strangely grounded.

The glacier left behind an aquifer that bubbles up into natural spring water ponds, in which Peter Fritsch and his team at Rushing Waters raise super fresh, clean, sweet rainbow trout. They only harvest when you place your order, then ship the fresh fish overnight the next day.

We smoke the fish ourselves, though it is also available pre-smoked. The key for this recipe is to keep the eggs soft-scrambled while folding in the cream cheese and arugula (rocket) at the very end.

In a medium mixing bowl, whisk the eggs until thoroughly combined. Heat an 8-inch (20 cm) nonstick frying pan over medium heat. Add the oil and trout. Cook for 15 seconds, then add the beaten eggs. Using a heatproof spatula, stir the eggs constantly and rapidly, in small circular motions, to produce a scramble with small, wet curds the texture of cottage cheese. Remove from the heat when the eggs are nearly cooked. Stir in the cream cheese and return to the heat, gently folding the cheese into the egg mixture. Taste for seasoning.

At the last moment, fold in the baby arugula (rocket), so it just wilts slightly in the scramble. Top with a few dill sprigs.

SERVES 2

6 eggs
1½ teaspoons blend oil
2¾ oz (70 g) smoked trout, flaked into pieces
2 tablespoons + 2 teaspoons cream cheese
Handful of baby arugula (rocket)
Dill sprigs
Salt

EGG SALAD
ON TOAST WITH
RADISHES AND DILL

Here we have classic flavors, with the addition of the fermented chile-citrus paste from Japan called yuzu kosho (page 21). This condiment gives anything a funky depth and sass. Our egg salad is made with jammy eggs, just set and still a little gooey, then mixed with aioli. So, yes, egg on egg on egg. Using softer eggs instead of hard-boiled makes for a creamier result, delightfully messy when prepping but delicious to eat.

SERVES 4

Egg Salad

¼ cup (1 oz/25 g) cornichons

1 tablespoon Roasted Garlic purée (page 246)

1 teaspoon capers

½ teaspoon green yuzu kosho

Grated zest of ⅓ lemon

¼ cup + 2 tablespoons (3 fl oz/90 g) Roasted Garlic Aioli (page 248)

1 teaspoon apple cider vinegar

1 teaspoon honey

1 tablespoon minced chives

8 eggs

Salt and black pepper

To Serve

4 pieces toasted rye bread

4 radishes, sliced

Dill sprigs

Maldon sea salt

Marash chile flakes

MAKE THE EGG SALAD

In a medium bowl, mix the cornichons, roasted garlic, capers, and yuzu kosho. Transfer the mixture to a cutting board and chop until the mixture is homogenized and paste-like. Return to the bowl and fold in the lemon zest, roasted garlic aioli, apple cider vinegar, honey, and chives.

Bring a medium pot of water to a boil over high heat. Add the eggs and cook at a steady simmer for 9 minutes. Remove from the heat and let the eggs sit 1 more minute in the hot water. Drain the eggs and run cold water over them to stop the cooking. Refrigerate the eggs for 30 minutes, until cold. Peel the eggs and chop thoroughly—they will be messy and jammy. Fold this mess into the aioli mixture, then season with salt and pepper.

TO SERVE

Divide the egg mixture among the rye toasts. Garnish with sliced radishes, dill, Maldon sea salt, and a sprinkle of Marash chile flakes.

POZOLE VERDE
BY MIRVELLA

10 02

Mirvella Mesa has worked at Lula as a cook since 1999. She's been with us since the days when we worked on top of stacked milk crates. One Halloween, I remember her children sitting in costumes at her feet, waiting for her to finish making a batch of pozole. Soups and stews of all kinds are Mirvella's specialty—from the Sweet and Sour Cabbage Soup (page 84) to the Chickpea and Fennel Tagine (page 36) to the endless seasonal variations.

I asked Mirvella to contribute a recipe of her own for this book—her Pozole Verde. She's made this dish for us many times over the years, and it became a special that regulars would often request we turn into a staple. We've done red pozole with chicken thigh, white pozole with celery root, and this favorite green version with pork shoulder. Mirvella has brought this recipe from her home to ours with love and kindness. She's the best.

NB: In this recipe we've used canned (tinned) hominy to speed things up. At the restaurant, we use the otherworldly dried hominy from Rancho Gordo, prepared to their specifications.

In a large stock pot, add 3 quarts (3 liters) water, the pork shank (hock), pork shoulder, half the white onion, half the garlic, the bay leaves, and 1 teaspoon of salt and bring to a boil. Reduce the heat to a steady simmer, and cook, skimming the foam off regularly, for 1½ hours, or until the pork is fork-tender. Strain the meat and reserve the stock. Let the pork cool, then break it all into large chunks by hand.

Heat 2 tablespoons of the oil in a large pot over medium heat. Add the tomatillos, serranos, poblanos, remaining onion, and remaining garlic. Sauté for 10 minutes, or until the onions are translucent. Add the pepitas, lettuce, spinach, cilantro (coriander), and epazote, and sauté for a further 3 minutes. Remove from the heat and allow to cool. Purée in a blender along with 3 cups (25 fl oz/750 ml) of the reserved pork stock.

Heat 2 tablespoons of the oil in a large stock pot over medium heat. Add the tomatillo mixture and cook for 10 minutes, stirring constantly. Add the hominy and cook for 10 minutes more. Add the oregano, reduce heat to low, and simmer for 10 more minutes. Add the pork and simmer for 15–25 minutes on low to let the ingredients meld together. Taste and adjust seasoning.

TO SERVE

Divide the hot pozole among 4 bowls. Top each with a poached egg, and serve the shredded cabbage, lime wedges, radishes, cilantro (coriander), tortilla chips, and avocado wedges alongside—the last of which (ahem), if you're like me and it's the one food you can do without, you may skip.

SERVES 4

11 oz (300 g) pork shank (hock)
1 lb (450 g) pork shoulder
2¼ oz (60 g) white onion, chopped
6 cloves garlic, minced
3 bay leaves
4 tablespoons blend oil
3 tomatillos (3 oz/80 g), diced
¾ oz (20 g) serrano peppers, deseeded and sliced
1¼ oz (30 g) poblano peppers, chopped
½ cup (2 oz/50 g) raw pepitas (pumpkin seeds)
1¼ oz (30 g) romaine lettuce
1 cup (1¼ oz/30 g) spinach
1 cup (1¼ oz/30 g) cilantro (coriander)
8 epazote leaves
1 lb/450 g canned (tinned) hominy (see NB)
2 teaspoons chopped oregano
Salt

To Serve
4 poached eggs
Shredded cabbage
Lime wedges
Sliced radishes
Cilantro (coriander) sprigs
Tortilla chips
Avocado wedges

LAKE WHITEFISH DIP WITH MELBA TOAST

05 15

"Whitefish" or "white fish?"

It took me a few years as a professional chef to get rid of my bias around the term "white fish." For us New Englanders, and I'm assuming for folks from both coasts, a "white fish" is simply any type of fish with flaky, pale-colored flesh, such as cod, halibut, haddock, sole, or fluke. But when I moved to the Great Lakes, I learned the hard way that whitefish is not a generic term at all and refers instead to the universally beloved *Coregonus clupeaformis*, or lake whitefish. This species is found in the cold freshwater of the Great Lakes (and a thousand lesser lakes, too, I suppose), with a mild, sweet flavor that offends no one and which happens to be great smoked.

This recipe is our homage to the smoked-fish-and-sour-cream dip you would find in a Wisconsin shore town but using a 50/50 mix of aioli and crème fraîche to keep the texture light and airy. We like a slice of thick, brittle Melba toast with this dip, but try potato chips (crisps) or a toasted French baguette.

MAKE THE WHITEFISH DIP

In the bowl of a stand mixer fitted with the whisk attachment, combine all the ingredients except the whitefish and salt. Whisk until uniform and smooth. Switch to the paddle attachment. Add the whitefish and mix on low, just until combined. Do not overmix or whip. Taste and add salt and/or more lemon juice as needed.

MAKE THE SUNFLOWER SEEDS

Set a medium sauté pan over medium-high heat. Add the sunflower seeds and oil and cook for 5 minutes, until fragrant and toasted. Season with salt, then transfer to a paper-towel-lined plate to cool.

MAKE THE CASCABEL CHILE OIL

Combine all the ingredients in a blender and purée on high speed until smooth. Strain through a fine-mesh sieve or tamis.

TO SERVE

Using either a platter or 4 individual plates, spoon the whitefish dip into the middle of the dish and press on it with the back of a large spoon, making a divot in the center. Drizzle the sunflower seeds around the dip, then sprinkle chives everywhere. Serve with the chile oil and Melba toast on the side.

SERVES 4

Whitefish Dip
¼ cup (2 oz/60 g) crème fraîche
¼ cup (2 oz/60 g) Roasted Garlic Aioli (page 248)
2 tablespoons Roasted Garlic purée (page 246)
Grated zest of ½ lemon
Grated zest of ½ orange
1 tablespoon distilled white vinegar
1 teaspoon lemon juice, plus extra if needed
1 teaspoon grated horseradish
¼ teaspoon red yuzu kosho
⅛ teaspoon black pepper
7 oz (200 g) smoked whitefish, cleaned of skin and bone, flaked
Salt

Sunflower Seeds
¼ cup (1½ oz/40 g) sunflower seeds
½ teaspoon blend oil
Salt

Cascabel Chile Oil
Scant 1 cup (7½ fl oz/225 g) blend oil
4 Cascabel chiles
2 cloves garlic, chopped
2 shallots (3½ oz/100 g), chopped
1 tablespoon sherry vinegar
¼ teaspoon salt

To Serve
1 tablespoon very thinly sliced chives
8 slices Melba toast

BLACK PEPPER SPAETZLE

I met Patrick in the summer of 2000 at the back door of the original kitchen at Lula, when he arrived alongside Greg Gunthorp from Gunthorp Farms. He was Greg's assistant and the entrance was unforgettable.

Patrick looked like an extra from *Almost Famous*, with long, wild Randy Rhoads-style curls. He was tall, wiry, maybe even gaunt, yet came through the door carrying a bin of pork shoulder and whole chickens with ease. He was wearing a stained sleeveless white shirt with tiger-claw-like tears in the fabric.

A few words later and I immediately knew I was in the presence of a brilliant man. His mind raced at supersonic speeds, almost faster than he could speak. I grew close to Patrick over the years. He lived quietly, studiously, a profoundly hopeful, healing soul at odds with the modern world. He donated his time to farmers like the Gunthorps because he believed in the mission of supporting organic agriculture and animal husbandry.

Patrick was also known to restaurant chefs because he had a side hustle sourcing specialized ingredients from around the world. Chefs who took the time to talk with him late at night when he made his deliveries found themselves in impromptu tasting sessions of otherworldly dandelion miso and golden mirin from Japan, fragrant whole buckwheat grains, tiny jars of mustard oil that burned the tip of your tongue, and fruity, sweet black walnuts.

I remember the crumpled brown paper bag that the walnuts came in. Like a young boy's lunch shoved in the pocket of his coat. These nuts came from the trees on a property eight hours north in Wisconsin, owned by an elderly couple who cracked the fruit by hand as a cure for the arthritis they both shared.

Black walnut shells are notoriously difficult to open. Folks have been known to drive over their harvest in a desperate attempt to crack the hard outer shell. Once harvested, the nut meat is distinctively fruity in taste and aroma, which is both its appeal and its demise. Nothing goes rancid quicker than black walnuts.

Look for fruit with a pleasant aroma like an apricot pit (stone). Store them in the freezer and use sparingly. In our recipe, we created a pesto to fold into a peppery, rye-based spaetzle. Served at brunch, with wintry flavors of rosemary, squash, and mushroom, the black walnut makes for an evocative and alluring dish.

I am sure Patrick is somewhere in the fields and forests of Wisconsin. Or maybe further away. He changed my life back in those days by sharing the idea that what you eat can save you. He believed that good food is good medicine and that knowing your farmer is the first step in knowing your world.

SERVES 4

Spaetzle
½ cup + 2 tablespoons (3 oz/80 g) all-purpose (plain) flour
3 tablespoons rye flour
½ teaspoon black pepper
¼ teaspoon dry mustard
½ teaspoon salt
1 small egg
⅓ cup plus 1 tablespoon (3½ fl oz/ 100 g) whole milk

Black Walnut Pesto
1 cup (1 oz/25 g) parsley, chopped
1 cup (4 oz/125 g) black walnuts, lightly toasted
¼ oz (10 g) chopped rosemary
½ cup (1¼ oz/35 g) grated Parmesan
Scant ½ cup (3¾ fl oz/110 g) olive oil
2 tablespoons lemon juice
1 clove garlic
¼ teaspoon salt

Delicata Squash and Maitake Mushrooms
4 tablespoons olive oil
2 tablespoons chopped rosemary
½ teaspoon cracked black pepper
Grated zest of 1 lemon
1 teaspoon salt
1–2 delicata squash (14 oz/400 g), sliced into 1-inch (2.5 cm) thick rounds, seeds removed
4 clusters maitake mushrooms (1½ oz/40 g)

Grilled Lemon Powder
2 lemons

MAKE THE SPAETZLE

In a medium mixing bowl, whisk together both flours, pepper, dry mustard, and salt. In a separate mixing bowl, whisk together the egg and milk. Fold the wet ingredients into the dry to create a smooth, thick batter.

Bring a large pot of water to a boil over high heat. Working in batches of about ½ cup (4 fl oz/120 g) at a time, spoon the batter into a spaetzle maker held over the pot of water (or pass the batter through the large holes of a colander). Cook the spaetzle in the boiling water for 30 seconds. Remove with a slotted spoon and transfer to a bowl. Repeat until all the batter is used.

MAKE THE BLACK WALNUT PESTO

Combine all the ingredients in a food processor fitted with the blade attachment, then grind into a paste.

MAKE THE DELICATA SQUASH AND MAITAKE MUSHROOMS

Preheat the oven to 375°F/190°C. Line 2 baking sheets with parchment paper.

In a mixing bowl, whisk together the olive oil, rosemary, pepper, lemon zest, and salt. Add the squash and mushrooms and toss to coat. Arrange on the prepared baking sheet, keeping the mushrooms and squash separate. Roast for 20–25 minutes, until the squash is tender.

MAKE THE GRILLED LEMON POWDER

Cut the lemons in half and grill on a gas or charcoal grill until very charred on all sides—literally almost burnt. Leave to cool, then transfer to a dehydrator until entirely dried, approximately 12 hours. Then grind to a powder in a spice grinder.

TO SERVE

Heat the butter in a large sauté pan over medium-high heat. Add the spaetzle and sauté, toasting in the butterfat, for 3 minutes, or until golden brown. Remove from the heat and toss with ¼ cup (2 fl oz/ 60 ml) pesto. Season with salt and lemon juice to taste.

If necessary, reheat the mushrooms in a low oven until warm.

Cook 1 egg per person in the style of your choosing; we do sunny-side up. Season the eggs with Maldon sea salt and pepper.

Spoon 1 tablespoon aioli on 4 separate plates. Divide the roasted squash, maitakes and spaetzle among the plates, layering with leaves of dandelion greens (about 5 leaves per plate). Top with the eggs, grated Parmesan, and grilled lemon powder.

To Serve

2 tablespoons butter
Lemon juice, to taste
4 eggs
4 tablespoons Roasted Garlic Aioli (page 248)
20 dandelion green leaves
1 tablespoon + 1 teaspoon grated Parmesan
Maldon sea salt
Salt and freshly ground black pepper

Image on page 76

POLENTA CAKES

08 21

We have been making some version of polenta cakes with hollandaise since we opened in '99—from spring romps with asparagus and salmon to autumnal versions with squash, brown butter, and sage.

This recipe came after a trip to the Green City Farmers' Market one August morning in the summer of 2021. Carmen peppers, grown by Jerry at Froggy Meadow Farm, are an American version of the *corno di toro* Italian varietal. Translated as "bull's horn," the name describes the pepper's unusually long, tapered, hooked body, which gives people the mistaken impression that this pepper is going to be hot. It's actually the sweetest, firmest, fleshiest pepper we know, and when I saw them at Jerry's stand I immediately asked if we could buy them all. That summer we tried to preserve as many as possible by marinating them in vinegar and oil (see *sott'olio*, page 202).

From Janie's Mill in Illinois, we sourced the intensely aromatic "bloody butcher" cornmeal, flecked with red and white varieties of heirloom corn. Combining this richly flavored, coarse polenta with a standard yellow cornmeal gave us both the flavor and textures we wanted.

Feel free to follow this recipe in whole or in part. The cakes could be served on their own, with a side of crispy bacon for a simple breakfast, with a steak for dinner, or with roasted vegetables for a hearty meat-free entrée.

The recipe for the sott'olio of Carmen peppers yields nearly a full quart. It's quite the process, so you might want to make a large batch and save the rest in the refrigerator for 7 days—for snacks or for spooning on bread or pasta. Save every ounce of that delicious oil!

SERVES 4

Polenta Cakes
3 cups (25 fl oz/720 g) whole milk
¾ teaspoon salt
1 cup (5½ oz/160 g) yellow cornmeal
½ cup (2¾ oz/70 g) red heirloom cornmeal
¾ oz (20 g) grated Parmesan
Vegetable oil, for greasing

Sott'olio Peppers
1 lb (450 g) Carmen peppers
Scant 1 cup (7½ fl oz/225 g) blend oil
2 shallots (3½ oz/100 g)
2 cloves garlic, sliced
1¾ tablespoons white wine vinegar
½ teaspoon salt
Cracked black pepper
Olive oil, to cover

Roasted Cauliflower
4 cups (12 oz/350 g) bite-sized cauliflower florets
2 teaspoons blend oil
Salt

Hollandaise
3¼ oz (90 g) butter
3 egg yolks
1 teaspoon Dijon mustard
¼ teaspoon lemon juice
Pinch of cayenne pepper

MAKE THE POLENTA CAKES

In a medium, heavy-bottomed saucepan, bring the milk, 2 cups (16 fl oz/475 g) water, and salt to a simmer over medium-high heat. Add both cornmeals in a slow, steady stream while whisking continuously to keep lumps from forming. Stir to a porridge consistency. Reduce heat to low and cook, whisking regularly, for 30–40 minutes, until the mixture thickens and pulls away from the edge of the pot as you stir. Depending on the cornmeal, you may need to add water or extend the cooking time. Add the Parmesan, then taste and adjust the seasoning.

Lightly oil a 9 × 9-inch (23 × 23 cm) baking dish. Spoon the polenta into the dish and spread out evenly. Cover with parchment paper and refrigerate for at least 4 hours. When thoroughly cold, punch out 8 circles with a 3-inch (7.5 cm) biscuit (scone) cutter.

MAKE THE SOTT'OLIO PEPPERS

Char the peppers on the stove by placing them directly on the gas flame. Use a pair of tongs to turn the peppers and char all sides. Place in a bowl and cover with plastic wrap (cling film). Rest for 30 minutes. Peel off the charred skin and remove the seeds. Cut into medium dice.

Meanwhile, heat the blend oil in a small saucepan over low heat. Add the whole shallots. They should be just covered in oil. Bring to a simmer, then reduce the heat. Cook slowly for 30 minutes until the shallots are super soft. Remove them from the oil with a slotted spoon and place in a medium mixing bowl. Add the sliced garlic to the same warm oil in the pan and cook slowly for 5 minutes, until soft. Transfer to the bowl with the shallots.

Add the peppers to the mixing bowl. Season with white wine vinegar, salt, and a little cracked black pepper. Taste and adjust seasoning if necessary; the peppers should be bright and punchy with flavor. Transfer to a lidded container and top with olive oil until covered. Refrigerate until ready to use.

MAKE THE ROASTED CAULIFLOWER

Preheat the oven to 450°F/230C°.

In a mixing bowl, toss the cauliflower florets with the blend oil and a little salt until coated. Arrange in an even layer on a baking sheet and roast for 10–15 minutes, or until lightly charred and tender, but not overcooked.

MAKE THE HOLLANDAISE

Melt the butter in a small saucepan over medium heat. Keep warm.

Fill a medium saucepan with 4 cups (35 fl oz/950 g) water and bring to a light simmer over medium heat. In a stainless-steel mixing bowl that will fit over the pot to create a double boiler, combine the egg yolks, Dijon mustard, lemon juice, and cayenne. Whisk vigorously, then place on top of the pot of simmering water. Allow the eggs to heat for a few minutes, whisking continuously, then slowly add the butter, a little at a time, whisking vigorously between each addition. Continue until all the butter is incorporated and the hollandaise is thick and coats the back of a spoon. Season with salt and set aside in a warm (but not hot) place.

TO SERVE

Preheat the oven to 350°F/180°C.

Place the polenta cakes on a parchment-lined baking sheet and heat in the oven for 3–5 minutes, until warmed through.

Warm 2 tablespoons of the oil from the sott'olio in a medium saucepan over medium heat. Add the roasted cauliflower and heat until sizzling. Add 1 cup of the sott'olio peppers, reduce the heat to low, and gently warm the vegetables.

Cook the eggs in your preferred style; we do sunny-side-up.

Place 2 polenta cakes on each of 4 plates. Spoon the cauliflower and pepper on the side. Place an egg on top of each plate and season with salt and pepper. Spoon the warm hollandaise on top. Garnish with hemp seeds, dill sprigs, and shavings of Parmesan.

To Serve

4 eggs
2 tablespoons hemp seeds
Dill sprigs
Shaved Parmesan
Salt and freshly ground black pepper

Image on page 77

CRISPY RED RICE
AND CHICKEN

0916

We've been serving brunch rice bowls for years in some kind of prescient fog, not realizing we were being trendy at all. I think the appeal of a crispy rice bowl is the variety of textures and flavors you can fit into a single bite. For this version, we layered pieces of tender, tangy chicken thigh with savory onion, bitter radicchio, and a hard-boiled egg.

Our preference for this dish is to use the chewy bite and nutty flavor of Camargue red rice from the Rhône river delta in France, a variety that developed its red hue through natural mutation. To get that extra crispness, we add crunchy puffed rice and do a kind of stir-fry at the end, folding in some of the ingredients, like the spring onion and the radicchio, as the very last step. We keep veggies out until the end because they are full of water, and the steam released in the sauté pan would turn all that rice from deliciously crisp to damp and mushy.

SERVES 4

Red Rice

1½ cups (10 oz/280 g) red rice
¼ cup (1 oz/25 g) coarsely chopped pistachios
2¾ oz (70 g) Fennel Soffritto (page 194)
¼ cup (1½ oz/40 g) finely diced dried apricots

Yogurt-Marinated Chicken

4 boneless chicken thighs (1 lb 2 oz/500 g)
¼ cup + 2 teaspoons (2¼ oz/70 g) Greek yogurt
1 tablespoon Aromatic Spice Mix (page 248)
½ teaspoon salt

Roasted Spring Onions

3½ oz (100 g) spring onion bulbs, halved
1 teaspoon blend oil
⅛ teaspoon paprika
1 teaspoon cava vinegar
Salt

Seasoned Yogurt

¾ cup (6 fl oz/175 g) Greek yogurt
Grated zest of ½ lemon
¼ teaspoon lemon juice

To Serve

2 tablespoons olive oil
Lemon juice, to taste
½ cup (3 oz/80 g) chicories (such as radicchio and similar), torn into bite-size pieces
¼ cup (¼ oz/10 g) spring onion tops, thinly sliced
2 hard-boiled eggs (simmer for 8 minutes, then rest in the hot water for 1 minute before transferring to an ice bath), halved
½ cup (¼ oz/10 g) cilantro (coriander) leaves
Pistachios, grated, to garnish
Salt

MAKE THE RED RICE

Bring 2 cups (16 fl oz/475 g) water to a boil in a medium saucepan set over high heat. Salt generously. Add the rice, reduce heat to low, cover, and cook until the rice is tender and has absorbed the water.

Transfer ½ cup (3½ oz/100 g) cooked rice to a baking sheet and spread out evenly. Follow directions for the Puffed Rice recipe on page 247. Set aside.

Mix the remaining cooked rice with the pistachios, soffritto, and dried apricots. Add the puffed rice to the mix.

MAKE THE YOGURT-MARINATED CHICKEN

In a mixing bowl, combine the chicken, yogurt, spice mix, and salt. Cover and marinate overnight in the refrigerator.

The next day, preheat the oven to 350°F/180°C. Arrange the chicken on a parchment-lined sheet tray (rimmed baking tray). Roast for 35 minutes, until cooked through. Leave the oven on. When cool enough to handle, dice the chicken into 1-inch (2.5 cm) pieces and set aside.

MAKE THE ROASTED SPRING ONIONS

In another mixing bowl, toss the onion bulbs with oil and season with salt. Spread on a baking sheet and roast in the oven for 10 minutes at 350°F/180°C. Return to the mixing bowl and allow to cool. Add the paprika and vinegar and toss to coat.

MAKE THE SEASONED YOGURT

Whisk all the ingredients together in a small bowl. Refrigerate until ready to use.

TO SERVE

Warm the red rice mixture in a small saucepan over medium heat. Add the olive oil, roasted chicken, and roasted spring onions. Heat until warmed throughout, stirring to prevent the mixture from sticking to the bottom of the pan. Season with salt and lemon juice. Transfer to a mixing bowl. Mix in the chicories and spring onion tops. Taste and adjust the seasoning.

Divide the seasoned yogurt among 4 bowls. Top with the rice mixture, half a hard-boiled egg, and cilantro (coriander) leaves. Garnish with grated pistachio.

Where we started—stirring a big, steaming
pot of vegetables into some kind of dream.

SWEET AND SOUR CABBAGE SOUP

09 99

The original Lula soup and the recipe I get asked for the most often. The key ingredient here is kecap manis, a syrupy Indonesian soy sauce sweetened with palm sugar, without which this cabbage soup would lose its unique flavor. We use ABC's medium-sweet soy sauce (kecap manis Sedang), both here and in the recipe for The "Tineka" Sandwich (page 30), which were staples from Lea's work in the Logan Beach days in the '90s.

Before we took over the cafe, when we sold soup out of Lea's little car, there was a particular day I remember, in the late summer of '98, when we had ten or twenty samples of this cabbage soup in the back seat. We drove uptown to Lincoln Square, Andersonville, and Rogers Park with the windows down, summer wind picking up the enigmatic scents of ginger, coriander, tomato, and soy. I imagined the sweet aromatics wafting down the city streets, even turning heads. We left samples with disaffected baristas all over town. *Let us know what you think!* we chirped before heading to the next cafe. When we got in the car to drive back home, *O-o-h Child* by Five Stairsteps came on the radio and we sang along. The chorus became a kind of anthem for us as we started to work together that year and make plans for Lula. "Things will get brighter soon."

Place a large pot over medium heat, add the oil and heat until shimmering. Add the onion, ginger, garlic, sambal, and coriander and cook over low heat until the onions are translucent and soft, 15–20 minutes. Add the kecap manis and cook for an additional 10 minutes, until reduced by half. Stir in the cabbage, tomatoes, coconut milk, and stock and cook until the cabbage is fork-tender, about 20 minutes. Season with vinegar and salt to taste. Garnish with cilantro (coriander) and chives.

SERVES 4

¼ cup (2 fl oz/60 g) blend oil
6¾ oz (190 g) red onion, finely diced
1¼ oz (35 g) minced ginger
1¼ oz (35 g) minced garlic
1 tablespoon sambal oelek
1¼ teaspoons ground coriander
¾ cup (6 fl oz/175 ml) kecap manis (sweet soy sauce)
1 lb 2 oz (500 g) green cabbage, large-diced
1 × 14 fl oz (400 g) can crushed tomatoes (passata)
1 × 14 fl oz (400 g) can coconut milk
2 cups (16 fl oz/475 g) Vegetable Stock (page 255)
Distilled white vinegar, to taste
Small bunch cilantro (coriander), leaves picked, to garnish
Small handful of chives, sliced, to garnish
Salt

WATERMELON GAZPACHO

08 08

Our watermelon gazpacho is a luxurious, mostly raw preparation of summer melons and cucumber—tangy, zippy, and alive—shaped into candy-like orbs floating in a chilled tomato broth. We use a slow-simmered and puréed soffritto to give our broth contrasting depth of flavor and body. In this case, the tomato recedes into a savory supporting role.

Eating a spoonful of juicy, crunchy, fruity spheres is pretty much the most fun you'll have with a bowl of soup. But you will need to do the work with a melon baller to make these shapes. To remove the skin from a melon, you'll find it best to trim a little bit off both the top and stem sides, to get the round shape to sit steadily on a flat board. It should look like this: (_) . Then use your knife to cut off the skin in long strokes from top to bottom, removing... (((and then))). And let this be the last time someone gives you a cooking tip about melons using parentheses.

MAKE THE COMPRESSED WATERMELON, CANTALOUPE, AND CUCUMBER BALLS

Cut the skin from the melons following the instructions above. Using a melon baller, scoop out all surface-level flesh from the watermelon, cantaloupe, and cucumbers. Remove any seeds, then reserve the different balls in 3 separate containers.

Remove the seeds from the remaining melon and cucumbers and reserve the flesh for the gazpacho base.

In a mixing bowl, stir together the lime juice, sugar, and spices until the sugar dissolves. Fold in all the fruit balls, then compress the mixture in Cryovac bags for 15 minutes. Alternatively, marinate the fruit in a bowl in the refrigerator for 30–45 minutes.

MAKE THE SHALLOT, SUNGOLD, GINGER SOFFRITTO

In a small pot, cook all the ingredients until tender and soft, 15 minutes. Purée in the blender on high speed until smooth. Reserve in a container in the fridge until ready for use.

MAKE THE GAZPACHO BASE

Combine all the ingredients in a large bowl with the soffritto. Purée in batches in a blender. Strain each batch through a fine-mesh strainer or tamis and set aside.

TO SERVE

Divide the melon-cucumber balls and the sungold tomatoes among 4 small soup bowls. Divide the serrano and shallot slices among the bowls, laying them on top of the fruit as though they just fell there. Pour in ½ cup (4 fl oz/120 g) gazpacho base along the side of each bowl, and garnish with edible flowers.

SERVES 4

Compressed Watermelon, Cantaloupe, and Cucumber Balls
1 red watermelon, sweet and seedless if possible
1 ripe cantaloupe melon
4 cucumbers, peeled
Juice of 3 limes
1 tablespoon granulated sugar
Small pinch ground coriander
Small pinch pink peppercorns

Shallot, Sungold, Ginger Soffritto
1 medium shallot (1½ oz/45 g), thinly sliced
1 cup (6 oz/175 g) sungold tomato
1 tablespoon finely chopped ginger
¼ teaspoon pink peppercorns
2 tablespoons olive oil

Gazpacho Base
3 lb (1.4 kg) watermelon flesh (reserved from above), roughly chopped
10 oz (280 g) cantaloupe flesh (reserved from above), roughly chopped
10 oz (280 g) cucumber flesh (reserved from above), roughly chopped
3 large ripe red tomatoes (1 lb/480 g), seeds removed, roughly chopped
8 mint leaves
Juice of 2 limes
1 teaspoon salt

To Serve
Generous 1 cup (6 oz/175 g) sungold tomatoes, halved
1 serrano pepper, sliced paper-thin
1 shallot, sliced paper-thin
Edible flowers

CHILLED **CARROT** SOUP WITH **CHAMOMILE** AND **BLACK LIME**

0816

We served this carrot soup in Milan in 2016, as part of an educational trip with our food education foundation, Pilot Light. I invite you to imagine our famous (but now deceased) host chef, an octogenarian giant of Italian fine dining, as he took a late tour of the event like a general inspecting his ranks. At our table he stopped to stare me down.

"What is that?!" he demanded, gesticulating vaguely with his finger. I couldn't tell whether he was disgusted, curious, or both.

"*Zuppa di carote*," I said proudly.

He took a demitasse of our soup and gave it a vexed swirl. On the table beside me all my mise en place was arranged for the evening's service.

"And what is that?" he said, pointing at the table.

Nervously I gathered up my ingredients to show him, beginning with our luscious "creamy" chilled vegan carrot soup, the tiny carrot flowers and chamomile I had brought from home in my carry-on luggage, the alien dark stone of a fermented black lime.

"No, no, no, that, that, what is that?" he demanded.

"Oh, yes, the chamomile oil," I said. "This is made by steeping fresh chamomile flowers and bay leaves and other aromatics at a low temperature."

He did not ask for a taste.

"I," he said with a pause, "like *olio d'oliva. Olive* oil."

He set down the demitasse of soup and walked straight off into a group of admirers.

"A photo!" they called. "Over here! Just one, please! Maestro!"

And with kindness, he obliged.

SERVES 4-6

Carrot Soup

3 tablespoons + 1 teaspoon grapeseed oil
1 lb 3 oz (560 g) carrots, peeled and sliced
4½ oz (140 g) shallots, sliced
6 cloves garlic
1 tablespoon chamomile tea
1 teaspoon coriander seeds
3 cups (25 fl oz/750 ml) Vegetable Stock (page 255)
Scant 1¼ cups (9 fl oz/285 g) sherry
1 tablespoon sherry vinegar
½ cup (3½ oz/100 g) sugar
4 cups (32 fl oz/950 ml) fresh carrot juice
1 tablespoon fresh lemon juice
¼ teaspoon xanthan gum
Scant ½ cup (3¾ fl oz/115 g) olive oil
Salt

Roasted Baby Carrots

10 oz (300 g) baby carrots, peeled
2 tablespoons olive oil
Salt

To Serve

Carrot Top Gremolata (page 251)
Chamomile Oil (page 246)
Fresh chamomile flowers
Cilantro (coriander) leaves
Black lime powder

MAKE THE CARROT SOUP

Heat the grapeseed oil in a stock pot over medium heat. Add the carrots, shallots, and garlic. Sauté for 10 minutes. Add the chamomile tea, 1 tablespoon of salt, and coriander seeds. Sauté for 10 minutes more. Add the vegetable stock and ¼ cup (2 fl oz/60 ml) of the sherry. Bring the liquid to a gentle simmer and cook for 45–60 minutes, until the carrots are fork tender and most of the stock has reduced. Allow to cool a bit, then purée in batches in a blender. Finish with the sherry vinegar and season with salt to taste. This is the carrot purée.

Heat the remaining sherry and the sugar in a small saucepan over medium-high heat. Simmer for 15 minutes, until reduced to ⅓ cup.

In a mixing bowl, stir together the carrot juice, carrot purée, sherry reduction, lemon juice, and 1 teaspoon of salt. Working in batches, purée on high with the xanthan gum. With the machine running, add the olive oil in a slow stream, as though you were making an aioli, until the soup becomes glossy and slightly thickened. Adjust salt to taste.

MAKE THE ROASTED BABY CARROTS

Preheat the oven to 350°F/180°C. Line a baking sheet with parchment paper.

In a small bowl, toss the baby carrots with olive oil and a little salt. Arrange on the baking sheet and roast for 25 minutes, until tender.

TO SERVE

In 4 separate bowls, place a little of each ingredient except the soup itself in a cute pile at the center of the bowl. At the table, pour the soup carefully into each bowl.

SWEET POTATO
MISO SOUP

10 14

Miso is one of our favorite ingredients to add to the base of puréed soups like this wintry sweet potato and apple bisque. Unlike in the soup served in Japanese restaurants, the miso here is not stirred in at the end. Instead, we let it caramelize in browning butter, where it develops deep nutty aromas and makes everything a stronger, darker, deeper, almost moody version of itself.

Sweet Potato Miso Soup

4 tablespoons high-fat, cultured butter
8½ oz (240 g) onion, sliced
6 oz (175 g) apples, peeled, cored, and sliced
1 cup (3¼ oz/90 g) mushroom stems
⅛ cup (2¼ oz/60 g) red miso
¼ teaspoon dark chile powder
¼ teaspoon black peppercorns
Scant 1 cup (7½ fl oz/225 ml) Brut cider
8 cups (64 fl oz/1.8 kg) Vegetable Stock (page 255)
1 lb 15 oz (880 g) sweet potato, peeled and cubed
1 teaspoon apple cider vinegar
½ teaspoon Worcestershire sauce
Scant 1 cup (7½ fl oz/225 g) heavy (double) cream
Salt

Roasted Mushrooms

2 large lobster mushrooms
2 tablespoons butter, melted
1 teaspoon salt

To Serve

¼ cup (1 oz/25 g) toasted pecans
Olive oil, for drizzling

MAKE THE SWEET POTATO MISO SOUP

Heat the butter in a large, heavy-bottomed stock pot over medium heat. As soon as it foams, add the onions and apples. Sauté for 5–7 minutes, until lightly caramelized, then add the mushroom stems, red miso, chile powder, and peppercorns. Let this all sizzle in the butter for 3–5 minutes, until deeply golden and caramelized (you want it to brown without burning, so control the heat accordingly). Add the cider to deglaze the pan, stirring to scrape up the browned bits. Simmer for 3 minutes to cook off the alcohol, then add the vegetable stock and sweet potatoes. Simmer for 1 hour, until the potatoes are complete and utter mush (we say "blown out"). Add the cider vinegar and Worcestershire sauce. Working in batches, blend the soup in a blender on the highest speed, letting it spin 15–20 seconds per batch. You want a smooth, velvety texture. Stir in the cream, season to taste with salt, and if it seems a little thick, feel free to add a little water.

MAKE THE ROASTED MUSHROOMS

Preheat the oven to 350°F/180°C. In a small mixing bowl, combine the mushrooms, melted butter, and salt. Place on a small baking tray or sauté pan in the oven and roast for 20–25 minutes, until tender but still firm. Cool, then slice.

TO SERVE

The soup is delicious by itself, but if you want to make it fancy, the textures of the wild mushrooms and nuts really bring out the early winter vibes of the sweet potatoes.

Preheat 4 soup bowls. Gently reheat the soup in a pot over medium-low heat, if needed. Ladle the soup into the bowls. Add the sliced roasted mushrooms across the top of the soup. Grate the pecans over the soup, and finish with a drizzle of olive oil.

CELERY ROOT AND ALMOND BISQUE

01 09

Though not cheap, Spanish Marcona almonds are the secret to the base of what is otherwise a simple puréed root vegetable soup. As I write, I can hear the voice of my mother after reading this recipe: You sure I can't just use regular almonds?

This depth of flavor comes from the gentle browning of the milk and nut fats in the soffritto, just like the brown butter in the Pasta Yiayia (page 26). As we sauté the Marcona almonds in butter with lemon and thyme, the aromas intensify and double upon themselves. The milk solids and sugars brown like caramel, and the nuttiness of both the butter and almonds seem to play against each other. This could not happen without the plump, moist, almost creamy flesh of real Marcona almonds. They give up their fragrance and evocative flavor to the butter, and the butter in turn infuses every ounce of this winter bisque. So no, Mom, regular almonds would just toast too fast and taste bitter.

You want to get the textures right here, so don't skip reading "Using your fancy blender" (page 21) and adjust with water if you need to. There's a fine line between an elegant bisque and some absurdly premium baby food.

SERVES 8

3 tablespoons butter
½ cup (3 oz/75 g) Marcona almonds
Grated zest of ½ lemon
3 thyme sprigs
10 oz (280 g) onions, sliced
6½ oz (180 g) celery, sliced
2¼ oz (55 g) leeks, white part only, washed and diced
6 cloves garlic
½ cup (4 fl oz/120 ml) dry vermouth
6 cups (48 fl oz/1.4 kg) Vegetable Stock (page 255)
1 small Parmesan rind
4 cups (1 lb ¾ oz/475 g) peeled and diced celery root (celeriac)
2 cups (10 oz/275 g) diced Yukon Gold potatoes
Lemon juice, to taste
1 x quantity Dill Gremolata (page 251)
Crème fraîche
Salt

Melt the butter in a large stock pot over medium heat. Add the almonds, lemon zest, and thyme. Sauté gently for 3–5 minutes, until the butter solids become golden brown (don't brown the almonds). When this "noisette" stage is reached, add the onions, celery, leeks, and garlic. Reduce heat to medium-low and cook for 20–25 minutes, stirring and taking care not to brown the vegetables, until the onions are translucent and soft.

Remove the thyme sprigs and discard. Season with salt. Add the vermouth and stir to scrape up any browned bits. Add the vegetable stock, 3 cups (25 fl oz/750 ml) water, and the Parmesan rind. Increase heat to medium and bring to a simmer.

Add the celery root (celeriac) and potatoes, reduce heat to low, and cook for 30–45 minutes, until the vegetables are total mush. You can add more water if necessary.

Remove the Parmesan rind. Working in batches, blend the soup in a blender on high speed until completely smooth. Strain through a fine-mesh strainer or tamis, then season with lemon juice and salt.

Serve warm with generous swirls of dill gremolata and crème fraîche.

Snacks at Lula are an important part of
the nightly seasonal menu—they spark the
appetite, make you crave the rest of the meal,
lift you up from your seat to reach across
the table, grab a last bite, and say: So hey,
what's next?

SN
A
CKs

SWEET CORN, CIPOLLINI ONION, AND RACLETTE TART

I'm from New Haven, Connecticut, where we have some of the best pizza outside Naples. I'm always telling visitors to my hometown that they have to try the "white pizza," a thin-crust coal-fired pie with clams, mozzarella, oregano, and garlic. I'm close to telling you about a twisted, hallucinogenic fever dream I once had which gave us the idea for this tart. It took place at Modern on State Street. I was sitting with my father, who was a boy of six. I was my normal age. But it is just too weird. Maybe corn connects to clams in my mind. Maybe sweet Midwest onions to the fresh chopped garlic. Gooey, Alpine raclette cheese to mozzarella. It was "Apizza," in another world. Maybe you were there . . .

MAKE THE CORN FILLING

In a medium stock pot, boil the potatoes in water until fork tender, then drain. Once the potatoes are cool enough to handle, pass through a ricer and set aside.

In a sauté pan, add the butter, onion, and garlic and sauté over low heat until translucent, 5–7 minutes. Raise the heat to medium and add the corn kernels. After 3 minutes, add the white wine and cream plus 1 teaspoon of salt, return the heat to low, and cook until reduced by about a quarter. Carefully add this hot mixture to a blender and purée, then pass the purée through a fine-mesh strainer or tamis.

In a mixing bowl, combine the strained corn mix with the mascarpone, remaining salt, pepper, and lemon juice. Fold this into the riced potato, using a sturdy whisk to make a smooth filling. Pass again through the strainer or tamis.

MAKE THE TART

Preheat the oven to 375°F/190°C, and grease a 13 × 4-inch (33 × 10 cm) rectangular tart pan (tin) with canola (rapeseed) oil spray or butter.

Roll out the tart dough to ½-inch (5 mm) thick. Place in the pan, then press with a gentle but insistent touch, so the tart dough sits inside snugly. Trim any excess with scissors, then press into the edge to create a crimped effect. Spray the surface of the tart lightly with oil, then line with a piece of parchment paper and top with baking beans. Blind bake for 15 minutes, then set aside to cool.

Once cool, fill the tart shell with the corn-potato filling. We pipe it in with a pastry (piping) bag, but you could also use an offset palette knife. The key here is to create a smooth surface. Top with the raclette, Gruyère, and sage leaves.

Bake until the tart dough and the cheese are golden brown, approximately 20 minutes.

MAKE THE ROASTED CIPOLLINI ONIONS

Cut the onions in half (keep the skin on) and toss with the oil, salt, and thyme. Place on a sheet tray (rimmed baking tray), cut side down, and roast for 30–45 minutes, until tender. When cool, separate into individual petals.

TO SERVE

Cut the tart into 4 servings, then top with 6–7 petals of cipollini onion, julienned sage, a squeeze of lemon juice, drizzle of olive oil, sprinkle of Espelette, and a little Maldon sea salt.

SERVES 4

Corn Filling

1 lb (450 g) Yukon Gold potatoes, peeled and cubed
2 tablespoons butter
½ onion (7 oz/200 g), sliced
2 cloves garlic, minced
4 ears sweet summer corn, shucked, cleaned, and kernels cut from cob (4 cups/1 lb/450 g)
⅓ cup (2½ fl oz/70 g) dry white wine
¾ cup (6 fl oz/175 g) heavy (double) cream
1½ teaspoons salt
¾ cup (5 oz/150 g) mascarpone
1 teaspoon Espelette pepper
1 teaspoon lemon juice

Tart

Canola (rapeseed) oil spray or butter, for greasing
1 × quantity Cornmeal Tart Dough (page 252)
½ cup (2 oz/50 g) shredded (grated) raclette
¼ cup (1 oz/25 g) shredded (grated) Gruyère
1 teaspoon chopped sage leaves

Roasted Cipollini Onions

16 cipollini onions (8 oz/225 g)
2 tablespoons olive oil
¼ teaspoon salt
4 thyme sprigs, leaves picked from the stem

To Serve

Julienned sage leaves
Lemon juice
Olive oil
Espelette pepper
Maldon sea salt

CHICKEN LIVER MOUSSE AND CARROT BREAD

The things I love about our chicken liver mousse are the things *not* in it. "The notes we don't play." We don't sear the livers, caramelize the onions, or deglaze with heavy doses of wine or brandy. Instead, our mousse is a custard of delicate, almost floral flavors with the rich texture of mascarpone. Our twist is tart dried apricots and a splash of white wine vinegar. Cooked like a pot de crème, in a covered water bath at low temperature, the mousse comes out of the oven with a barely gelled texture that thickens as it cools. Despite the care you take, the surface might gray a little in the oven. Simply skim this layer off and dig into that sultry pink pâté.

Tasting the apricot and champagne vinegar together, we thought to accent it with vadouvan, or "French curry," an east-west mashup of traditional Indian spices with dried onion, shallot, and parsley. For our version, we use the delicious fried shallots found in Asian markets, which lend an addictive crunch. One batch will make plenty extra to keep around for topping breakfast potatoes, roasted cauliflower, grilled meats, or a buttery popcorn snack. And what cuter accessory to pair with such a sophisticated mousse than a slice from a miniature loaf of savory carrot bread?

SERVES 10

Chicken Liver Mousse

¼ cup (2¼ oz/60 g) dried apricots
½ cup (4 fl oz/120 g) brandy
2 teaspoons brown sugar
1 cup (11¼ oz/315 g) chicken livers
5 egg yolks
½ teaspoon salt
1 tablespoon champagne vinegar
⅛ teaspoon "pink" curing salt
5 oz (150 g) butter, diced and softened
Scant 1 cup (7½ fl oz/225 g) heavy (double) cream
Vegetable oil spray

Carrot Bread

5 tablespoons chicken fat
5 oz (150 g) butter, diced and softened
Generous ¾ cup (5¾ oz/165 g) granulated sugar
6 eggs
1¾ cups (9¼ oz/260 g) flour
¼ teaspoon curry powder
1½ teaspoons baking powder
1 teaspoon salt
¼ cup (2 fl oz/50 g) carrot juice
1¼ cups (10 oz/280 g) crème fraîche

To Serve

Butter, for toasting
Sliced Pickled Carrots (page 247), to garnish
5 cups (9 oz/250 g) mustard greens, to garnish
8 tablespoons Vadouvan Spice Mix (page 248), to garnish
Olive oil, to garnish
Maldon sea salt, to garnish

MAKE THE CHICKEN LIVER MOUSSE
Preheat the oven to 275°F/135°C.

Combine the dried apricots, brandy, and brown sugar with ½ cup (4 fl oz/120 g) water in a small saucepan over low heat, then simmer until the liquid has reduced by half. Transfer to a blender and purée at high speed until smooth.

Next add the livers, egg yolks, salt, champagne vinegar, and pink salt to the blender. Blend again on high. Once the mixture is emulsified, add the butter, and then, 1 tablespoon at a time, the cream. You're going to need a ladle or blender plunger to really get this mixture to "spin." You'll also need to work quickly so the butter and cream don't melt and/or break.

Prepare five 4-ounce (120 g) ramekins by coating each with vegetable oil spray. Pour the blended mousse into the ramekins. Cover with plastic wrap (cling film). Place the covered ramekins in a roasting pan (tin), then add enough water to the pan to cover three-quarters of the ramekin height. Bake in the oven until the mousse has barely set, about 30 minutes.

Remove from the water bath and leave to cool. The mousse will set further as it cools, so fear not if it is slightly jiggly when first removed from the oven. Chill to set.

The chicken liver mousse can be stored, wrapped, in the fridge for up to 1 week.

MAKE THE CARROT BREAD
Preheat the oven to 350°F/180°C.

In a stand mixer fitted with the whisk attachment, cream the chicken fat, butter, and sugar, adding 1 egg at a time until a silken texture is achieved.

Combine the flour, curry powder, baking powder, and salt in a separate bowl, then add to the wet ingredients in the mixing bowl. Combine at medium speed until thoroughly mixed. Add the carrot juice and crème fraîche and mix. The batter should be smooth and runny.

Grease five 6 × 3-inch (15 × 7½ cm) loaf pans (tins). Pour the batter into the pans and place on a sheet tray (rimmed baking tray). Bake for 35 minutes until golden.

TO SERVE
Slice the carrot bread loaves. Heat a sauté pan or griddle and add a small pat of butter. Toast the carrot loaf slices until golden brown. Divide the mousse among 10 plates, garnish with pickled carrots, mustard greens, some vadouvan spice mix, olive oil, Maldon salt, and serve with slices of carrot bread.

GRILLED **STRAWBERRIES** WITH **FENNEL** AND BURRATA

This is a super simple summer take on that faddish 2010s ingredient—burrata. I, too, fell mad in love for this distant cousin of buffalo milk mozzarella, which makes a milky wonder of literally anything you pair with it. For this combination, I was thinking of the tomato-mozzarella skewers my family used to make when I was a kid. We were the kind of Americans who on the Fourth of July served caprese "kabobs" alongside the hot dogs and burgers. We'd skewer "ciliegine" mozzarella balls with fresh cherry tomatoes from my stepfather's garden, then dress the whole thing in store-bought Italian dressing.

This dish is playful and fun to cook and the juice from the grilled strawberries . . . like, who knew? Grilled strawberry "jus" is intense, reduced, essential *strawberriness*. Basically an elixir of the gods. With a hint of smoke and char, it drips down into the chilled burrata and makes for a beautiful summertime treat.

MAKE THE STRAWBERRY SKEWERS

Soak four 3-inch (7.5 cm) wooden skewers in water for 1 hour before grilling. Carefully insert a skewer into a strawberry through its thickest cross-section. Then repeat four times to create one skewer. Repeat with the remaining skewers.

MAKE THE STRAWBERRY GLAZE

Combine all the ingredients in a small sauce pot over medium heat and cook until reduced by half. Pass through a fine-mesh strainer or tamis, then set aside to cool.

MAKE THE SHAVED FENNEL SALAD

Combine all the ingredients in a small bowl.

TO SERVE

Preheat a gas or charcoal grill to medium. Brush the strawberries with the glaze and cook until the fruit is lightly charred. The strawberries should be juicy, yet still firm. Continue to glaze while cooking and immediately after removing from the grill.

Place half a ball of burrata on a plate, cut side up and exposed. Give the cheese a robust shot of Maldon sea salt and crushed black pepper. Lay a grilled strawberry skewer alongside the cheese. Top with a teaspoon of honey, drizzled across both. Then garnish with the fennel salad and anise hyssop. If there's any delicious olive oil left in the fennel mixing bowl, spoon that across the whole thing, too.

SERVES 4

Strawberry Skewers
20 strawberries

Strawberry Glaze
1 medium shallot (1¼ oz/35 g), sliced
¾ cup (6 fl oz/170 g) red verjus
¼ cup (3 oz/80 g) honey
9¼ oz (260 g) strawberries
5 black peppercorns
Small pinch chile flakes
¼ cup (2 fl oz/60 g) white balsamic vinegar

Shaved Fennel Salad
¼ fennel bulb, shaved on a mandoline
Juice of ½ lemon
2 tablespoons olive oil
Salt, to taste

To Serve
2 balls chilled burrata (1 lb/450 g), halved
4 teaspoons honey
Anisse hyssop leaves and flowers
Maldon sea salt and freshly ground black pepper

BABY CORN WITH
BLACK GARLIC AIOLI

08 17

The baby corn in this recipe comes from Tracey Vowell, farmer at Three Sisters Garden in Kankakee, Illinois. Tracey was once a chef for the Frontera Hospitality Group and then became a farmer herself, growing, among many other specialties (pecans, notably), the trio of corn, beans, and squash for which her farm is named. While still a chef, Tracey also helped chef Rick Bayless build his Frontera Farmer Foundation. It is a nonprofit organization that has helped many new farmers with capital improvements over the last decade.

In February 2022, a large fire broke out in the barn that Tracey shared with her neighbor, in which they had stored seeds, storage crops, heavy machinery, and a generation's worth of tools. A group of us gathered to raise money so Tracey could harvest corn again the following year. It just shows the cyclical powers of good karma—that the chef who helped so many farmers in need was herself the recipient of a helping hand.

The friendships between the people who grow our food and our team of chefs have transformed our lives for the better. For me, it gives cooking a spiritual value, a resonance, something like the energy one feels taking a deep breath in a forest, exchanging what you don't need for what you do. "Know your farmer" may be a phrase in vogue, but for us it's more than a slogan—it's existential; it's the sense that we are continuing each other's breaths, that we are in a community, part of a story bigger than ourselves.

This dish appears on our menu in some form every August when Tracey delivers her miniature ears of corn. It will be very difficult to find such a product, though you can request your local farm pick some early corn for you. Just make sure you ask in June. Regardless, the same recipe will be delicious with a full-sized variety of summer corn. The recipe makes enough to serve on a platter, likely more than you'll need.

MAKE THE BLACK GARLIC AIOLI

In a saucepan over medium heat, add the butter, oil, and leeks. Cook gently until the leeks soften, 15–20 minutes. Add the black garlic, smashing it into the leeks with the tines of a fork. Cook for an additional 5 minutes. Add the fresh garlic, 1 tablespoon capers, and preserved lemon, then a scant ½ cup (3½ fl oz/100 g) water and the white verjus. Continue to cook until the leeks are fully tender and the liquid is reduced by half, stirring frequently. Add the paprika and black olives. Transfer to a blender and purée until smooth. Place in the refrigerator for 20 minutes to cool.

In a blender, combine the aioli base, remaining capers, egg yolks, lemon juice, 2 tablespoons of water, pickle liquid, and salt. Once fully puréed, drizzle in the oil in a steady, constant stream until the aioli is fully emulsified and thick.

TO SERVE

You can cook the corn however you'd like. You can roast it in the oven, boil in water, or grill on the barbecue. We grill ours over Japanese charcoal, with the corn still inside its husk. The miniature corn from Tracey's farm takes about 5–6 minutes to cook over a hot bed of coals, though your timing will depend on the size of the corn.

When they're cooked, we peel back the hot husks to reveal the cob, then we schmear the aioli on the hot kernels. Spread about ½ tablespoon aioli on each ear of corn and scatter a tablespoon of ricotta salata and a few oregano sprigs over each. Finish with a squeeze of lemon juice and a sprinkle of Maldon sea salt.

SERVES 6+

Black Garlic Aioli

1 tablespoon butter

1 tablespoon olive oil

2¼ oz (55 g) leeks, white part only, washed and sliced

1¾ oz (45 g) cloves black garlic

2 cloves garlic

1 tablespoon + 1 teaspoon capers

1 tablespoon preserved lemon, chopped

¼ cup (2 fl oz/60 g) white verjus

¼ teaspoon paprika

4 cured black olives

2 egg yolks

1 tablespoon lemon juice

1 teaspoon pickling liquid from Pickled Thai Chile (page 247)

¼ teaspoon salt

Scant 1 cup (7½ fl oz/225 g) grapeseed oil

To Serve

Baby corn, as many as you wish, cleaned of silk but with husks on

1 tablespoon shaved ricotta salata per ear

Oregano sprigs

Lemon juice

Maldon sea salt

CHICKPEA SOCCA
WITH **APPLE** AND **HONEY**

0918

A socca is farinata by another name, a crêpe-like chickpea snack originally from the Italian Riviera. Our version is more pancake than flatbread, especially since our kitchen is set up for brunch with a large cast iron gas griddle. Instead of baking the traditionally unleavened batter in the oven, we add yeast and cook it like pancakes on the griddle, creating something more like a chickpea blini.

This is a great gluten-free snack and can be served with caviar if you're feeling luxe.

MAKE THE SOCCA

Add all the ingredients except the vegetable spray to a blender with a generous 1 cup (8 fl oz/255 g) water and purée for 4 minutes. Transfer to an airtight container and rest at room temperature for 2 hours. (At this point you can refrigerate for up to 8 hours, but bring the batter back to room temperature before using it.) Heat a nonstick skillet (frying pan) or griddle to medium, greased with a generous amount of vegetable spray. Scoop 2-ounce (50 g) dollops of batter into the pan, cooking them like pancakes. Flip when crispy, about 2 minutes per side.

MAKE THE CHICKPEA CRUMBLE

Heat the oil in a deep fryer or large, heavy pot to 350°F/180°C or until a cube of bread browns in 30 seconds. Drain and dry the chickpeas by spreading out on paper towels, then fry the chickpeas until dark golden and crispy, 2–3 minutes. Drain on paper towels and season with salt. Crush the toasted caraway in a mortar and pestle, then crush the fried chickpeas with a mallet or the bottom of a mixing bowl. Combine the chickpeas and the caraway, then add the grated and dried ginger and granulated onion. Check for seasoning.

MAKE THE CHARRED APPLE HONEY

Toss the diced apples with the olive oil in a stainless-steel mixing bowl. On a gas or charcoal grill, char the apples until lightly browned and smoky, 5–7 minutes. Transfer the apples to a small pan with the honey and ginger, and heat on medium until simmering, then turn down the heat to its lowest setting and allow to simmer for at least 1 hour. Strain through a fine-mesh strainer or tamis.

MAKE THE COMPRESSED APPLE

If, like me, you don't have a Cryovac machine at home, simply toss all the ingredients together. If you do have a Cryovac, toss all the ingredients together, add them to a Cryo bag and compress at a high setting.

TO SERVE

Top each pancake with a spoonful of ricotta, a scattering of apple slices, a sprinkle of chickpea crumble, and a drizzle of charred apple honey. Garnish with thyme sprigs.

SERVES 4

Socca
¾ cup (3½ oz/100 g) chickpea flour
1 tablespoon alternative gluten-free flour
½ teaspoon active dried yeast
¼ teaspoon salt
2 teaspoons baking powder
Vegetable oil spray

Chickpea Crumble
1 cup (4½ oz/135 g) canned (tinned) chickpeas
1 teaspoon toasted caraway seeds
½ teaspoon grated fresh ginger
¼ teaspoon ginger powder
½ teaspoon granulated onion
Salt

Charred Apple Honey
1 apple (7 oz/200 g), peeled, cored, and diced
1 tablespoon olive oil
1 cup (11¾ oz/340 g) honey
¼ oz (10 g) piece of fresh ginger, peeled and sliced

Compressed Apple
3¾ oz (115 g) apple, halved and thinly sliced
2 tablespoons olive oil
Small pinch salt
1 tablespoon lemon juice
1 teaspoon thyme leaves

To Serve
160 g (5½ oz) Ricotta (page 254, or shop-bought)
Thyme sprigs

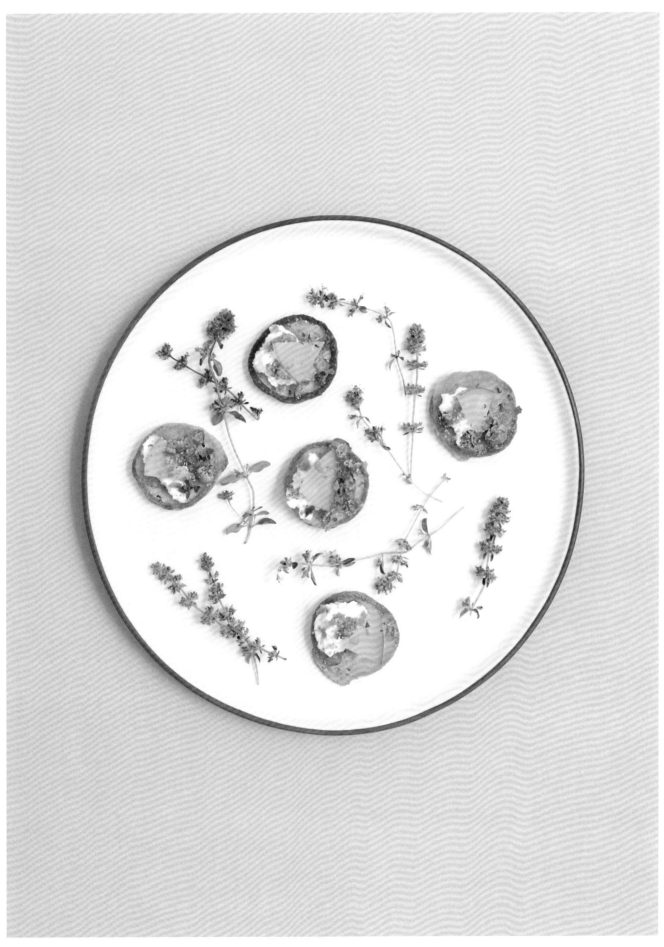

LAMB TARTARE

04 12

It may seem counterintuitive, but I think one of the best ways to foist lamb on people who normally find it "gamey" is to serve it raw. Guests who don't usually eat lamb are often surprised by their reaction to the clean, fresh, neutral taste of a raw loin dressed with bright acidic condiments, spices, and olive oil. We've surprised more than one hesitant holdout by this springtime preparation, which uses green garlic and preserved lemon to tighten the thematic connections of lamb to the season.

You'll want to use a neutral olive oil here, something buttery and smooth, as the green garlic will do that bitter, spicy, grassy work for you. There are a couple of key factors to making a good tartare. The first is temperature. Anytime you cut or grind meat, it needs to be just this side of frozen. You can chill the lamb in the freezer for 10–15 minutes before you begin—just make sure it's super cold. Chilled meat cuts cleanly and resists the tendency to rip. Second, your knife needs to be scalpel-sharp. Under the duress of a dull blade, even terrifically fresh, tender, chilled meat will end up like half-chewed cud, which, I know, is like the worst mixed metaphor ever. You want to dice the meat by slicing lengthwise down the loin in ⅛-inch (3 mm) thick slabs, which should then be laid flat on their sides and sliced again into ⅛-inch (3 mm) thick strips, then cut perpendicularly into ⅛-inch (3 mm) cubes, creating an exceptionally small dice. Once the entire loin is diced, chill it again, then return it to the cutting board (cold) and run your (sharp) knife back and forth through the meat several times, chopping firmly and forcibly down.

Dukkah is a North African spice and nut mix that literally means "to pound," and should be a texture somewhere between a powder and a granola, giving a dynamic crunch and flavor boost to the tartare.

SERVES 4

Tartare Dressing

Scant ¼ cup (1½ fl oz/50 g) olive oil
¼ cup (1¼ oz/35 g) thinly sliced
  green garlic, white part only
  (tops reserved)
¼ teaspoon each coriander and cumin
  seeds, toasted and ground
1½ tablespoons capers, chopped
1½ teaspoons minced shallots
1 tablespoon chopped preserved lemon
  rind (pith removed)
¼ cup (1¼ oz/35 g) green olives,
  chopped
3 teaspoons white soy sauce

Green Garlic Oil

1 cup (1 oz/25 g) parsley
½ cup (2 oz/50 g) reserved green garlic
  tops (from above), chopped
1¼ cups (10 fl oz/300 g) olive oil

Preserved Lemon Aioli

2 egg yolks
¼ oz (10 g) preserved lemon, seeds
  removed
1 tablespoon lemon juice
1 clove garlic
¾ cup + 1 tablespoon (7 fl oz/200 g)
  grapeseed oil
Salt (optional)

Almond Dukkah

1 teaspoon fennel seeds
1 teaspoon black peppercorns
1 teaspoon cumin seeds
2 teaspoons coriander seeds
½ cup (2¼ oz/60 g) toasted whole
  almonds
¼ cup (1¼ oz/30 g) sunflower seeds,
  toasted
1 tablespoon thyme leaves
1 teaspoon salt
2 tablespoons white sesame seeds
½ teaspoon Aleppo pepper

MAKE THE TARTARE DRESSING

In a small saucepan, combine 1 tablespoon olive oil and the green garlic, then cook over low heat until tender, about 5 minutes. Set aside to cool, then transfer to a mixing bowl and stir through the remaining ingredients. Leave to chill in the refrigerator.

MAKE THE GREEN GARLIC OIL

Bring a small pot of water to a boil and fill a bowl with a 50/50 mix of ice and water. Cook the parsley and green garlic tops for 1 minute in the boiling water, then shock in the ice water bath. Remove the parsley and garlic, then squeeze out the excess water by wrapping the vegetables in cheesecloth and wringing them dry. Transfer to a blender with the olive oil and purée on high for 1 minute. Strain through a fine-mesh strainer or tamis.

MAKE THE PRESERVED LEMON AIOLI

In a blender, combine the egg yolks, preserved lemon, lemon juice, garlic, and 2 tablespoons water. Purée on high until thoroughly combined. Then stream in the grapeseed oil slowly until a thick emulsion forms. It is unlikely that you'll need salt due to the preserved lemon, but taste and adjust if needed.

MAKE THE ALMOND DUKKAH

In a dry sauté pan, toast the fennel seeds, peppercorns, cumin, and coriander until fragrant, 2–3 minutes. Set aside to cool. Grind in a mortar and pestle until crushed but not ground. Chop the almonds, sunflower seeds, and thyme by hand until they are a homogenous crumble. Transfer to a bowl and add the spices, salt, sesame seeds, and pepper.

TO SERVE

Chill 4 plates. Dice the lamb with a sharp knife (see recipe introduction). In a bowl, mix the lamb with the tartare dressing, parsley, lemon juice, salt, pepper, and half the green garlic oil. Plate in a ring mold in the center of each plate, then top with dots of the preserved lemon aioli, almond dukkah, sumac, mint leaves, and a drizzle of the remaining green garlic oil. Serve with toasted bread or pita.

To Serve
_____

12 oz (350 g) lamb loin, trimmed of fat, chilled
2 teaspoons chopped parsley
2 teaspoons lemon juice
Sumac
Mint leaves
Toasted bread or pita
Salt and frehly ground black pepper

_____

Image on page 108

FAVA BEAN DIP
WITH **PITA**

This is a creamy hummus dip made with fresh fava beans. Sounds wildly demanding, right? Do we force a team of interns to peel thousands of tiny, fingertip-numbing fava beans and then purée them into a mash? Well, no, we're not like that. Instead, we have a hack. We make this dip by substituting white beans in the base, along with tahini, and then adding a bright purée of herbs and favas. This gives us the texture, color, and flavor that we need without the thousands of hours of work.

Back in my early days of being a chef, I used to swear by an aphorism from Chef Judy Rodgers of San Francisco's Zuni Café, who said, "Stop, think, there must be a harder way." She used this mantra to guide her vision of artisanal cooking that skipped no step, took no shortcut, bought nothing "pre made." Judy was responding to the food culture of convenience and mass consumption coming out of the 1970s and '80s. Chefs were "rediscovering" the lost processes of the craft. And thank god they did. The chefs of that era (I'm thinking of Paul Bertolli in his seminal *Cooking By Hand*) saw the threat posed to our traditional food ways by modern food, the danger that time-honored techniques and the wisdom of generations past might actually become extinct. For a time, it was a badge of honor to make cooking, even simple cooking, difficult, time-consuming, and arduous. As this ideology rose in U.S. kitchens, we saw a flourishing of house-made bread and charcuterie, fermented foods, extruded pasta, etc. Things that took time, that were "hard to make."

But today I'm wary of the idea. Or at least I question its place in restaurants. Because there is always someone on this side of the wall making those "hard" things. And maybe hard isn't always best. Pasta, for instance. Yes, we make our own, but we also buy pasta from people who've become experts in making it over hundreds of years. And whom we want to support.

Sometimes, a hack is worth the time you get back in your life and the time you don't take from someone else's. I love fava beans. I love them enough to blanch and peel them for this recipe. Or this one, too (page 212). But I'm not above using a can of white beans to give me back some time.

SERVES 4

Fava Bean Dip
1½ cups (3 oz/80 g) green garlic tops
½ cup (½ oz/15 g) parsley
6 cups (1¾ lb/800 g) fava beans, raw, in shell
¾ cup (6 oz/175 g) canned (tinned) cannellini beans, drained and rinsed
Scant ½ cup (3¾ fl oz/110 g) blend oil
1 oz (25 g) Parmesan, grated
1 tablespoon Roasted Garlic purée (page 246)
⅛ cup (1¼ oz/30 g) tahini
2 tablespoons lemon juice, plus extra if needed
Salt

Pita
1 teaspoon (5 g) active dried yeast
2½ cups (310 g) bread flour
Scant ½ cup (2¾ oz/70 g) whole wheat flour, plus extra for dusting
½ tablespoon salt
1 tablespoon granulated sugar
¼ cup (1¾ oz/45 g) natural yogurt
1 tablespoon olive oil, plus extra for greasing

Anchovies
Scant ½ cup (3¾ fl oz/110 g) grapeseed oil
⅛ oz (6 g) lemon peel
⅛ oz (6 g) lime peel
3 thyme sprigs
10 white anchovies (3 oz/80 g)

Szechuan Chile Crisp
1 tablespoon Szechuan chile flakes
½ tablespoon grated fresh ginger
½ teaspoon sugar
1 teaspoon white soy sauce
¼ oz (10 g) green garlic, white part only, thinly sliced
1 tablespoon thinly sliced shallots
3 tablespoons blend oil

MAKE THE FAVA BEAN DIP

Bring a pot of water to a boil and salt generously. Fill a small bowl with a 50/50 mix of ice and water. Boil the green garlic tops and parsley for 30 seconds, then immediately plunge into the ice water. Next, do the same with the fava beans, cooking for 30 seconds until tender, then "shocking" them in the iced water. Peel the fava beans and split them into two portions. Reserve ¼ cup (1¼ oz/30 g) favas for garnish, then combine the remaining portion with the parsley and green garlic tops.

In a blender, purée the cannellini beans and oil together on high. Add the Parmesan, roasted garlic, and tahini. Blend until smooth. Next add the green vegetables, 1 teaspoon salt, and lemon juice and blend again until smooth. Pass through a fine-mesh strainer or tamis. Taste for seasoning and adjust with salt or lemon juice.

MAKE THE PITA

In the bowl of a stand mixer, combine a scant 1 cup (7½ fl oz/220 g) warm water (~107°F/42°C) and the yeast, allowing it to activate for 10 minutes. Mix the flours, salt, and sugar together in a separate bowl. Add these dry ingredients to the mixer bowl using the dough hook attachment. Add the yogurt and olive oil. Mix for 7 minutes, until everything is incorporated and the dough forms a ball. Grease another vessel with olive oil in which to rest the dough. Cover and leave in a warm place for 30 minutes. It should double in size. Punch the dough down and roll into 12 balls of 2 oz (50 g). Place on a floured sheet tray (baking tray). Proof for another 20–30 minutes, then roll them to ¾-inch (1.5 cm) thick, again using plenty of flour.

Preheat a pizza stone in the oven at its highest setting. Brush the rolled dough with a light coating of olive oil. Place on the pizza stone and close the oven door. After 2 minutes, flip them over. Cook for an additional 2 minutes until charred and puffed. Store in clean dish (tea) towels in a warm place until ready to use.

MAKE THE ANCHOVIES

Gently heat the oil, lemon and lime peel, and thyme in a pan. Steep for 10 minutes, then leave to cool. Pour the mixture over the anchovies in a nonreactive container. Chill overnight to marinate.

MAKE THE SZECHUAN CHILE CRISP

In a mixing bowl, combine the Szechuan chile with the ginger, sugar, and soy. In a small saucepan over low heat, sauté the garlic, shallot, and oil gently without any caramelization or color. When the vegetables are soft, raise the flame to medium and allow the caramelization to begin. Just as the vegetables turn golden brown, pour them over the chile mix.

TO SERVE

Transfer the dip to a serving bowl. Heat the pita in the oven if needed. Slice the anchovies into ¼-inch (5 mm) pieces. Mix the parsley, reserved favas, anchovies, lemon juice, and lemon "agrumato" olive oil in a mixing bowl. With the back of a spoon, create a divot in the dip. Spoon this fava bean mixture into the divot, then drizzle with the chile crisp and extra oil. Grate the pistachios over the top, and finish with oxalis and nasturtium leaves.

To Serve
1 tablespoon chopped parsley
1 teaspoon lemon juice
2 teaspoons lemon "agrumato" olive oil, plus extra for drizzling
2 teaspoons pistachios
Oxalis and nasturtium leaves

Image on page 109

OYSTERS WITH ROSE MIGNONETTE

We source our oysters from the cold waters of the northeast—places like Nova Scotia and Prince Edward Island in Canada. I'm partial to the Pink Moon variety, though that might be because I like the Nick Drake reference. Most of the smaller specimens from that region are perfect for this lightly floral, citrusy mignonette.

MAKE THE MIGNONETTE

Combine all the ingredients together in a nonreactive bowl.

TO SERVE

Shuck the oysters and serve dotted with the mignonette and garnished with a snipped chive.

To prevent all their precious liquor spilling out, it's helpful to set the oysters on a bed of dried beans (or ice). Here we use dried chickpeas and dried rose petals.

SERVES HOWEVER MANY YOU WANT

Mignonette
¼ preserved lemon or mandarin, pith removed, minced incredibly small
1¼ oz (30 g) shallots, very finely minced
1½ teaspoons honey vinegar
1 tablespoon red wine vinegar
½ teaspoon dried rose petals, ground
Salt and freshly ground black pepper

To Serve
Oysters, washed
Snipped chives, to garnish

CRISPY SPRING ONION, CHICKPEAS, AND RAITA

0718

At sixteen I got my first job bussing tables at New Haven's beloved Japanese restaurant, Miya's. One night the sushi chef went back home to Japan. There was simply no replacement in town. (The chef-owner's son, Bun Lai, my age at the time, would eventually take over the restaurant and become one of the country's best sushi chefs and a leader in the sustainable fish movement.)

No raw fish made for some quiet nights at the restaurant, sharing bowls of soup and tempura with the proprietor, Bun's mother, Yoshiko Lai. I would sit in the tatami room as Chef Lai told me stories of a perilous life's journey from Japan to the U.S. This was one of the first times I remember being really struck, aesthetically, by the beauty of food and of its connection to a life story. I picked out the sweet negi in the tempura, my favorite. The green of the scallion appeared through a tenuous, brittle layer of batter. Chef Lai spoke softly and carefully. I saw the young mother with a suitcase and a child. It was the transparency, things obscured and revealed, that I found so arrestingly beautiful—then and now.

This dish is a mashup—part Japanese inspiration, Indian technique, Levant and Sicilian flavors—and yet it is familiar because in the end it's fried onions and dip. You want an onion small enough to pick up with your fingers but that still has a sweet, juicy bulb and tender, edible green top. We slice them lengthwise with the root end intact. Once dropped into the fryer, the onions start to unfold, batter finding its way inside the layers of petals, wild crispy tendrils left everywhere in-between.

SERVES 4

Batter
1 cup (4 oz/120 g) chickpea flour
2 tablespoons cornstarch (cornflour)
1 tablespoon + 1½ teaspoons baking powder
½ teaspoon salt
¼ teaspoon cayenne
¼ teaspoon ground cumin
¼ teaspoon ground coriander

Chickpeas
¼ cup (1½ oz/40 g) fresh green chickpeas, shelled
½ tablespoon finely chopped mint
½ tablespoon finely chopped parsley
1 clove garlic, grated
1 tablespoon pistachios, finely chopped
Grated zest of 1 lemon
2 tablespoons olive oil
Salt

Raita
½ cup (3½ oz/100 g) natural yogurt
1 teaspoon very thinly sliced chives
2 oz (50 g) Persian cucumber, finely grated
1 clove garlic, grated
1 tablespoon lemon juice

To Serve
1 lb (450 g) spring onions, root end trimmed, sliced lengthwise
Sumac
Fennel pollen
Salt

MAKE THE BATTER

In a medium mixing bowl, gently whisk all the ingredients together with 1 cup (8 fl oz/250 g) water, then rest at room temperature for 20 minutes.

MAKE THE CHICKPEAS

Bring a pot of water to a boil and salt generously. Fill another small bowl with a 50/50 mix of ice and water. Cook the fresh chickpeas in salted water for 30 seconds, then immediately chill in the ice water bath. Peel the tender skins, combine with the remaining ingredients in a mixing bowl, and season to taste. Set aside.

MAKE THE RAITA

Combine all the ingredients in a bowl and chill in the refrigerator.

TO SERVE

Heat the oil in a deep fryer or heavy large pot to 350°F/180°C, or until a cube of bread browns in 30 seconds. Prepare a sheet tray (baking tray) lined with a paper towel, suitable for holding the onions in a single layer. Place the batter in a wide bowl suitable for dipping onions. Dip the spring onions in the batter, one at a time, taking care to immerse them fully. Remove using tongs. Allow any excess batter to drip off, but do your best to get them into the fryer quickly and carefully, making sure that multiple onions don't fuse together en masse. Turn carefully (again with tongs) as they fry, so they are an even golden brown on all sides, 2–3 minutes, depending on the size of the onion. Drain on the towel-lined tray, making sure to keep them separate from each other. Season generously with salt and sumac while still hot.

Place the raita in a small bowl, topped with a gentle sprinkle of fennel pollen.

Plate the spring onions next to the raita and spoon the green chickpeas over the onions. Serve quickly. It's all so much better warm.

PLUMS AND RICOTTA WITH MINT ZA'ATAR

While we often make our own ricotta at Lula, there are many terrific artisan producers in the United States. Two in particular come from my hometown of New Haven, Connecticut. Both Calabro and Liuzzi make the kind of curdy, strained-yet-creamy product that isn't available at your big chain grocery store.

A few months before my grandfather died, he told me about his first job as an apprentice at a cheesemaker in New Haven. He was 102 when he told me this story from the head of a crowded table, which was to be his last Thanksgiving with us all. I could barely hear him over the ruckus of his great-grandchildren playing under the table, tying shoes together, pinching toes. He said he was "eleven, twelve, maybe nine" when he got his first job cutting curd in giant tanks of milk heated by a coal fire. Then he would stretch mozzarella by soaking the curds in whey heated to a near boil until the curds softened and became malleable, all while standing on a crate because he was too short to reach the vat unaided. He shaped bocconcini and braids and "cherries" (ciliegine, page 100) with his bare hands. I asked him if it hurt. He held up as evidence the thick, rough hands I'd known since I could remember. "A bit," he said. "But you get used to it . . . Do you make cheese at your restaurant?" he asked. I nodded. "Rigot'?" He smiled approvingly. "Ever make muzz'?" No, I said. He put his hand on my forearm and leaned in, about to find a memory. His eyes seemed to cast out somewhere deep into the past. "The boss there at the shop," he said, squeezing my arm. This boss sat on a stool by the door. He couldn't remember his name, but he could remember that the man was not kind.

MAKE THE MINT ZA'ATAR

Combine all the ingredients together in a small bowl.

TO SERVE

Plate the ricotta first. Using a large spoon or scoop, press a divot in the top, then fill it with the marigold honey, a drizzle of olive oil, and a sprinkle of Maldon sea salt. Next to the ricotta layer place slices of plums, another drizzle of olive oil, and top with the za'atar and a sprig of mint. Place the crackers on the plate alongside the ricotta.

SERVES 6

Mint Za'atar
2 tablespoons za'atar
1½ teaspoons chopped mint leaves
2 tablespoons olive oil

To Serve
1¼ cups (12 oz/350 g) Ricotta (page 254)
6 tablespoons Marigold Honey (page 252)
Olive oil, for drizzling
8 plums, sliced into thin rounds
Mint sprigs
1 x quantity Olive Oil Crackers (page 252)
Maldon sea salt

PARSNIP **SFORMATO** WITH **FIG** AND **MATSUTAKE**

10 22

My favorite Italian culinary terms are a kind of kinetic poetry, expressing movement and process—not outcome.

A sformato is a type of savory soufflé or flan, baked in a vessel and then turned out to be served on its own. Unmolded. Unformed. In Italian grammar, the "s" works as a privative, negating the meaning of its base.

To me, the English "unmolded" sounds like a wet hunk of clay. But a sformato still has form. In Italian, the word seems to speak to this tension, telling the story of the way the soufflé maintains its shape, tenuous and fragile as a sandcastle tower.

This delicate custard is made of parsnips and served with matsutake mushrooms, autumn fig, Parmesan, and mugolio, a syrupy, balsamic-like condiment made from the nectar of pine buds. As matsutake are pine-loving mushrooms, it made sense to use this unusual (and embarrassingly cheffy) ingredient, though you can substitute with a high-quality aged balsamic vinegar to the same effect.

MAKE THE PARSNIP PURÉE

Preheat the oven to 350°F/180°C. Peel the parsnips, then toss them in the olive oil and salt. Wrap them individually in foil, place on a sheet tray (baking tray) and roast in the oven for 1 hour or until soft. Add the parsnips and any residual oil to a blender with 1 cup (8 fl oz/250 g) water and blend on high.

MAKE THE SFORMATO

Reduce the oven temperature to 250°F/120°C. Place the parsnip purée and all the other ingredients (except the vegetable oil spray) in the blender and purée on high until smooth. Spray five 3-ounce (80 g) silicone molds and then fill each one with the sformato base. Bake until slightly puffed and starting to pull away from the edges, approximately 40 minutes. Set aside to cool, and when cool to the touch use an offset spatula to loosen the souffles from the molds. Turn them out carefully onto a silpat-lined tray.

MAKE THE SAGE VINAIGRETTE

Combine all the ingredients in a blender and purée on high. Pass through a fine-mesh strainer or tamis.

TO SERVE

If necessary, gently reheat the sformato in the oven. Place on 4 individual plates. Drizzle the sage vinaigrette over the top, then add sliced figs and a little mugolio. Top with alternate shavings of matsutake and Parmesan. Finish with sage leaves, a drizzle of olive oil, and a little Maldon sea salt.

SERVES 4

Parsnip Purée

6 oz (175 g) parsnips
½ tablespoon olive oil
¼ teaspoon salt

Sformato

1 egg
½ cup (3½ fl oz/100 g) heavy (double) cream
1 tablespoon gluten-free flour
½ teaspoon salt
1 clove garlic, grated
¾ oz (20 g) Parmesan, grated
Vegetable oil spray

Sage Vinaigrette

1½ cups (1½ oz/40 g) parsley
½ cup (¼ oz/10 g) sage
¾ cup (6 fl oz/170 g) grapeseed oil
1 tablespoon cider vinegar

To Serve

2 fresh figs, sliced
A few drops mugolio
1¼ oz (30 g) matsutake, cleaned and shaved
¾ oz (20 g) Parmesan, shaved
Sage leaves
Olive oil, for drizzling
Maldon sea salt

CHANTERELLE TOAST WITH CAVIAR, DILL, AND RYE

11 20

For eighteen months during the pandemic, with our dining room closed, all our food had to "travel" to be reheated at home. The team developed hundreds of recipes for boxes, deli cups, foil packs, and paper bags, closing our collective eyes against the images of our creations spinning in some godforsaken microwave. All I wanted to do was put food on plates; to see someone actually chew. And then, as if this wasn't challenge enough, I was asked to come up with an appetizer for a charity gala that could be delivered to guests a full twenty-four hours in advance. It had to be both reheatable and "three-star." So this DIY caviar toast came to be.

We prepared a sott'olio (page 202) of chanterelle mushrooms and delivered it to guests in a mini mason jar, with even cuter glass ramekins of crème fraîche, caviar, and dill. The guests could then heat the mushrooms on their own and spoon the warm, marinated chanterelles over a freshly toasted piece of rye, topping it all with the different garnishes.

I was alone prepping fifty of these jars late one November night. There's something particularly eerie about being alone in a commercial kitchen after a restaurant is closed, never mind being alone in one closed *possibly for good* in the middle of a global pandemic. With the dining room dark and the kitchen brutally lit, you hear sounds, you see things. I remember suddenly feeling that I wasn't alone. I looked across the pass, to the bar where the stools had been flipped over for a cleaning crew that never showed after that last service on Sunday, March 15, 2020. I sensed someone rushing through the dining room, someone who seemed to know their way through the thick forest of tables and chairs, but who seemed frightened and cold. Even today, I'll swear on something precious that I saw this ghost, but maybe it was just the echo of all the busy nights our dining room once knew. (And that—thankfully—we'd soon know again.)

SERVES 2-4

Chanterelle Sott'olio

Scant ¼ cup (2 fl oz/50 g) olive oil, plus extra if needed

1½ cups (2¾ oz/70 g) pearl onions, peeled

½ cup (1¾ oz/45 g) garlic cloves, peeled and sliced

4 cups (11½ oz/320 g) chanterelles, cleaned and trimmed

¼ teaspoon salt, plus extra to taste

Scant ¼ cup (2 fl oz/55 g) white wine

4 strips lemon peel

1 teaspoon thyme leaves

1½ teaspoons dill leaves

⅛ teaspoon cracked black pepper

Small pinch chile flakes

To Serve

2 tablespoons Garlic Aioli (page 248)

2 thick slices rye bread, lightly toasted

2 teaspoons caviar

2 teaspoons crème fraîche

Dill sprigs

Maldon sea salt and freshly ground black pepper

MAKE THE CHANTERELLE SOTT'OLIO

In a sauté pan large enough to hold the mushrooms, heat the olive oil. Sauté the pearl onions and garlic over low to medium heat, cooking until very tender, about 15 minutes. Remove the onions and garlic and strain them of oil, reserving both oil and aromatics.

Add the chanterelles and salt to the pan and cook over a medium heat. As the mushrooms cook, they will release water and shrink. As the water is cooked out of the mushrooms, return the onions and garlic to the pan, then deglaze with the white wine and reduce by one quarter. Add the oil back to the pan and bring to a very gentle simmer, until the mushrooms are tender. Add the lemon peel, thyme, dill, black pepper, and chile flakes. Fold together, taste for seasoning, and place in a mason jar. Top with fresh olive oil if needed.

TO SERVE

Spread the garlic aioli over the bread slices and then spoon over the chanterelles. Top with caviar, a drizzle of crème fraîche, and then Maldon sea salt, pepper, and dill.

BURRATA AND BUTTERNUT DIP

12 20

If you've read the section on "Using your fancy blender" (page 21) and feel like you're ready for a real-world exercise, follow this recipe for a rich squash and burrata purée. Use the weights as a guide but trust your instincts here—too much liquid and the dip will be formless and wet; not enough and the purée won't spin properly in the carafe. Good "spin"—the centrifugal path of a purée moving inside the blender's carafe—is necessary for proper emulsification. If you don't get it right, especially with the dairy in this recipe, the dip will seem grainy, even curdled. A dip with a high-end ingredient like burrata needs to be supple, luxurious, so smooth it glistens.

I recognize an ingredient like xanthan gum isn't an everyday staple. But of all the emulsifying agents commonly used in modern kitchens, it's the most readily available, safe, neutral in taste, and relatively easy for an amateur. The gum is a soluble fiber that thickens in a similar way to a slurry in gravy (though not by the same method). We use it to tighten sauces that might otherwise "break," the term we use when a formerly creamy, unctuous sauce separates into its component parts.

You'll need something to dip into this, like crackers or crostini. We add a little bitter green frisée salad and winter truffles over the top, then serve a big pile of salty, herby breadsticks alongside

MAKE THE BUTTERNUT SQUASH BURRATA DIP

Preheat the oven to 350°F/180°C. Halve the squash lengthwise and scoop out the seeds. Brush with the 2 tablespoons of olive oil. Sprinkle with ½ teaspoon of salt. Place the garlic cloves in the cavity of the squash and push the cloves and star anise directly into the squash's flesh. This technique, often done on hams, is called "studding." Roast the squash, flesh side up, on a sheet tray (rimmed baking tray) until extremely tender, then scoop out the flesh with a spoon, scraping every last bit from the skin.

Reserve the squash flesh, then dispose of the cloves and star anise. If the garlic stays in there, all the better.

Add the burrata, ricotta, black pepper, and lemon zest to a blender and start blending, using the bottom of your ladle or the approved "plunger." Make sure you're getting a decent spin (page 21). Add the xanthan gum and blend on high for 30 seconds, then add the squash, lemon juice, and remaining salt and olive oil. Blend first on low, then increase the blender's speed until you reach the highest level. Purée until very smooth and thick. Add water to the purée only if absolutely necessary, and if so, in 1 teaspoon increments. Chill before serving.

TO SERVE

Scoop the butternut squash burrata dip into a small bowl, and scatter with the frisée, truffle, and olive oil. Set the grissini on the side.

SERVES 10

Butternut Squash Burrata Dip

1 small butternut squash (1 lb 10½ oz/750 g)

¼ cup (2 fl oz/60 g) olive oil, plus 2 tablespoons for brushing

1 teaspoon salt

4 cloves garlic

½ teaspoon cloves

1 tablespoon star anise

1 ball (8 oz/225 g) burrata

¼ cup (2 oz/50 g) Ricotta (page 254, or shop-bought)

⅛ teaspoon black pepper

½ teaspoon grated lemon zest

¼ teaspoon xanthan gum

2 teaspoons lemon juice

To Serve

¼ head frisée (6 oz/175 g), leaves picked

1 black or white truffle, grated or sliced as you wish

1 tablespoon olive oil

8 oz (225 g) grissini

Our salads at Lula are chilled, crunchy, bright,
full of texture and intrigue. They aspire to be
the raw expression of a season, of a day, in
its pure and honest form. Served just as they
came out of the ground. Well, not exactly.

FIRST SPRING SALAD WITH ASPARAGUS 05 14

For us Midwestern chefs, April is the cruelest month. All winter long, trapped in the root cellar, you wait for something bright and green to come with the thaw. You see the Los Angeles chefs with their goddamn peas and expect your due, too. But who among us Chicago chefs hasn't felt true despair picking through a soggy harvest of wild mustard—which, let's be frank, is really a weed—the one fresh vegetable at the Chicago market in April.

I've decided it's not really spring until we get asparagus. Ours comes from Mick Klüg Farm in Saint Joseph, Michigan, sometimes in late April, sometimes not until May. But then, what joy! Asparagus picked fresh is one of those ingredients that has no correlative. It's a Persephonean leap, a shoot, a blossom pushing through the earth in a hungry reach for the sky. Tasting asparagus raw in the field is a revelation, both because of the incredibly sweet, grassy flavor and the vision of all these shoots springing forth with such verve. Natural sugars in the stalk turn quickly to starch. So when the asparagus first arrives, we rush to create new dishes with other fleeting, hopeful things—sunflower, salmon, the sharp bitter spike of wild greens.

Every year we call these dishes "First Spring Salad." We want to remind people of the moment they're in, and where they're at, what it means to us who waited all winter long, of the origin of the word "spring" as an "opening." All you LA chefs should frankly abstain from using the word. What is spring to someone who gets green garlic all year long and melons in May?

Because the puffed salmon skin takes time to prepare, consider substituting it with cured or smoked salmon. This would make for a nice salad for the first dinner at which you can leave the windows open—it goes great with a warming breeze.

MAKE THE SUNFLOWER TAHINI

Place all the ingredients in a blender with ¼ cup (2 fl oz/60 g) water and blend on high until smooth. If still grainy, pass through a fine-mesh strainer or tamis. Adjust the thickness with water; you want something schmearable.

MAKE THE SALMON SKIN

Using a chef's knife, trim and scrape any fat or meat off the salmon skin without tearing it. Set flat in a dehydrator until fully dry and crisp, approximately 24 hours.

Heat the oil in a deep fryer or large, heavy pot to 350°F/180°C or until a cube of bread browns in 30 seconds. Add the salmon skins to the oil for 45–60 seconds, until puffed up. Drain on a paper towel and season with salt and Espelette pepper.

MAKE THE ASPARAGUS

Bring a pan of water to a boil and salt generously. Fill another small bowl with a 50/50 mix of ice and water. Cook the fresh asparagus in salted water for 30 seconds, then immediately chill in the ice water bath.

Preheat your grill. Toss the blanched asparagus in olive oil and salt. Grill until the edges are charred but the asparagus is still firm. Set aside to come to room temperature.

TO SERVE

Chill 4 plates or a serving platter. Spoon the sunflower tahini onto the plate(s) in a thick swoosh. Add the asparagus and dandelion greens, then top with the artichoke vinaigrette, nasturtium oil, salmon skin, nasturtium leaves, and a squeeze of lemon juice.

SERVES 4

Sunflower Tahini
½ cup (2¾ oz/75 g) sunflower seeds
6 canned (tinned) artichoke hearts (3 oz/80 g)
4 cloves Roasted Garlic (page 246)
2 tablespoons tahini
¼ cup (2 fl oz/60 g) blend oil
Small pinch each of ground cinnamon, cayenne, and black pepper
¼ teaspoon ground cumin
1 tablespoon nutritional yeast
1½ teaspoons honey
2 tablespoons lemon juice
1 teaspoon Dijon mustard
½ teaspoon salt

Salmon Skin
8 pieces (2 oz/50 g) salmon skin
Salt and Espelette pepper

Asparagus
1 bunch (8 oz/225 g) asparagus, peeled from tip down and trimmed of its butt
2 tablespoons olive oil
Salt

To Serve
Baby dandelion green leaves
1 × quantity Artichoke Vinaigrette (page 250)
1 × quantity Nasturtium Oil (page 246)
Nasturtium leaves and/or other spring greens
Lemon juice, to taste

"SO MANY RADISHES"

0614

Sometime in the early '80s, my mother bought one of those "it slices, it dices" machines advertised on late-night TV and promptly cut her finger shaving button mushrooms for a coquilles Saint Jacques. That's what you get for being fancy. I was downstairs sitting on the carpet in front of the TV. She called out, "Help, someone, Help!" I sat up and saw the impression the rug had left on my hands and elbows from lying there since noon.

Don't worry. Italian moms exaggerate. My mother's cut was minor, but it's true that I've seen more than a few nicks when using a mandoline. Here's some practical advice: 1) Your finger is worth more than whatever you're cutting. 2) A mandoline is a razor; buy them cheap and replace when dull. 3) Pay attention. This last rule is very important. Mandolines make slicing so impossibly easy, you forget what you're doing, leading to absolute failures of attention. Most cuts come from people who have finished slicing the thing they set out to slice and then continue slicing mindlessly, no matter the consequence.

This recipe was our favorite from the summer of 2014. It's a riff on the classic duo of radishes and butter. The beauty is all in the presentation, how you slice the radish thin enough for it to be pliable yet thick enough to hold up to an elaborate stacking technique. I like to press the radish slice between my fingers once or twice to soften it enough to bend while maintaining a crisp concave shape.

Brillat-Savarin was named after the nineteenth-century gastronome Jean Anthelme Brillat-Savarin. The cheese is a triple-cream, soft-ripened cow's milk from Burgundy with a natural, bloomy rind. With the sourness of rhubarb echoing the faint sourness of the cheese itself, and the fatty triple cream cut by the peppery crunch of the radish, the flavors and textures of this dish speak to the first warm days of early spring.

MAKE THE RHUBARB SAUCE

Combine the rhubarb, vermouth, and honey in a pan. On a medium-low heat, simmer until the rhubarb is tender, about 15–20 minutes. Add the Espelette and lemon juice, then transfer to a blender. Purée on high until smooth. You may need a splash of water to blend.

MAKE THE POACHED RHUBARB

Simmer the vermouth, honey, Espelette, and vinegar in a small pan until the honey melts and the liquid is reduced by half. Add the rhubarb and simmer gently, just under a boil, until the rhubarb is tender but not soft, about 15 minutes. Remove from the heat and allow to cool.

MAKE THE PICKLED SPRING ONIONS

In a small stainless-steel or nonreactive pan, simmer the vinegar, sugar, salt, and ¼ cup (2 fl oz/60 g) water until the sugar and salt dissolve. Cool to room temperature, then pour over the spring onions. Marinate for at least 1 hour, then strain and combine the pickled spring onions and poached rhubarb.

TO SERVE

Chill 4 plates. Using the back of a wide spoon, spread the Brillat Savarin in a circle on the plate. Drizzle the rhubarb sauce over the cheese, then spoon the rhubarb and onion mix on top. Using a mandoline, shave the radishes to approximately ¹⁄₁₆-inch (1.5 mm) thick (see recipe introduction). Plate the radish slices one by one, in layers, and build a kind of nest. Drizzle with the olive oil, lemon juice, a small pinch of Maldon sea salt and Espelette, and poppy seeds. Place the crackers on the side.

SERVES 4

Rhubarb Sauce

1½ cups (6 oz/175 g) roughly chopped rhubarb

Generous ¼ cup (4¼ fl oz/130 g) sweet (red) vermouth

1 tablespoon honey

⅛ teaspoon Espelette pepper

2 tablespoons lemon juice

Poached Rhubarb

Scant 1 cup (7½ fl oz/225 g) sweet (red) vermouth

1 tablespoon honey

⅛ teaspoon Espelette pepper

1 tablespoon red wine vinegar

3 stalks (3½ oz/100 g) rhubarb, peeled and sliced into ½-inch (1 cm) segments

Pickled Spring Onions

¼ cup (2 fl oz/60 g) champagne vinegar

1 tablespoon granulated sugar

Small pinch salt

2 oz (50 g) spring onions, thinly sliced, tops and bottoms

To Serve

2¾ oz (75 g) Brillat Savarin

8–16 radishes per serving, depending on size

2 teaspoons olive oil

Lemon juice

¼ teaspoon poppy seeds

1 x quantity Olive Oil Crackers (page 252)

Maldon sea salt and Espelette pepper

CUCUMBER AND **PLUM** **SALAD** WITH **BASIL**

Plums and cucumbers are seasonal sisters. Wait for them to appear together at the market and then pick out matching sizes so neither dominates the other. We want sibling rivals, not bullies. At Lula we use a vacuum sealing machine to compress the cucumbers in the basil oil, which forces the oil into the cells of the cucumbers and transforms them into translucent, jade-like jewels. At home I toss the basil oil with the cucumbers before layering the fruit one atop the other.

Once again, the idea of theme and variations on an ingredient in our dishes made us think of the preserved Japanese plum called umeboshi, which acts as a bitter, salty foil to all the summery flavors in this dish.

MAKE THE UMEBOSHI VINAIGRETTE

In a stainless-steel bowl, whisk all the ingredients together.

TO SERVE

In a mixing bowl, add the cucumbers, basil oil, and salt to taste. Spoon yogurt into the center of a bowl and schmear with the back of the spoon. Lay cucumbers and plums on top of each other, alternating each. With every layer, drizzle over a teaspoon of vinaigrette and a sprinkle of Maldon sea salt. Finish with a drizzle of basil oil (you can use what's left behind in the bowl) and a few fresh basil leaves.

SERVES 4

Umeboshi Vinaigrette

1 tablespoon umeboshi, finely chopped

1 serrano pepper, seeded and finely chopped

½ teaspoon minced preserved lemon rind

2 tablespoons champagne vinegar

1 tablespoon minced shallot

1 teaspoon granulated sugar

2 tablespoons olive oil

To Serve

6 medium (1 lb 4 oz/560 g) cucumbers, sliced ½-inch (1 cm) thick

2 tablespoons Basil Oil (page 246)

Scant ¼ cup (1¾ oz/50 g) natural yogurt

3 medium red plums (5 oz/150 g), sliced ½-inch (1 cm) thick

Purple basil leaves

Maldon sea salt

Salt

BEET AND STRAWBERRY PANZANELLA

So—thinking about my relationship to panzanella, the task at hand when writing a cookbook. As you may know, panzanella is a Tuscan salad of tomatoes, onions, oil, vinegar, and crusty bread, in which the juices of the tomato act like a kind of dressing, but here we swap a few of those ingredients for something unexpected and new, though still full of summery juices: beets (beetroot) and strawberries.

First, I thought about writing an ode to the panzanellas I had while living in Italy. (Like this one night when I crashed a party at the Tuscan villa of a publishing magnate, a movie-set house with its own bell tower, an ancient library where the first book I opened was a legit signed first edition of *The Stranger*, and a kitchen with a jolly octogenarian chef who fed me my first utterly transformative melon-prosciutto combo (page 140) and a panzanella of the gods.) But instead I am thinking about my father-in-law, Ivan Tshilds. He passed away at 91 as I was working on this book. He lived his final years in our home with me and Lea and the kids. During the quarantine of 2020, with the chef of the house oddly unemployed, I cooked dinner every night for the family. No matter the meal, I would always serve a large leafy salad with vinaigrette and big hunks of toasted sourdough, since, like the rest of the country, I had time to make my own. After the meal, Ivan would ask for the empty salad bowl. There would be left a puddle of vinaigrette—cider-thyme, yuzu citronette, a creamy white balsamic. Ivan was tall, with long, thin, clumsy arms. He'd reach across the table, slop his toasted bread down in the pool of vinaigrette, in all that tangy, punchy, pucker-inducing oil, and just let it soak for a few minutes before popping the crouton joyfully in his mouth. I never saw such devious delight as his when soaking a piece of crunchy bread. I'm sure he'd be delighted as well by this salad's many flavors and textures, the strawberries both fresh and dried, the pecans and crunchy bitter greens, the vinegar-soaked croutons.

The truth is, when I make this salad, or any panzanella, this is what I think of now.

MAKE THE DRIED STRAWBERRIES
Place the strawberries in a dehydrator at 165°F/ 74°C and dry until the fruit is shriveled and chewy, but not dry or brittle.

MAKE THE VINAIGRETTE
Place all the ingredients in a medium bowl and whisk together without trying to emulsify the vinaigrette (keep it "broken").

MAKE THE TOASTED PECANS
Preheat the oven to 375°F/190°C. Line a sheet tray (baking tray) with parchment paper. Roast the pecans on this tray for 10 minutes, until fragrant but not browned. Leave to cool, then roughly chop.

TO SERVE
You need two mixing bowls—one bigger than the other.

First, schmear the goat cheese on 4 chilled plates. Set aside.

In one of the mixing bowls, combine the croutons, pecans, dried strawberries, mint, half the vinaigrette, half the lemon juice, and salt.

In the second bowl, combine the beets (beetroot), fresh strawberries, radicchio, remaining vinaigrette, quarter of the lemon juice, and salt.

Taste both halves and adjust salt and/or lemon juice accordingly.

Marry the two halves in the larger bowl. You've done this extra step to keep the contrast of texture and color, so that not everything is stained red, so just mix the panzanella once, gently, preferably with your hands. Don't overmix or overhandle. Divide the salad ingredients between the 4 plates and drizzle olive oil over everything.

SERVES 4

Dried Strawberries
10 oz (280 g) fresh strawberries, washed, dried, trimmed, and cut in half if large

Vinaigrette
¼ cup (2 fl oz/60 g) honey vinegar
1 tablespoon distilled white vinegar
1 tablespoon white balsamic vinegar
1 small shallot (1 oz/25 g), minced
1½ tablespoons minced chives
⅓ cup plus 1 tablespoon (3¼ fl oz/95 g) olive oil
Pinch red chile flakes

Toasted Pecans
½ cup (2½ oz/65 g) pecans

To Serve
½ cup (3½ oz/100 g) Whipped Goat Cheese (page 253)
6 oz (175 g) Sourdough Croutons (page 253)
4 mint sprigs, leaves only, torn by hand
Juice of ½ lemon
1 x quantity Roasted Beets (page 255)
3½ oz (100 g) fresh strawberries cleaned and quartered
1 small head radicchio (9oz/250 g), cored, leaves separated
Olive oil, for drizzling
Salt

ASIAN PEAR AND RADICCHIO SALAD WITH PECORINO TOSCANO 09 21

It was a rainy morning in September when I bumped into Michael Thompson—beekeeper at Chicago Honey Co-op and a well-loved guru at the Green City Market—as he rode through Logan Square on a loaded cargo bike. Michael apparently knows my tastes well. He stopped to tell me of an urban farm near Garfield Park with a patch that was filled, fence to fence, with small heads of radicchio.

"I immediately thought of you," he said. "And there you were."

We ended up buying the entire garden's worth and running this salad for, alas, just two nights. But it was memorable for the circumstance and for the dressing we created for our lucky find—a vegan poppy seed dressing that really messed with your mind. It was the perfect tangy foil. I got the idea to use aquafaba, the leftover liquid from cooking chickpeas, from Sarah and Sara of Kismet Restaurant in Los Angeles, and the way the starchy water made the verjus emulsify with the olive oil tricked most people into thinking we'd added buttermilk or yogurt. But, no, this dressing is dairy free. Then we antagonists had to shave pecorino Toscano all over the top.

Verjus is the highly acidic juice of unripe grapes. In the Middle Ages it was more common than vinegar in dressings and sauces. We use it here as part of a trio of acids that includes distilled white vinegar and cider vinegar. I love the way a mix-and-match approach to acids pulls back the assertive flavors of some vinegars (cider and sherry are particular offenders) without forfeiting the grip on your tongue. To me, verjus, especially the white variety, has a gentleness that other vinegars don't, and yet still hits all the high notes. As we say, it makes things pop.

Parsnip Chips
2 parsnips (8 oz/225 g), peeled
Salt and freshly ground black pepper

White Poppy Seed Dressing
1½ oz (35 g) shallot, minced
2 oz (50 g) garlic, minced
2 oz (50 g) fennel, minced
¼ tablespoon minced fresh ginger
1 teaspoon salt
Generous ½ cup (4½ fl oz/135 g) white verjus
1 teaspoon distilled white vinegar
1½ teaspoons cider vinegar
2 teaspoons Dijon mustard
Grated zest of 1 lemon
1 tablespoon honey
1 bunch parsley, chopped
3 tablespoons aquafaba
1 tablespoon white poppy seeds
1 cup (8 fl oz/225 g) blend oil
Scant ½ cup (3¾ fl oz/110 g) olive oil

To Serve
2 heads radicchio (1 lb 5 oz/600 g), cleaned and leaves separated
1 Asian pear (7 oz/200 g), halved, cored, and sliced
Lemon juice, to taste
4 oz (120 g) pecorino Toscano, shaved
1 teaspoon white poppy seeds
Salt and cracked black pepper

MAKE THE PARSNIP CHIPS
Heat the oil in a deep fryer or large, heavy pot to 300°F/150°C, or until a cube of bread browns in 30 seconds.

Using a vegetable peeler, create strips of parsnip by "peeling" long, wispy strands along the entire length of the root. Deep fry the parsnip pieces for 3–5 minutes, taking care to move the pieces around and fry them evenly. Drain on a paper towel-lined tray. Season with salt and pepper.

MAKE THE WHITE POPPY SEED DRESSING
In a mixing bowl, combine the shallots, garlic, fennel, and ginger with salt, verjus, and vinegars. After 15 minutes, add all the remaining ingredients except the oils. Whisk heartily; you're trying to get some air into the mixture and begin the emulsification process. Then whisk in the oils as though making an aioli. You should have a rich, creamy dressing.

TO SERVE
In a large salad bowl, dress the radicchio leaves and pear with the dressing, adding an additional splash of lemon juice. Taste and adjust the seasoning with salt and fresh cracked pepper. Build the salad in layers on 4 plates, with the leaves and pear alternating with shaved pecorino, white poppy seeds, and parsnip chips.

"TOMATO TONNATO"

08 14

For me, growing up in an Italian household meant eating foods like garlic broccoli and "sausage stuffed bread," so I have no personal connection to a dish like vitello tonnato. It reminds me of the private school kids in my hometown who'd go skiing for winter break. The boys with turned-up collars and lift tags still hanging from the zippers on their parkas. My nemeses.

Vitello tonnato, the Piedmontese dish of cold veal in a velvety, mayo-based tuna sauce, has always felt too luxe (and less passionate) than the Italian food I knew. But as I got older, I recognized tonnato sauce as the ultimate umami condiment, and truly soulful. So, while I wish I could say our dish is a Neapolitan salvo against the north, grudges are not held here. The real reason this dish happened at all was pure accident.

It was a hot night in August, late after service on the line. There were all these random tops and bottoms of gorgeous, ripe heirloom tomatoes from Leaning Shed Farm on the cutting board. Chef de cuisine Sarah Rinkavage made an improvisatory snack. She dipped some tomato in the anchovy aioli from our fregola dish and gave a giddy smile. *I got an idea*, she said.

NB: Don't expect a tomato to be delicious just because you bought it at a farmers' market or because the grocery store called it an heirloom. Neither provenance is a synonym for quality. I've learned that exceptional care and stewardship of tomato crops aren't exactly common practice. You'll need to learn which vendors have the passion. Find the ones who riff on the merits of one tomato versus another. Who are willing to hand-select a perfect choice based on the time of day. You want someone who talks about cool mornings with gravitas. Who tells you he picked the tomatoes in the dark because they were ready, that they couldn't wait till morning. Maybe the clichés about art and suffering become real when you work with tomatoes. Because while nearly all farmers at the markets need the income from a lucrative crop, there are few who grow true masterpieces. And they have suffered. One told me he slept in a tent on his farm for twelve years because he was so focused on the crop.

Store your tomatoes in a cool place, but not in the fridge. Do not squeeze or stack them, which means never, ever pile them up in a bowl. Store flat, stem-side down. Cut tomatoes with a sharp knife only, in a single long, steady stroke, like a sushi chef slicing tuna. No sawing. No serrated knives, though that would be better than a dull straight edge. Serve immediately after cutting.

SERVES 4

2 cups (16 fl oz/475 g) canola (rapeseed) oil
1 tablespoon capers
1½ lb (680 g) heirloom tomatoes, stem end removed
16 cherry tomatoes
Lemon juice, to taste
4 teaspoons olive oil
1 × quantity Tonnato Sauce (page 250)
Dill seed
Maldon sea salt and cracked pepper, to taste

In a small pan, heat the oil to 350°F/180°C. Add the capers, fry until crisp, 3–5 minutes, then drain on a paper towel.

Chill 4 plates. Cut the larger tomatoes into ½-inch (1 cm) thick slices. Cut the cherry tomatoes in half. As you slice, lay each piece of tomato flat on its side, separately, on a large plate or tray or on the edge of your cutting board. Season each slice with Maldon sea salt and black pepper, then a quick squeeze of lemon juice. Taste one to make sure you're getting the salt right. Drizzle olive oil over everything.

Divide the tonnato sauce between the 4 plates, spooning it into the centre, and press down with the back of the spoon. Carefully transfer the tomato slices and cherry tomatoes to the 4 plates, overlaying them slightly. Sprinkle the final layer of tomatoes with dill seed and fried capers.

LOBSTER, TOMATO, AVOCADO, AND RED QUINOA

0919

SERVES 4

Here's a simplified version of a composed salad created by chef Morgan O'Brien for the dinner menu in 2019. Sometimes dishes like these come out of the economic realities of running an independent, low-key joint that still wants to buy ingredients like lobster. We can't afford to serve whole tails or claws at Lula, so instead we imagined a summer salad in which the shellfish was the accent, not the star. Morgan dressed tomatoes with morsels of poached lobster and a self-reflective tomato oil. The fatty avocado brought a creamy finish without using any actual dairy at all.

If you buy the lobster already cooked, a speedy cook could have this ready for a picnic in thirty minutes. Make the oil for the pantry and keep it on hand for an August night when you want to watch the fireflies from the stoop. Please choose small, firm tomatoes so you can toss them freely in the oil without them breaking apart.

And yeah, if you want to match, you might want to change into something red.

Lobster Tails

3 lemon slices
2 tarragon sprigs
3 cloves garlic
Scant ½ cup (3¾ fl oz/115 g) white wine
2 lobster tails (8 oz/225 g)

Seasoned and Fried Quinoa

½ cup (2¾ oz/85 g) red quinoa
1 clove garlic, grated
1 teaspoon olive oil
Lemon juice, to taste
Salt

To Serve

4 large heirloom tomatoes (6 oz/180 g), sliced ¼-inch (5 mm) thin
14 red cherry tomatoes, halved
2 tablespoons Pimenton-Tomato Oil (page 246)
Lemon juice, to taste
Tarragon leaves, torn
Mint leaves, torn
½ avocado (3½ oz/100 g), diced
2 tablespoons olive oil
Wood sorrel, chervil, and tarragon leaves
Salt and freshly ground black pepper

MAKE THE LOBSTER TAILS

In a nonreactive stock pot, bring 4 cups (32 fl oz/950 g) water, lemon, tarragon, garlic, and wine to a simmer. Add the lobster tails and reduce the heat to a low simmer. Cook for 8 minutes. Cool, then remove the meat from the shell and slice into 1½-inch (4 cm) chunks.

MAKE THE SEASONED AND FRIED QUINOA

In a small saucepan, bring 1 cup (8 fl oz/ 250 g) water to a simmer and cook the quinoa until tender, about 18–20 minutes. Drain and dry on a paper towel-lined tray. Reserve ¼ cup of the quinoa for frying and set aside—it needs to air-dry for at least 30 minutes. Season the rest of the quinoa with garlic, olive oil, lemon juice, and salt and set aside.

Heat the oil in a deep fryer or large, heavy pot to 350°F/180°C, or until a cube of bread browns in 30 seconds. Fry the reserved quinoa until crisp, about 90 seconds. You'll need some kind of fine-mesh sieve or strainer to remove it from the oil. Season with salt.

TO SERVE

In a large stainless-steel mixing bowl, add the tomatoes, pimenton-tomato oil, salt, pepper, and lemon juice. Taste for seasoning and adjust. Then add the lobster, mix once or twice, and taste again. Then add the seasoned cooked quinoa. Mix and, yes, taste again. Add the tarragon, mint, and fried quinoa. Mix once. Fold in the avocado and olive oil. Carefully transfer to a serving bowl and top with wood sorrel, chervil, and tarragon leaves.

CANTALOUPE WITH
CHIMICHURRI

In the ancient walled city of Lucca in Tuscany, Lea and I waited for an hour outside a popular trattoria with our two young children. After a day spent at the beaches in Lerici and two-plus hours in the car, they were in that state of restless fatigue we parents call "overtired." The two-year-old stalked the rim of a fountain basin like a cat. The six-year-old counted skips across the piazza and back, and across again. My poor wife seemed to have fallen asleep standing up.

When we were finally brought to our table around 10 o'clock, the children were at a restraint-worthy stage of madness. I ordered all the antipasti and attempted to calm nerves with descriptions of what we were about to eat.

Issy, I told my daughter. Your favorite. Prosciutto!

Ismene loved prosciutto. With melon! I exclaimed.

She gave a skeptical look. I don't want fruit. I want food, she said.

You're going to love it, you'll see.

A simple plate of prosciutto and Tuscan melon was set on the table and we all dug in, my daughter first. She shoved thin slices of ham in her mouth, one atop the other.

No, no, I said. Eat the melon with the prosciutto. Like this. Trust me.

I wrapped the ham around a slice of melon and set it in her little hand. She closed her eyes defiantly, pinched her nostrils shut, and took a bite.

A look of pure transformative joy came across her face. A smile I can still remember.

Dad, she said. You are such an amazing chef! How did you ever think of this combination?

I rest my case. Good melon is indeed good on its own. But with salty, savory, fatty things, the combination casts a magic spell. Inspired by this night, we paired beautiful cantaloupe from Seedling Farm with shaved ribbons of ricotta salata, a chimichurri of the vibrant, cilantro (coriander)-adjacent herb papalo, and spiced pumpkin seeds. Serve on a hot summer day when you're truly at your wits' end.

SERVES 2

Compressed Melon

1 large cantaloupe (1¾ lb/800 g), trimmed of its skin, quartered, and deseeded
Scant ¼ cup (1¾ oz/50 g) lemon juice
2 tablespoons lemon "agrumato" oil
1½ teaspoons granulated sugar

Chimichurri

1 cup (¾ oz/20 g) papalo, chopped
2 cups (1½ oz/40 g) cilantro (coriander), chopped
2 tablespoons minced shallots
2 cloves garlic, minced
Scant ½ cup (3¾ fl oz/110 g) olive oil
2 tablespoons rice wine vinegar

Pepita Crumble

¾ cup (3¾ oz/115 g) pumpkin seeds
1½ teaspoons butter
¼ teaspoon granulated sugar
¼ teaspoon Espelette pepper
Salt, to taste

To Serve

2 tablespoons lemon juice
2 teaspoons olive oil
Radish slices
8 slices ricotta salata
Papalo leaves, mint leaves, cilantro (coriander) leaves, basil leaves, edible flowers
Maldon sea salt

MAKE THE COMPRESSED MELON

Cut one quarter of the melon into ½-inch (1 cm) thick slices. In a bowl, whisk the lemon juice, oil, and sugar. Toss with the melon slices and compress in a Cryovac machine, if you have one. Otherwise, set aside and chill. Slice the remaining melon in shapes of similar thickness.

MAKE THE CHIMICHURRI

Mix the herbs, shallot, and garlic together on a cutting board and chop them all finely together (yes, I know they're already chopped). Add the olive oil and rice vinegar and chop again to combine. You're going for a pesto-y quality here.

MAKE THE PEPITA CRUMBLE

Preheat the oven to 350°F/180°C. Grind all the ingredients in a food processor to a crumble consistency. Bake on a parchment-lined tray until the pumpkin seed mix is golden and fragrant, about 10–15 minutes.

TO SERVE

Toss the compressed/chilled and raw melon slices with the lemon juice and olive oil. Plate and top with the chimichurri. Garnish with radish slices, ricotta salata, pepita crumble, Maldon sea salt, and as many herbs and flowers as you wish.

WINTER
CITRUS SALAD

02 16

One night my son stops to ask, quoting *National Geographic*, did I know that humans developed an ability to taste bitterness as protection against consuming toxic plants in the wild. If this is true, I say, why do we love bitter things so much?

He shrugs. You like bitter things. I don't.

It's true I love radicchio in all its forms (see pages 80, 132, 134, 182). Maybe bitter foods heighten our senses while we eat, casting back to an instinctive understanding that what we eat might kill us.

Because I do feel, not to be dramatic, heightened physiological senses when eating bitter things. They are a foil to other tastes on the tongue. Without bitterness, sweet things are saccharine, vapid, cloying. Without bitterness, fatty things would taste plump and numb as a swollen lip.

All this to explain why I love bitter chicory with sweet citrus. Chicory here refers not to the root used in New Orleans coffee but rather to the cultivated leaf chicories that blossom into "greens" of myriad shapes, colors, and textures. Very few farms specialize in growing these vegetables in all their variegated splendor—tardivo, Castelfranco, radicchio bianco, endive, frisée, rosa di gorizia, Treviso, rosa di Veneto, puntarelle, rosso di Chioggia—it's just too much work, so most of us are limited to round red radicchio at the grocery store. This salad will bring life to the brutal winter months, making you feel like you're truly living on the edge.

NB: On cutting citrus for salads. I like to use a small, thin knife for citrus. Trim the top and the bottom of the citrus, slicing just the top ⅛ inch (3 mm), to create a flat surface on which the fruit can stand upright. Starting at the apex, carve the fruit down along its side, trimming it of rind and pith. You want smooth, long strokes here. Do not leave any white pith on the flesh. Trim as needed.

For supremes: Use a paring knife to separate the fruit flesh from the membrane by cutting on either side of each segment. Chefs usually hold the fruit in their nondominant hand while doing this, but you can lay the fruit on its side on a cutting board.

For slices: Follow the same instructions, but laterally slice ¼-inch (5 mm) rounds from the fruit.

Dress the radicchio, endive, and frisée leaves with the honey vinaigrette in a mixing bowl. Season with salt and pepper to taste.

In a serving bowl, layer the dressed bitter greens, the wheels and segments of citrus, and the goat cheese. Garnish with a grating of pistachios.

SERVES 2

2 cups (3 oz/80 g) various radicchio leaves, such as Treviso, sugarloaf, Castelfranco, etc.

1 cup (1 oz/25 g) endive leaves

½ cup (¼ oz/10 g) frisée leaves

6 tablespoons Honey Vinaigrette (page 249)

"Wheels" of citrus:

  4 slices Cara Cara oranges

  6 slices blood oranges

  ½ cup (1½ oz/40 g) mandarin supremes

1¼ oz (35 g) aged goat cheese, such as Idiazabel, shaved thin

2 tablespoons shelled pistachios

Salt and freshly ground black pepper

BRUSSELS SPROUT
SALAD
WITH CASHEWS

10 14

Seems like every fall (autumn) we ask: are we going to do this to ourselves again? Another shaved Brussels sprout salad? And yet every fall we agree that shaving these tiny, rock-hard cabbages is worth the effort and risk to our fingers. Don't worry, you'll have it easy with a party of four. It's when you serve fifty of these salads a night that the task just makes you want to collapse right there on your cutting board.

Thinly shaved raw Brussels make a terrific seasonal base for coleslaw-like salads. They're a somewhat bitter, sweet after a frost, fun to eat, juicy, crunchy, neutral base. It's important to season them first so they break down just a bit and soften, which makes for a better marriage of dressing and vegetable. Over the years we've changed the "set" many times, but we almost always deep fry individual leaves as garnish and add lots of salty, funky, creamy, fruity, and nutty elements. You want textures and bold flavors here, for a little surprise and discovery as you eat.

Some ideas from years past include smoked trout with orange, rye, and dill; apple with poppy seed, crème fraîche, and caviar; blackcurrants with pecan, arugula (rocket), and mint. But when it came time to pick my favorite it was the Brussels with the Asian pear and lime that came to mind, with the subtle funk of a fish sauce vinaigrette, fatty cashews, and cool mint.

SERVES 4

Cashew Cider Sauce
½ cup (2½ oz/65 g) cashews, lightly toasted
⅓ cup plus 1 tablespoon (3½ fl oz/ 100 g) apple cider
1 teaspoon salt

Black Lime Cashews
2 egg whites
1 tablespoon sugar
1 teaspoon salt
1½ cups (7 oz/200 g) cashews
1 black lime, grated

Fried Brussels Sprouts
6–8 Brussels sprouts (3½–4½ oz/ 100–135 g)
Salt

Shaved Brussels Sprouts
20 Brussels sprouts (12 oz/340 g)
2 teaspoons salt

To Serve
1 Asian pear (7 oz/200 g)
Lime juice, to taste
1 × quantity Fish Sauce and Lime Vinaigrette (page 250)
2 cups (3½ oz/100 g) Sourdough Croutons (page 253)
Mint leaves, torn
Grated black lime
Salt

MAKE THE CASHEW CIDER SAUCE
In a blender, purée the cashews, cider, and salt on high speed for at least 1 minute, or until as smooth as possible. Pass through a fine-mesh strainer or tamis.

MAKE THE BLACK LIME CASHEWS
Preheat the oven to 350°F/180°C.

Using an electric hand-held mixer or stand mixer with the whisk attachment, beat the egg whites to stiff peaks, then add the sugar and salt. Gently fold in the cashews. Spoon the mixture onto a silpat-lined baking tray, using the back of a spoon or spatula to spread the nuts in an even layer. Toast in the oven until golden brown, 15–20 minutes. When cool, roughly chop, and season to taste with grated black lime.

MAKE THE FRIED BRUSSELS SPROUTS
Heat the oil in a deep fryer or large, heavy pot to 350°F/180°C, or until a cube of bread browns in 30 seconds. Using a paring knife, carefully peel each layer from the Brussels sprouts, removing leaves from their core one by one, until you have 24 whole leaves. You can use whatever waste you have during this process for the salad.

Deep-fry the leaves in batches until they are crisp, 3–5 minutes. Drain on a paper towel-lined tray and season with salt.

MAKE THE SHAVED BRUSSELS SPROUTS
Using a mandoline or sharp knife, slice the Brussels as thin as possible. Ten minutes before you're about to make the salad, season them with salt. The slicing can be done ahead, but don't season until you're almost ready to serve.

TO SERVE
Dice the Asian pear into ½-inch (1 cm) cubes, then season with lime juice. In a large mixing bowl, combine the shaved Brussels with the Asian pear, vinaigrette, and croutons. Mix thoroughly, then taste for seasoning. Correct with salt and an additional squeeze of lime juice. Add the mint to the Brussels mix, then transfer to a serving platter. Drizzle the cashew cider sauce over everything. Top with the black lime cashews, the fried Brussels leaves, and a healthy grating of black lime.

SUGAR SNAP PEA
TABBOULEH

07 15

This salad of grains, hemp seeds, and sugar snap peas is a summer party dish, best enjoyed on a picnic table in the sun. Here it's served with cups of romaine and meant to be scooped up with one's fingers. At Lula, we paired it with lamb ribs braised for hours and then glazed quickly over a charcoal fire.

When fresh and properly cleaned, few vegetables are more delicious than sugar snap peas. Juicy, sweet, crunchy, with a full-on July vibe. Snap peas have two fibrous strings running along the seams that hold these green envelopes together. These, if not removed, really suck to eat. To prepare the peas, first make sure the ones you have are worth the effort—they should be firm and sweet, with actual budding peas inside them. It's easy to mistake English peas (the ones you shuck) with sugar snap peas (fully edible husks). Even produce guys mix them up. So, taste first and go by the principle that a good snap pea should live up to its name. Next, rinse your peas in iced water. With a paring knife, remove the strings by making a small diagonal incision at the tip where the pea was attached to the vine, but don't cut all the way through. You want to hold the tip in your hand, string still attached. Then use your thumb and forefinger (don't put down the knife) to remove the string by pulling the cut tip down along the inner spine of the pea. This move pulls the string off completely. Then flip and do it again, from the other direction, starting again with the vine tip and pulling the string down along its backside.

MAKE THE SNAP PEAS

You're preparing two kinds of snap peas: sliced for texture ,and a "pesto" to dress the bulgur. Bring a pot of water to a boil and salt generously. Fill another small bowl with a 50/50 mix of ice and water. Cook the peas in salted water for 30 seconds, then immediately chill in the ice water bath. Slice two-thirds of the beans cleanly on the bias and set aside.

Chop the remaining snap peas super finely and mix with all the herbs and celery leaf. Add the chopped garlic and oil and return to the cutting board. This is messy, but keep chopping everything together until the mixture resembles a homogenous paste, a "pesto." Add the lemon juice and zest. Transfer this mixture to a bowl and top with the remainder of the oil.

MAKE THE BULGUR

You're preparing both regular cooked bulgur, and a puffed bulgur.

Bring a scant ¾ cup (5¾ fl oz/ 165 g) water and the ¼ cup (2 oz/50 g) bulgur to a boil in a small pot with a tight-fitting lid. Reduce the heat to a low simmer and cook, covered, for 10 minutes. Remove from the heat and allow the pot to rest, still covered, for an additional 5 minutes. Fluff the bulgur with a fork, then set aside.

Heat the oil in a small stainless-steel skillet (frying pan) until very hot but not smoking. Add the 1 tablespoon bulgur. Shake the pan as you would when making popcorn. The bulgur will make the tiniest puffs of white—don't expect popcorn. It's less dramatic. Pour onto a paper towel-lined plate. Sprinkle with a pinch of salt.

TO SERVE

Mix the sliced snap peas, snap pea "pesto," regular bulgur, puffed bulgur, tomato jam, hemp seeds, and ground cardamom together in a bowl. Season with salt and pepper and add the lemon oil, olive oil, and lemon juice. Mix and taste for seasoning. Set a 5-inch (12.5 cm) ring mold on a plate and fill with the tabbouleh salad, pressing down firmly with the back of a spoon. Grate a little horseradish over the salad, then sprinkle a pinch of hemp seeds over the top. Drizzle with olive oil. Plate the romaine leaves next to the salad as a self-service scoop.

SERVES 4

Snap Peas

1 cup (9 oz/250 g) sugar snap peas, cleaned and prepared (see recipe introduction)

2 tablespoons minced Italian parsley

2 tablespoons minced mint leaves

2 tablespoons minced celery leaf

1 clove garlic, finely chopped

2 tablespoons olive oil

Grated zest and juice of 1 lemon

Salt

Bulgur

¼ cup (2 oz/50 g) + 1 tablespoon bulgur wheat

2 teaspoons canola (rapeseed) oil or similar

Salt

To Serve

1 × quantity Golden Tomato and Shallot Jam (page 251)

1 tablespoon hemp seeds, plus extra for sprinkling

Pinch ground cardamom

1 tablespoon lemon "agrumato" oil

1 tablespoon olive oil, plus extra for drizzling

Lemon juice, to taste

Fresh horseradish, for grating

1 head romaine lettuce (1 lb 5 oz/ 600 g), washed and leaves separated into "cups"

Salt and freshly ground black pepper

ZUCCHINI, FETA, YUZU, AND SWEET CORN

07 12

One takeaway from the several meals that I had at Charlie Trotter's and Blackbird in Chicago in the early 2000s was how to use a flavor in multiple textures, layers, and forms on one plate. I particularly remember this dish that was like the Platonic form of fennel, intensely resonant, like an orchestra playing one note and me finding endless nuance within the droning sound. There was fennel shaved raw, compressed, puréed, geléed, candied—all in tiny dots and swirls and crispy shapes around the plate, surrounding sea scallops, I think.

The same ways of thinking are here in a much more shabby-chic, Lula-style farmers' market salad of summer squash, sweet corn, tomatoes, and feta. We use corn both grilled and in a mustardy aioli. Zucchini (courgette) both raw and roasted. Textures and flavors as theme and variations.

Mix and match the varieties of summer squash—whatever you can find at the market. Patty pans, romanesco, yellow, crookneck, zephyr.

The nasturtium leaves and flowers used here belong to the mustard family. They're lightly spicy and peppery, almost like arugula (rocket). Paired with the mustard in the aioli it's another example of flavors repeating and doubling up on themselves.

SERVES 4

Sweet Corn Aioli
2 ears corn, kernels removed
 (8 oz/225 g)
1 tablespoon butter
1 egg yolk
1 teaspoon Dijon mustard
3 cloves Roasted Garlic (page 246)
1 teaspoon green yuzu kosho
1½ teaspoons yuzu juice
⅛ teaspoon salt, plus extra to taste
Scant 1 cup (7½ fl oz/225 g) blend oil

Roasted Zucchini
2 tablespoons butter
2 medium zucchini (courgette)
 (14 oz/400 g), cut on the bias
8 thyme sprigs, leaves only
1 tablespoon lemon juice
Salt and freshly ground black pepper

Grilled Corn Kernels
1 ear of corn, shucked and cleaned
 of silk
1 tablespoon olive oil
Salt and freshly ground black pepper

To Serve
5 tablespoons Yuzu Kosho Vinaigrette
 (page 250)
Lemon juice, to taste
3 small summer squash (7 oz/200 g),
 shaved on a mandoline
10 gooseberries or sungold tomatoes
 (2¾ oz/75 g), halved
½ cup (2 oz/50 g) feta, crumbled
Basil leaves
Nasturtium leaves and flowers
Sumac, for sprinkling
Salt and freshly ground black pepper

MAKE THE SWEET CORN AIOLI
In a small saucepan over a medium flame, cook the corn and the butter together for 5 minutes, then leave to cool. Add the cooked corn to a blender with the egg yolk, 2 tablespoons water, mustard, roasted garlic, yuzu kosho, yuzu juice, and salt. Blend on high for 30 seconds, then add the oil in a cautious, steady stream, until the aioli emulsifies and thickens. Pass through a fine-mesh strainer or tamis. Adjust for seasoning.

MAKE THE ROASTED ZUCCHINI
In a large sauté pan, heat the butter until foaming, then add the zucchini (courgette). Season with salt, pepper, and thyme. Cook until barely done, not too brown, just tender yet still crisp and vital, about 3–5 minutes. Cool on a tray in a single layer and drizzle with the lemon juice.

MAKE THE GRILLED CORN KERNELS
Preheat a gas or charcoal grill or griddle pan. Brush the whole corn with oil and season with salt and pepper, then grill over a medium-high heat until charred. Leave to cool, then cut the corn from the cob and set aside. Alternatively, you can roast the seasoned corn in a 400°F/200°C oven to achieve a similar roasty flavor.

TO SERVE
Schmear the aioli on the base of a serving bowl. In a separate bowl, toss the roasted zucchini (courgette) with the vinaigrette, season to taste with lemon juice, salt, and pepper, then add the corn, shaved squash and gooseberries or tomatoes. Plate on top of the aioli in a chic but messy pile. Top with feta, then scattered leaves of basil and nasturtium. Finish with a sprinkle of sumac.

Our warm plant-based dishes are not necessarily vegetarian, but they do put veggies center stage. Using a variety of cooking techniques, we pull textures and flavors from the ingredients, with the goal of surprising both your eyes and your palate.

VEGETABLES

SNAP PEAS
WITH RADISHES AND
OYSTER BUTTER

0618

Glazing a vegetable is a kind of "three chords and the truth" moment in cooking. Vegetable, water, butter. Three ingredients, nothing more. Done right, you have a luscious, creamy sauce that makes vibrant jewels of spring vegetables like radishes and peas. But without the touch, it can easily become a sloppy, drippy mess. In this recipe we do a quick glaze by blanching the snap peas and braising the radishes ahead of time, so the only cooking you do before serving is the glaze itself. Without added sugar and with a butter made of briny oysters and fragrant herbs, this glaze comes across more savory and umami-rich than most.

Elderflower can be found fresh in Chicago for about two or three weeks in July, right when these snap peas are at their finest. We get ours from Seedling Farm, or by luck on foraging walks through the city. Really nothing is prettier than these tiny white flowers dancing around on a plate of bright green peas.

MAKE THE OYSTER BUTTER

Heat 2 tablespoons of butter in a small pan. As the butter foams, add the spring onion bulbs, sauté for 30 seconds, then add the vermouth. Sauté for 2 minutes, add the oysters, sauté for an additional minute, then transfer to a mixing bowl and set aside.

Once cool, mix in the lemon zest and juice, preserved lemon, garlic, spring onion tops, parsley, and capers. Transfer this mixture to a food processor and pulse for 30 seconds. Blend with the softened butter cubes, pulsing until all the ingredients are mixed together into a compound butter.

This recipe will make a good-sized batch of oyster butter. You can freeze it for later use. Also, it's amazing on grilled steak.

MAKE THE ROASTED SPRING ONIONS

Preheat the oven to 400°F/200°C. Toss the spring onions with the olive oil and season with the salt. Lay cut-side down on a parchment-lined sheet tray (rimmed baking tray) and roast in the oven for 15–20 minutes until tender.

MAKE THE BLANCHED SNAP PEAS

Bring a pot of water to a boil and salt generously. Fill another small bowl with a 50/50 mix of ice and water. Cook the snap peas in salted water for 30 seconds, then immediately chill in the ice water bath. Leave half of the peas whole and slice the other half into rounds.

MAKE THE BRAISED RADISHES

Heat the butter in a small saucepan until it foams, then bloom the elderflower in it for 15 seconds. Add the radishes and salt, and sauté for 1 minute, just to coat. Add the vegetable stock and braise until tender, about 3–5 minutes. As soon as the radishes are done, remove from the heat, transfer from the pan to a tray and keep them in a warm place.

TO SERVE

In a small pan, bring 2 tablespoons water to a simmer. Add the whole peas and the roasted spring onion bulbs. Toss in the oyster butter and emulsify by shaking the pan and swirling the vegetables around. "Loosen" the emulsion with more water if necessary to prevent the sauce from becoming too tight or caramelizing. Once you have a luscious, creamy, shiny glaze, add the spring onion tops and the sliced peas. Season with the lemon juice and salt. Add the braised radishes just before plating, so the sauce doesn't turn pink.

Divide among 4 plates and top with basil and as much elderflower as possible.

SERVES 4

Oyster Butter

2 tablespoons butter, plus
  ¾ cup (6 oz/175 g) butter, cubed
  and softened
¾ oz (20 g) spring onion bulbs, sliced,
  plus ½ oz (15 g) spring onion tops,
  chopped
2 tablespoons dry vermouth
13 oysters (3 oz/80 g), shucked
Grated zest of 1 lemon
1 tablespoon lemon juice
1½ teaspoons preserved lemon
1 clove garlic
½ oz (10 g) chopped parsley leaves
½ teaspoon capers

Roasted Spring Onions

7 oz/200 g spring onions, halved
1 tablespoon olive oil
⅛ teaspoon salt

Blanched Snap Peas

2½ cups (8 oz/225 g) snap peas
Salt

Braised Radishes

2 tablespoons butter
1 teaspoon elderflower
2 cups (11 oz/300 g) radishes, cleaned
  and halved
¼ teaspoon salt
½ cup (4 fl oz/120 g) Vegetable Stock
  (page 255)

To Serve

1 tablespoon spring onion tops
1 tablespoon lemon juice
¼ teaspoon salt
Basil leaves
Elderflowers

WHITE ASPARAGUS
WITH PROSCIUTTO
AND WALNUT

0418

In this crunchy, mouth-watering dish, daikon and white asparagus play along like cousins. Both sweet, naturally juicy, with a hint of bitterness and spice, the radish and asparagus are like the apples and celery in a Waldorf salad. They seem to jump around in your mouth, dressed with a simple vinaigrette of lemon, olive oil, and fish sauce, which, in my opinion, should be promoted to be one of the "mother sauces." Ham and walnuts continue with the Waldorf theme, but here we char the walnuts a bit before using them in a couple different ways: crumbled over the top after a light pickle and blended into a craveable horseradish aioli. This gives everything a little smoky edge.

MAKE THE CHARRED WALNUTS
Heat a sauté pan over a medium-high flame and add the walnuts. Toast dry, tossing them continuously until the outsides lightly char. Transfer to a cooling rack or tray.

MAKE THE WALNUT-ROSEMARY CRUMBLE
Heat the oil in a deep fryer or large, heavy pot to 350°F/180°C, or until a cube of bread browns in 30 seconds. Add the rosemary and fry. It will sizzle and crisp up quickly, so pay attention and remove as soon as the leaves turn a darker shade of pine green.

Next, in a small pot, heat the vinegar, sugar, and salt until the sugar dissolves. Mix the shallots with two-thirds of the charred walnuts in a stainless-steel or nonreactive bowl and then stir in the hot vinegar mix. Rest for 30 minutes. Then drain and discard the liquid from the charred walnut mix and add the toasted walnuts and fried rosemary. Transfer this to a cutting board and hand-chop with a chef's knife until it becomes a crumble.

MAKE THE HORSERADISH AIOLI
Place the egg yolks, remaining charred walnuts, lemon juice, horseradish, mustard, and ¼ cup (2 fl oz/60 g) water into a blender. Purée until you have a homogenous, smooth mixture, then start streaming in the oil, slowly at first, until a thick emulsification forms. Season with salt.

MAKE THE FISH SAUCE VINAIGRETTE
Whisk all the ingredients together in a bowl.

MAKE THE POACHED WHITE ASPARAGUS
Peel the stalks of white asparagus. Bring a shallow pot of water to a boil and season with salt. Fill a small bowl with a 50/50 mix of ice and water. Drop the asparagus into the pan of boiling water and poach until just tender, but still with a slight crispness, 2–5 minutes. Transfer to the ice bath to cool, then dry on paper towels. Slice into small coins and set aside.

TO SERVE
In a stainless-steel or nonreactive mixing bowl, toss the white asparagus coins with the daikon coins, fish sauce vinaigrette, salt, and olive oil. Spoon the horseradish aioli onto the bottom of each plate. Top with the asparagus-daikon mix in a ring mold. Lay the prosciutto pieces over the asparagus. Drizzle the honey over this and top with the walnut crumble and mache leaves.

SERVES 4

Charred Walnuts
¾ cup (2¾ oz/70 g) walnuts

Walnut-Rosemary Crumble
¼ cup (6 g) rosemary
3 tablespoons cava or white wine vinegar
1 tablespoon granulated sugar
⅛ teaspoon salt
2 tablespoons shallot, brunoise
½ cup (2½ oz/60 g) toasted walnuts

Horseradish Aioli
2 egg yolks
1 tablespoon lemon juice
2 tablespoons grated horseradish
½ tablespoon Dijon mustard
Scant 1 cup (7½ fl oz/225 g) blend oil
⅛ teaspoon salt

Fish Sauce Vinaigrette
1 tablespoon lemon juice
1 teaspoon fish sauce
2 tablespoons olive oil

Poached White Asparagus
22 stalks (10 oz/280 g) asparagus

To Serve
2 pieces daikon (11 oz/300 g), peeled, trimmed, cut with a 1-inch (2.5 cm) ring cutter, then sliced
¼ teaspoon salt
1 tablespoon olive oil
4 slices prosciutto
1 teaspoon honey
Mache leaves

RED WINE BEETS WITH BLACKBERRY AND RED ONION

08 10

Beets, blackberry, basil, cream. A favorite theme from which to make delicious variations.

Is it a stretch to call the combination iconic? Who knows where it came from first, but I most associate it with Alain Passard of L'Arpège in Paris and the "beets and berry" dishes Jeremy Fox has done over the years in California. Wizards both.

Our version has some unique twists of its own, mostly in the vinaigrette created from dehydrated blackberries, which we use to dress the beets, and which concentrates their purple color.

Maybe it's the color, the red on black on red, staining the white spaces of the plate and the crème fraîche. Maybe it's that you expect the berries to be sweet and the beets to be earthy but it's the other way around. Maybe it's the way the dish expresses a moment in summer before the days become too long, when the first root vegetables are baby-sized and tender and the basil peppery fresh. Maybe it's that a blackberry cut in half may be the most beautiful thing on earth. I don't know, but it's definitely icon status in my world.

MAKE THE DRIED BLACKBERRIES

Place the blackberries in a dehydrator on high until totally dried out, about 35 hours. Let cool, then blend to a dust.

MAKE THE BEETS

In a Dutch oven or similar (must be heavy and have a lid), heat the butter and add the beets (beetroot), thyme, and black peppercorns. Then add the soy, red wine, red wine vinegar, 2½ cups (20 fl oz/ 600 g) water, and the salt. Cover the pot and simmer low and slow, using a heat diffuser if necessary, until the beets are tender, approximately 1 hour.

Remove the beets from the pot, leave to cool, then peel. Slice into bite-sized morsels.

MAKE THE DRIED BLACKBERRY VINAIGRETTE

In a blender, combine the dried blackberries and the olive oil on high until no large chunks remain. Transfer to a bowl, then add the remaining ingredients.

MAKE THE SUMAC POWDER

Combine the dried blackberries and sumac in a small bowl.

TO SERVE

Toss the onion petals in the sumac powder to coat them. In a separate mixing bowl, dress the beets in the vinaigrette, seasoning with salt and lemon. On a platter or individual plates, spoon the crème fraîche in a centralized puddle. Top loosely with the beets, the fresh blackberries, the petals of onion, and the basil. Drizzle the additional vinaigrette over the top and add a sprinkle of Maldon sea salt.

SERVES 4

Dried Blackberries
2½ cups (12 oz/350 g) blackberries

Beets
2 tablespoons butter
1 lb 5 oz (600 g) baby beets (beetroot), ends trimmed, washed
4 thyme sprigs
1 teaspoon black peppercorns
Generous ⅓ cup (2¾ fl oz/80 g) soy sauce
Scant 1 cup (7½ fl oz/225 g) red wine
2 tablespoons red wine vinegar
1 tablespoon salt

Dried Blackberry Vinaigrette
½ cup (½ oz/15 g) Dried Blackberries (see above)
Scant 1 cup (7½ fl oz/225 g) olive oil
1½ teaspoons Indonesian medium sweet soy sauce (we use ABC)
1 teaspoon aged balsamic vinegar
1 teaspoon balsamic vinegar

Sumac Powder
1 tablespoon Dried Blackberries (see above)
1 teaspoon sumac

To Serve
Roasted Cippolini Onions, divided into petals (page 255)
Lemon juice, to taste
2 tablespoons crème fraîche
10 fresh blackberries (3 oz/80 g), halved
Purple basil leaves
Maldon sea salt, for sprinking
Salt

POTATOES WITH
SMOKED TROUT
AND PEACH TAHINI   07 16

Potatoes go with butter.
Trout goes with butter and almonds.
Almonds go with peaches.
Peaches go with brown butter.
Brown butter goes with sesame.

As we swirl these kinds of thoughts around, flavors start to orbit our central ingredient (in this case, new potatoes from Green Acres Farm) like wayward moons. They have their own momentum, but something else happens as they spin. They grow by adding supporting elements, the lemon and coriander, the thyme and sesame. Then, on that day, Beth from the farm just happens to show up with an early batch of shishito peppers. We add them by chance and all the orbits change.

A finished dish is a tension between harmony and contrast, of sweet and smoky and salty, of texture, too, but it's also about the connections the flavors have in our experience, in our minds, in culinary culture and tradition, and the connections made, literally, face-to-face that day. Take a point of access, something familiar to many, i.e. peach and almond. Then leap from one ingredient to another until you have a dish that is composed both of comforting, familiar combinations, and the surprise contrasts that happen when you link ingredients at either end of the thought. Potato and peach. Trout and tahini.

In this, as with other Lula dishes, we push the limits of what can reasonably connect, all while remaining satisfying and unequivocally delicious. We're less interested in the risk and more fascinated by the experience of rediscovering. We strive to create dishes that bring a delight back to the familiar things—like how falling in love with the same person over and over again can still feel like something new.

Speaking of new, for a long time I thought "new" potatoes referred only to baby red potatoes in the grocery store. But when I became a farmers' market regular and discovered the first freshly dug potatoes of the year, with their wispy skins and unique colors and shapes, I understood that new potatoes were really just about another precious moment in time.

SERVES 4

New Potatoes
16 small new potatoes (11¾ oz/340 g)
5 thyme sprigs, leaves picked
1 tablespoon olive oil
¼ teaspoon salt
Freshly ground black pepper

Peach Tahini
1 lb (450 g) peaches, skin-on, pitted
1 tablespoon olive oil
2 tablespoons tahini
3 cloves Roasted Garlic (page 246)
2 tablespoons lemon juice, plus extra
  as needed
¼ teaspoon coriander seeds
¼ cup (1¼ oz/40 g) Brown Butter
  (page 170)
¼ teaspoon salt, plus extra to taste

Shishito Peppers
1 tablespoon canola (rapeseed) oil
20 shishito peppers (5 oz/150 g)

Brown Butter Vinaigrette
½ cup (3 oz/85g) Brown Butter
  (page 170)
Grated zest and juice of 1 lemon
8 thyme sprigs, leaves picked
1 teaspoon honey

Almond Crumble
1 tablespoon butter
¾ cup (3½ oz/100 g) whole almonds
5 thyme sprigs, leaves picked
¼ teaspoon ground coriander
¼ teaspoon cracked black pepper
¼ teaspoon dried lemon peel
1 tablespoon white sesame seeds
¼ teaspoon salt

MAKE THE NEW POTATOES

Preheat the oven to 425°F/210°C. Toss the potatoes with the thyme leaves, oil, salt, and a little pepper. Roast on a parchment-lined sheet tray (rimmed baking tray) for 30–40 minutes, until fork tender. When cool, slice each one in half.

MAKE THE PEACH TAHINI

Preheat the oven to 375°F/190°C. Toss the peaches in the olive oil in a mixing bowl. Place on a parchment-lined sheet tray and roast for 1 hour or until thoroughly cooked. Leave to cool, then chop roughly. Put all the ingredients into a blender with ¼ cup (2 fl oz/60 g) water and blend on high. It will need assistance to blend smoothly (page 21). When done, pass through a fine-mesh strainer or tamis. Taste for seasoning and adjust salt or lemon juice, if needed.

MAKE THE SHISHITO PEPPERS

Heat a cast iron skillet or heavy frying pan over very high heat until nearly smoking. Add the canola (rapeseed) oil. Immediately, yet with caution, add the peppers and sear on high heat until lightly charred, approximately 2–3 minutes. Leave to cool, then slice thinly and perpendicularly, discarding the stems.

MAKE THE BROWN BUTTER VINAIGRETTE

Place all the ingredients in a mixing bowl and whisk to combine.

MAKE THE ALMOND CRUMBLE

Heat a sauté pan over a medium flame. Add the butter and almonds and sauté until fragrant and golden, just 1–2 minutes, then add the remaining ingredients. Swirl everything around as the butter froths and foams, but do not brown. Reduce the heat if necessary. Once toasty and richly golden, remove from the pan to a tray to cool. Once cool, roughly chop by hand.

TO SERVE

Dollop the peach tahini in the center of each plate. Using the back of the spoon, schmear the tahini in a smooth, thick circle. In a medium sauté pan or sauce pot, warm the potatoes, slowly and gently, with the brown butter vinaigrette. Taste for seasoning and add salt if necessary. Remove to a mixing bowl and add the shishito peppers, trout, diced peaches, chives, almond crumble, lemon juice, and pepper. Toss and then plate on top of the tahini. I add dill flowers, though you'll have to be in the right place at the right time for that, too.

To Serve

¼ cup (1½ oz/35 g) smoked trout, torn into bite-sized pieces
¼ cup (1½ oz/35 g) diced fresh peach
1 tablespoon chives, sliced super thin
1 teaspoon lemon juice
2 flowers of fresh flowering dill (optional)
Few robust cracks black pepper
Salt

Image on page 160

HASSELBACK
SWEET POTATO WITH
BLACK LENTILS

12 19

The retro but now faddish hasselback technique is said to have originated in a Stockholm restaurant, the Hasselbacken, in the 1940s. It refers to the process of cutting a potato into Pringle-thin slices without cutting all the way through, making a sculptural showpiece of a vegetable not known for its glamor. The hasselback technique isn't just for looks, though—it gives the potato increased surface area and dynamic edges that, when roasted, broiled (grilled), and glazed in a hot oven, showcase the homely root as though it were an expensive cut of meat.

Vegan dishes like this one deserve a star, something "center of the plate," and when you use this simple but impressive technique, a potato can front like a diva just as much as any brawny, bone-in, dry-aged steak.

That said, there are many types of sweet potato and we recommend a variety called the Beauregard, mainly for its long, narrow shape and the deep orange of its flesh.

MAKE THE BLACK LENTILS

Rinse the lentils in cold water, then drain. Add the lentils with 1⅔ cups (14½ fl oz/ 420 g) water to a medium pot with a tight-fitting lid and bring to a boil. Reduce the heat to a gentle steady simmer and cook, covered, for 10–15 minutes or until tender. Strain through a fine-mesh strainer and spread the lentils out on a tray to cool. Reserve ½ cup (3½ oz/100 g) of lentils for the fried lentils (see below). In a mixing bowl, toss the remaining cooked lentils with the yuzu kosho, figs, red onion, olive oil, salt, and lemon juice.

MAKE THE FRIED LENTILS

Heat the oil in a deep fryer or large, heavy pot to 350°F/180°C, or until a cube of bread browns in 30 seconds. Fry the reserved lentils until crisp, 2–4 minutes, then drain on paper towels. At the restaurant, we use a small fine-meshed colander with a long handle, so you can literally drop the lentils inside the colander into the oil, then remove them easily. Season with salt.

MAKE THE SEAWEED POWDER

Preheat the oven to 325°F/165°C. Lay the dulse on a sheet tray (rimmed baking tray) and toast in the oven for 10 minutes. Leave to cool, then grind to a powder in a spice grinder or blender.

MAKE THE HASSELBACK SWEET POTATO

Preheat the oven to 375°F/190°C. Place the sweet potatoes on a cutting board between two chopsticks. The chopsticks will prevent you from cutting all the way through the potato, providing a physical stop for the knife, which, by the way, needs to be surgically sharp. Make parallel slices in the sweet potatoes every ⅛ inch (3 mm), but only go three-quarters of the way through the potato. The cuts should be precise and clean. Trim the ends. Carefully brush the potatoes with oil and sprinkle with salt. Wrap them individually in aluminum foil and bake in the oven for 45 minutes.

MAKE THE SWEET POTATO SAUCE

Peel the potatoes, dice, and rinse in cold water for 30 minutes. Juice the potatoes, then strain the juice through a fine-mesh strainer or tamis. Transfer the strained juice into a sauce or stock pot and bring to a simmer, stirring constantly. Reduce by half and strain a second time. Cool, then transfer the juice to a blender with the remaining ingredients. Purée and set aside.

MAKE THE YUZU LACQUER

Whisk the yuzu juice and olive oil together in a mixing bowl.

SERVES 4

Black Lentils
½ cup (3¾ oz/110 g) black lentils
½ teaspoon green yuzu kosho
3 dried figs, finely chopped
1 tablespoon red onion, brunoise
1½ tablespoons olive oil
¼ teaspoon salt
1 teaspoon lemon juice

Fried Lentils
½ cup (3 oz/80 g) cooked lentils (reserved from above)
Salt

Seaweed Powder
1 cup (¾ oz/20 g) dulse

Hasselback Sweet Potato
4 sweet potatoes (2¼ lb/1 kg), scrubbed clean
2 tablespoons olive oil
2 teaspoons salt

Sweet Potato Sauce
5 sweet potatoes (3 lb/1.4 kg)
1 tablespoon olive oil
⅛ teaspoon xanthan gum
⅛ teaspoon salt
1 teaspoon lemon juice

Yuzu Lacquer
3 tablespoons yuzu juice
3 tablespoons olive oil

MAKE THE YUZU AIOLI

Place all the ingredients in a blender with 3 tablespoons water and purée on high until smooth.

TO SERVE

Combine the cooked and fried lentils in a mixing bowl, check for seasoning, adding lemon juice or salt if necessary. Set aside.

Reheat the sweet potato sauce and set aside somewhere warm. Meanwhile, using a pastry brush, glaze the potatoes with the yuzu lacquer and reheat in the oven. Continue to brush the potatoes with the lacquer as they reheat; as the yuzu reduces on the surface of the potato it will make you understand why we call this a lacquer. You will likely need to urge the perforated slices of the potato to separate, pushing them apart to create more surface area and places for the lacquer to penetrate. Remove the potatoes and turn on the broiler (grill). Brush again with the lacquer and then place the potatoes under the broiler to lightly brown and crisp the edges and skin.

Spoon the yuzu aioli into the center of a large platter or 4 individual plates. Place the potatoes on the aioli, then spoon the sweet potato sauce around the potatoes. Cover the potatoes with the mixture of crispy and cooked lentils. Sprinkle the plate with seaweed powder.

Yuzu Aioli

8 oz (225 g) firm tofu
1 tablespoon Roasted Garlic purée
  (page 246)
1 tablespoon yuzu juice
⅛ teaspoon salt

To Serve

Lemon juice, to taste
Salt

Image on page 161

BUTTERNUT SQUASH WITH 'NDUJA AND AGED GOUDA

0916

'Nduja is a fatty, funky, spreadable pork sausage originally from Calabria, Italy, made from the "fifth quarter" leftovers of a pig after its more valued parts have been sold off by the butcher. Ours is made here in Chicago by Tempesta Artisan Salumi, run by a family that has been in the restaurant business for generations, and whose youngest members had the vision to make 'nduja the traditional way, with Calabrian chiles and a high proportion of fat. The result is pure funk, with a sweet, nearly buttery texture, and addictively delicious. Even if you don't follow this recipe, please buy some 'nduja and spread it on grilled bread, fold it into your morning eggs, toss it with pasta, or add it to a buttery sauce for fish.

In this recipe, we purposefully "break" the sausage by submitting it to a hot skillet (frying pan) before tossing it with roasted winter squash. The little bits of pork crisp up in the fat and seem to get more flavorful with every minute on the stove, as the rendering lard releases the fragrance and umami of fermented chile and garlic. 'Nduja is unmistakably the product of resourceful folks struggling through conquest and poverty.

Although it takes place in Basilicata, and not Calabria, the piece of art that really brought this point home for me is Carlo Levi's memoir *Christ Stopped at Eboli*, and especially the film version directed by Francesco Rosi. If you want to understand what it might have been like for the people of southern Italy, who made sausages like this, meditate on the scene where the townspeople butcher a pig in the square, where certainly nothing went to waste, and where the purpose of the cooking could not be more at odds with where we are today.

SERVES 2

Roasted Butternut Squash
1 butternut squash (3¼ lb/1.5 kg)
2 tablespoons olive oil
2 teaspoons salt
Freshly ground black pepper, to taste

'Nduja Vinaigrette
½ cup (3¾ oz/115 g) 'nduja
1 tablespoon chopped shallots
1 teaspoon chopped garlic
1 tablespoon sherry vinegar
6 tablespoons blend oil

Fried Pumpkin Seeds
2 tablespoons blend oil
⅓ cup (2 oz/50 g) pumpkin seeds
¼ teaspoon paprika
⅛ teaspoon salt

To Serve
2 tablespoons Roasted Garlic Aioli (page 248)
½ oz (15 g) aged gouda, shaved
¼ oz (10 g) dill

MAKE THE ROASTED BUTTERNUT SQUASH
Separate the "neck" of the butternut squash from the round bottom section. Peel both, then slice the neck crosswise into circles ¾-inch (1.5 cm) thick. Cut the bottom section in half, scrape out the seeds, then cut the halves into wedge-shaped pieces. You should have approximately 6 "rounds" and 9 "wedges."

Lay out the squash rounds and wedges on a sheet tray (rimmed baking tray). Brush with olive oil and season with salt and pepper. Roast until just tender, 15–20 minutes, as they will be cooked again later.

MAKE THE 'NDUJA VINAIGRETTE
Combine all the ingredients in a food processor and purée until smooth.

MAKE THE FRIED PUMPKIN SEEDS
In a sauté pan or skillet (frying pan), heat the oil, then add the pumpkin seeds. Toast over medium-high heat until fragrant, glossy, and golden-green. Season with paprika and salt. Set aside on a paper towel-lined tray.

TO SERVE
In a large sauté pan or rondeaux that will fit all the squash, add the 'nduja vinaigrette, breaking it up with a wooden spoon, then let it melt, before adding the squash to the pan. Cook over medium-high heat until the edges of the squash crisp and the broken vinaigrette starts to turn golden brown. Baste the squash with the hot vinaigrette, continuing to allow it to brown. On a platter, schmear or dot the roasted garlic aioli. Top with the roasted squash and remaining vinaigrette from the pan, followed by the aged gouda, fried pumpkin seeds, and dill.

CARROTS,
PLUMS, AND DILL

We experimented with using shio koji, the mold responsible for Japanese fermented products like miso, soy sauce, and sake, to marinate meats like pork shoulder and quail before we started using it on vegetables. But this idea really took hold for us. These hearty carrots from Butternut Sustainable Farm in southwest Michigan have the strength of character to stand up to a night spent in this mysterious, umami-rich culture. The enzymes in the shio koji will tenderize and season the carrots, making them quick to cook and delicious to eat.

Marinate the carrots with the shio koji in a foil-wrapped package or tight container overnight, or for 12 hours in the refrigerator.

Preheat the oven to 350°F/180°C. Remove the carrots from the foil, then rinse or wipe off the shio koji and pat dry. Toss the carrots with olive oil in a mixing bowl. Then transfer to a sheet tray (rimmed baking tray) and par-roast in the oven until just tender, 7–10 minutes.

Place the par-roasted carrots in a medium sauté pan and toss with butter, lemon juice, and salt. Return to the stove over medium heat and glaze in the butter and lemon juice for 1–2 minutes. Schmear the dill aioli over 2 plates, then place the roasted carrots on top. Garnish with party crunch, plum slices, and dill sprigs.

SERVES 4

1 lb 5 oz (600 g) baby carrots, tops
   removed, lightly peeled or scrubbed
2¼ oz (60 g) shio koji
4 tablespoons olive oil
2 tablespoons butter
Lemon juice, to taste
¼ cup (3½ oz/100 g) Dill Aioli
   (page 249)
6 teaspoons "Party Crunch"
   (page 248)
2 plums, sliced
Bunch of dill
Salt

FINGERLING POTATOES
WITH SALT COD
AND GRAPES

09 19

In this recipe we use baccalà, or salt cod, in the same way you might use hunks of bacon in a breakfast hash. We cut the soaked salt cod into "lardons" and crisp them up in the pan to flavor this dish of roasted fingers, mushrooms, roasted onions, and fresh green grapes. Since you must soak salt cod for at least a day before using it, this step takes a bit of foresight; just skip it if you'd like and use pancetta or slab bacon instead.

My favorite thing about putting grapes in savory preparations is the way the sweet-sour juice bursts over the hot, fatty, rich elements of a dish. These local grapes, which ripen in the first weeks of September, are frank little reminders of the sweet joys of summer just when you need it the most.

SERVES 4

Confit Potato
___

1½ cups (12 fl oz/350 g) olive oil

1½ cups (12 fl oz/350 g) canola (rapeseed) oil

1 lb (450 g) fingerling potatoes, washed and dried

6 cloves garlic

6 pearl onions

1 teaspoon black peppercorns

5 thyme sprigs

4 rosemary sprigs

Chanterelles
___

1½ cups (4 oz/120 g) chanterelles, cleaned

1 shallot (¾ oz/20 g), thinly sliced

2 tablespoons butter

¼ cup (2 oz/50 g) salt cod, soaked overnight and cut into ½-inch (1 cm) lardons

2 tablespoons chopped parsley

Lemon juice, to taste

Salt, to taste

Grape and Pearl Onion Mix
___

Reserved pearl onions from confit (see above)

⅛ cup (1¼ oz/30 g) green grapes

1 oregano sprig, leaves picked

¼ teaspoon grated lemon zest

1 tablespoon olive oil

To Serve
___

2 tablespoons butter

1½ tablespoons za'atar, plus extra to garnish

Lemon juice, to taste

Salt, to taste

MAKE THE CONFIT POTATO

Heat the oils in a pot wide enough to hold all the potatoes (wide and shallow is best). Once the oil reaches 190°F/88°C, add the potatoes, garlic, pearl onions, peppercorns, and herbs. Simmer gently, maintaining a temperature of 190–200°F/88–93°C, cooking until the potatoes are tender, approximately 30–45 minutes depending on size. Strain the potatoes and pearl onions from the oil and set aside to cool. Discard the herbs. When cool enough to handle, the potatoes should be sliced into ¼-inch (5 mm) rounds.

MAKE THE CHANTERELLES

Heat a medium sauté pan until very hot, but not smoking, and add the chanterelles—yes, dry. Reduce the heat to medium and stir. The heat will extract water from the mushrooms and in a few moments you should have a little pool of mushroom "jus" in your pan. Let that liquid cook off and, just as the last droplets evaporate, add the shallots and butter. Cook until golden brown and tender, 3–5 minutes, then add the salt cod, parsley, and lemon juice to taste. Taste for seasoning; it might need a little salt but remember that the salt cod is, well, salty.

MAKE THE GRAPE AND PEARL ONION MIX

Cut the pearl onions in half and separate the layers into "petals." Cut the grapes in half. Mix all the ingredients gently in a bowl. Place the mixture on a sheet tray (rimmed baking tray) and heat in the oven, or in a separate small pan, until just sizzling but not broken down.

TO SERVE

In a large pan, heat the butter and add the confit potatoes. Sauté gently for 3–5 minutes, then add the za'atar. Add the chanterelle mix and toss together. Taste for seasoning and add more lemon or salt if needed. Plate the mushroom-potato mix in a serving bowl and top with the grapes and onions. Sprinkle a little more za'atar over the top and serve.

CAULIFLOWER
WITH BROWN BUTTER
HOLLANDAISE

12 18

Citrus and butter—it's a savory creamsicle.

SERVES 4

MAKE THE SPICE MIX

Grind all the ingredients in a mortar and pestle and set aside.

MAKE THE ROASTED CAULIFLOWER

Preheat the oven to 425°F/220°C. Slice the cauliflower into 2-inch (5 cm) steaks, reserving any smaller florets. You should get about 8 steaks. Place the steaks on a parchment-lined sheet tray (rimmed baking tray) and the smaller florets on a separate tray. Spray both with olive oil, then season with a generous sprinkle of the spice mix.

Roast until golden brown and tender, approximately 25 minutes. Obviously, the smaller tray will finish first. Keep an eye on both and reduce the oven temperature if necessary. You want a deep golden color, veering on toasty brown in spots, with crispy edges, tender texture, but not blown out.

MAKE THE BROWN BUTTER

Make the brown butter by cooking the butter in a small pan on a medium heat until toasty and brown. Remove from the heat and keep warm.

MAKE THE BROWN BUTTER HOLLANDAISE

Add the ingredients to a blender with 3 tablespoons of water and purée for 30 seconds, then slowly stream in the brown butter as though you were making an aioli. Once thickened, keep warm until ready to use.

MAKE THE BROWN BUTTER CRUNCH

Melt the butter in a small pan and stir in the milk powder. Allow it to toast, stirring, for 3–5 minutes, then transfer to a dehydrator and dry out to a crunchy crumble. Add the nutritional yeast and party crunch and stir to combine.

TO SERVE

On each of 4 warm plates, lay out 2 steaks and 2 florets of cauliflower. Spoon 5 white grapefruit supremes over each plate of cauliflower, then top with hollandaise, brown butter crunch, tarragon, and a dusting of lemon powder.

Spice Mix

2 teaspoons pink peppercorns
1 teaspoon black peppercorns
½ teaspoon Aleppo pepper
½ teaspoon dried lemon peel
1 tablespoon salt

Roasted Cauliflower

1 head cauliflower (2 lb/900 g)
Olive oil spray

Brown Butter

1¼ cups (10 oz/285 g) butter

Brown Butter Hollandaise

4 egg yolks
¼ cup (2 fl oz/60 g) white grapefruit juice
2 tablespoons lemon vinegar
¼ teaspoon xanthan gum
¼ teaspoon salt
Small pinch Aleppo pepper

Brown Butter Crunch

2½ oz (75 g) butter
1¼ oz (30 g) nonfat dried milk powder
3 tablespoons nutritional yeast
½ cup (2¼ oz/60 g) "Party Crunch" (page 248)

To Serve

20 white grapefruit supremes (page 48)
Tarragon leaves
Grilled Lemon Powder (page 74), for dusting

WHITE SWEET POTATO ROSTI WITH MATSUTAKE AND PEAR 11 17

These rosti came to the menu at Lula with a lavish pile of white matsutake mushrooms shaved on top. I loved the way the homely fried potato crunched beneath lacy wisps of elegant mushroom. Talk about high/low. It's like wearing Wranglers with Chanel. They're basically a hash brown. Serve them with good bacon and a sunny-side egg on one of those late mornings when you're trying to reconnect to better instincts.

It's not common to use a Japanese sweet potato for rosti, but like everyone else, we fell hard for the Murasaki variety (white flesh, purple skin) that you see on many menus these days. The hype is real, and the simplicity of a rosti seems to bring out the uniquely nutty flavors of the Murasaki. That said, a russet will do just fine and might be somewhat easier to handle.

No other vegetable has been studied more than the potato. For the curious, there are full-on dissertations about the relationships between starch, water, heat, caramelization. The goal is predictably the same: crunchy and golden on the outside, soft and creamy at the center. Rosti don't use flour or egg to bind them. Instead, the starch in the potato and the fat from the butter do the work. Your rosti could fall apart if you're less than cautious, but they won't be any less than delicious.

There's much debate about whether to boil the potatoes first. At Lula, we cook them in a controlled water bath at 140°F (60°C) for 20 minutes. A brief poach like this alters the texture of the potatoes, making them more golden, more crisp, and more inclined to keep their form.

MAKE THE PEAR SOUBISE

Heat 1 tablespoon oil and the leeks in a small saucepan over low heat, covered, for 7 minutes. Add the white wine, cook for 10 minutes, then add the pears, ginger, horseradish, and 1 cup (8 fl oz/250 g) water. Cover and cook until tender, adding more water if necessary. Leave to cool.

Add the tofu and xanthan gum and blend in a high-speed blender until smooth, then stream in the remaining blend oil. Season with salt and lemon juice to taste.

MAKE THE ROSTI

Poach the potatoes in a water bath for 20 minutes (optional, see recipe introduction), then chill in the refrigerator. Shred (grate) the potatoes in a food processor or using the large holes of a box grater. Place the potatoes in a tall container and set in the sink, then run cold water over the potatoes to rinse them. Every 3–5 minutes, agitate the potatoes to prevent them from clumping and to release starch. Continue washing until the water runs clear.

Strain the potatoes and dry thoroughly. Then, expel residual water from the shredded potatoes by squeezing them as hard as you can. Set the wrung-out potatoes on fresh paper towels. Do this a handful at a time. The drier the potatoes, the crispier the rosti.

Place 1 cup of the shredded potatoes in a mixing bowl. Add a quarter of the Parmesan, 1 tablespoon of clarified butter, season with salt and pepper, and mix. Using your hands, shape into a small patty, then repeat with the remaining ingredients. Cook the rosti on a griddle, or an 8-inch (20 cm) heavy frying pan or nonstick pan will also work, until golden brown and cooked through.

TO SERVE

In a small mixing bowl, combine the matsutake mushrooms, olive oil, lemon juice, and salt. Place a rosti onto each of 4 plates, topped with 1 tablespoon of pear soubise, the matsutake mushrooms, and a drizzle of oil.

SERVES 4

Pear Soubise

4 tablespoons blend oil
1 leek (3½ oz/100 g), white part only, chopped
Scant ½ cup (3¾ fl oz/110 g) dry white wine
2 pears (10 oz/280 g), peeled and chopped
½ teaspoon minced fresh ginger
1 tablespoon + ½ teaspoon chopped peeled fresh horseradish
2 tablespoons soft tofu
Pinch xanthan gum
Lemon juice, to taste
Salt

Rosti

2 medium Japanese white sweet potatoes (14 oz/400 g)
1 oz (25 g) Parmesan, grated
4 tablespoons clarified butter
Salt and freshly ground black pepper

To Serve

2–3 matsutake mushrooms, cleaned and shaved
1 tablespoon olive oil
Lemon juice, to taste
Salt

To borrow from Sophia Loren, "Everything you see I owe to Pasta Yiayia." These dishes follow that guide—a little bit of tradition, old-school technique, and some kind of delightfully surprising, unexpected, "outside" flavor.

PASTA & ONE RISOTO

PAPPARDELLE WITH WALNUT BOLOGNESE

09 21

Here is a long and possibly intimidating recipe. Let's parse it out.

First, to save some time, feel free to buy the pasta from an artisan source. Second, while the process for the sauce has a lot of steps, they are basic steps that anyone can do—put one foot in front of the other and you'll get there. The recipe is not long because we're trying to be difficult; rather, it's because we want this Bolognese to have texture, which comes from adding ingredients in several stages, including walnuts and tomatoes two separate times, to prevent the amalgam from a fate as soggy mush.

What makes a dish like this work is not the sauce or the pasta, necessarily, but rather the technique at the end that marries those two elements. Think of this step as an emulsification. Just as you make an aioli by whisking oil into an egg, here you "whisk" cold butter and cheese into the hot Bolognese by a vigorous shaking of the pan until the sauce becomes creamy and unctuous. It is a literal suspension of fat (butter, cheese) in water (the sauce). In Italian culinary language, this process is called *mantecare*. Once again, a compelling Italian culinary term is an action word—in this case, a verb with a root belonging to the word for lard, referring to this process of emulsifying butter and cheese into a pasta sauce or risotto at the end. To make the emulsification stick to the pasta itself you'll need to adjust the thickness of the Bolognese with starchy pasta water and toss, swirl, toss, swirl. Really this is an athletic move, tossing the pasta in the pan as the cheese and butter combine with the Bolognese and attach themselves to each strand of dough. You might find your forearms sore the morning after making this recipe.

The result you're looking for is a kind of transformative unity between these elements—a holy ghost of cooking. Flipping the noodles while adjusting the thickness of the sauce with additional pasta water is the art of the *primi*. When it's right, the sauce will cling to the pasta without clumping. Each strand will be dressed with just the right amount of delicious Bolognese, able to be pulled and twirled independently of the others. Without the right touch, this marriage can easily "break" and collapse into a greasy, wet mistake.

This recipe will make more than you need. The sauce can be saved in the refrigerator for up to 7 days and frozen for much longer. The pasta can be refrigerated and used the next day.

SERVES 4

Pappardelle
3½ cups (1lb/450 g) "00" flour, plus extra for dusting
5 eggs
Coarse semolina, for dusting

Walnut Bolognese
15 oz (420 g) canned whole San Marzano tomatoes, drained
6½ oz (185 g) onion, finely diced
14 cloves garlic, chopped
3½ oz (100 g) carrots, diced
3½ oz (100 g) celery, diced
3½ cups (1½ lb/675 g) oyster mushrooms
Generous ½ cup (4¼ fl oz/130 g) olive oil
1 tablespoon tomato paste
1½ cups (5 oz/150 g) walnuts, toasted and finely chopped
Scant 1 cup (7½ fl oz/225 g) red wine
1 tablespoon red miso
Scant 1 cup (7½ fl oz/225 g) Vegetable Stock (page 255)
Parmesan rind (approx. 3 oz/85 g)
Small pinch ground nutmeg

Tomato Purée
11 oz (300 g) San Marzano tomatoes
1 clove garlic, grated
1 tablespoon olive oil
Pinch chile flakes

MAKE THE PAPPARDELLE

To the bowl of a standing mixer with the hook attachment, add the flour and eggs and mix for 5 minutes. The dough should come together in a ball, but if it seems a little too dry or crumbly you can add a splash of water. Turn the dough out onto a clean surface and knead for 1 minute, until it forms an elastic ball. Wrap in plastic wrap (cling film) and let sit for 1 hour or overnight.

Set a pasta machine to the widest roller setting. Flatten the dough into smaller pieces no more than 2 inches (5 cm) wide Run through the machine, dusting lightly with flour. Repeat 3 times. Reduce the settings on the roller by the smallest increment possible. Run the piece through the roller repeatedly, each time narrowing the setting until the dough is $\frac{1}{16}$-inch (1.5 mm) thick or just translucent. Return the machine to the widest setting for the next ball of dough. Repeat the process until you have all the dough rolled into flat sheets. Dust with flour.

Cut the sheets into 1½-inch (4 cm) ribbons. Dust gently with semolina.

MAKE THE WALNUT BOLOGNESE

Pass the tomatoes through a food mill, then transfer to a small saucepan and bring to a simmer over medium heat. Reduce by half, then set aside.

In a food processor fitted with the chopping blade, pulse the onion, garlic, carrots, and celery. Remove and set aside. Grind the mushrooms in the food processor in the same way. Set aside.

In a large sauce pot or rondeaux, add the olive oil with the onion, garlic, carrots, and celery and sweat the vegetables until translucent. Add the tomato paste. Stir and continue to cook for 3–5 minutes, until the tomato paste is incorporated with the vegetables.

Next, add the mushrooms to the pan and continue to stir and sweat until all the water released by the mushrooms is cooked out. Add two-thirds of the walnuts, stir, and keep cooking. After 5 minutes, add the red wine and the reduced tomatoes. Cook for 5 minutes, then add the miso, stock, Parmesan rind, and nutmeg. Cover the pot and let cook for another 40 minutes, stirring occasionally, and checking to make sure the sauce doesn't dry out. Add splashes of water if it starts to stick, but maintain a low and consistent heat. Add the remaining walnuts, stir to combine, then taste for salt as needed.

MAKE THE TOMATO PURÉE

Pass the tomatoes through a food mill and season with garlic, olive oil, and chile flakes. Set aside.

TO SERVE

Cook the pasta in a large pot of salted boiling water until al dente; depending on the dryness of the pasta, this could be 2–6 minutes.

Meanwhile, in a sauté pan large enough to hold the pasta, add the Bolognese, tomato purée, and a splash of pasta water. Heat and stir. Add the butter and swirl the pan to emulsify it into the sauce. Pull the pasta just as soon as it's done and add to the pan with the Parmesan and the parsley. Vigorously stir and flip and swirl the pasta in the sauce, emulsifying the butter and the cheese. If the sauce gets too tight, add another splash of pasta water. Season with salt and lemon juice to taste. Top with additional Parmesan and a drizzle of olive oil.

To Serve
1½ tablespoons butter
2 tablespoons grated Parmesan, plus extra for sprinkling
1 teaspoon chopped parsley
Lemon juice, to taste
Olive oil, for drizzling
Salt

Image on page 178

SPAGHETTI WITH CLAMS, SQUASH BUTTER, AND KALE

12 14

I had my first spaghetti alle vongole in a strip mall in West Haven, Connecticut, close to the shore but far from anywhere you'd actually want to fish. We'd sit in the tall brown leather booths at Lorenzo's Ristorante while my father reminisced about Savin Rock, the boardwalk-style amusement park that once made this pier Connecticut's Atlantic City. The vongole came with soup, salad, and bread. It tasted briny and sweet at the same time. Grassy from fistfuls of chopped parsley. I can still feel the way the olive oil slicked my lower lip and chin. There was a racetrack over there, my dad said, pointing in the direction of the parking lot. You could watch without paying from the top of the fence. Lorenzo came out to talk with us in a cook's shirt stained with tomato sauce. He'd been raised here, too.

When my father passed, it was Lorenzo who offered to host the repast, giving me a "F&F deal" on the same room he gave us for my father's mother when she died. More than a few guys came in full-length fur coats. At the same table three different Louies ate cavatelli with broccoli rabe, ziti with sausage, and the classic spaghetti alle vongole.

This, however, is a wintertime "vongole," served far from the shore. We fly our clams in from the East Coast, but then take all sorts of Midwestern liberties, adding ham, squash, and kale. In the end clam pastas get most of their flavor from the liquid released as the clams steam open. You want to save that just as soon as it's released. Make sure you don't destroy the clam meat itself by overcooking them at the outset. And since you're working with salty ingredients here— both the clams and the ham—back off from salting the pasta water and taste carefully as you go. Do not overcommit yourself. Salt is one promise you can't break.

SERVES 4

Squash Butter
1 small butternut squash (1 lb 2 oz/ 500 g)
2 cloves garlic
2 tablespoons olive oil
¾ teaspoon salt
8 oz (225 g) butter, softened
½ teaspoon lemon juice

Serrano Ham Soffritto
1 cup (5 oz/150 g) finely diced serrano ham
2¾ oz (70 g) onion, diced
1 tablespoon olive oil
3 cloves garlic, sliced

Braised Kale
7 cups packed (5½ oz/165 g) lacinato kale, roughly chopped
2 tablespoons olive oil
1 clove garlic, thinly sliced
½ tablespoon thinly sliced Fresno peppers
2 tablespoons white wine
½ teaspoon lemon juice

Breadcrumbs
3 oz (80 g) baguette, crust removed, diced
¼ cup (2 fl oz/60 g) olive oil
2 cloves garlic, grated
2 tablespoons chopped parsley
1 teaspoon lemon zest

MAKE THE SQUASH BUTTER

Preheat the oven to 400°F/200°C. Cut the squash in half lengthwise and scoop out the seeds. Put the garlic cloves in the cavities and drizzle the olive oil and ½ teaspoon salt over the squash. Place on a sheet tray (rimmed baking tray) lined with parchment paper and roast until fully tender, about 45 minutes. Using a large spoon, scoop out the squash flesh from the skins and place in a food processor bowl. Leave it there for 5 minutes to cool, then add the butter, lemon juice, and remaining ¼ teaspoon salt. Process until smooth.

MAKE THE SERRANO HAM SOFFRITTO

In a small sauce pot over low-medium heat, render the serrano ham. Just get it going enough to pull out a decent amount of fat, then add the onion and olive oil. Cook over low heat until the onion is soft and translucent. Add the garlic and cook for 3 more minutes. Set aside.

MAKE THE BRAISED KALE

Bring a pot of (unsalted) water to a boil and fill another small bowl with a 50/50 mix of ice and water. Blanch the kale for 30 seconds, then shock in the ice water bath. Once chilled, squeeze out the excess water and dry the kale on a paper towel-lined tray.

Heat the olive oil in a sauté pan, add the garlic and Fresno peppers, and sauté over medium-high heat for 2–3 minutes. Add the kale and sauté for an additional 3 minutes, then add the wine. Braise the kale until tender, approximately 5 minutes, allowing the wine to reduce. Season with lemon juice. Again, no salt. It might seem a bit underseasoned but that's okay.

MAKE THE BREADCRUMBS

Toss the bread pieces in a mixing bowl with the olive oil and garlic. Then, in a large sauté pan or rondeaux, sauté gently, tossing and mixing often so the bread doesn't burn. Cook until golden and lightly crisp. Depending on how dry the bread is, you may need additional olive oil.

Remove from the heat and add the parsley and lemon zest. Cool the mix directly on a cutting board and give the breadcrumbs another healthy chop with your knife. The reason you don't do this in a food processor is because you're looking for an uneven texture and crumb.

TO SERVE

Cook the spaghetti in a pot of (unsalted) boiling water. In a separate saucepan or rondeaux large enough to hold all the cooked pasta, cook the clams in the white wine with the lid on over medium-high heat. As the clams open, pull them out right away and set aside while the others catch up. Once all the clams have opened, reserve the cooking liquid, then add the oil and soffritto to the pan. Sauté for 1 minute, then add the kale. Sauté for an additional 1 minute, allowing the flavors to meld.

While these are cooking, pick half the clams from the shell and roughly chop them. Set aside. Add the squash butter and the clam "juice" to the pan, shaking the pan to emulsify them. When the pasta is very al dente, strain but reserve the cooking water. Add the pasta to the pan and finish cooking in the squash butter-kale mixture, adding a little pasta water if necessary to keep a loose, saucy consistency. Add the parsley and lemon juice. Toss the whole and chopped clams back in to reheat. Plate in a large bowl or divide among 4 smaller ones. Top with the breadcrumbs and grated Parmesan.

To Serve

12 oz (350 g) dried spaghetti
36 clams (2¼ lb/1 kg)
Scant ⅔ cup (4½ fl oz/135 g) white wine
3 tablespoons olive oil
3 teaspoons chopped parsley
Juice of ½ lemon
Grated Parmesan, to taste

Image on page 179

SQUID INK
FREGOLA SARDA

This dish came from one of the most beautiful nights of my life. When my children were very young, we traveled with our extended Chicago Greek family to Athens, Sparta, and Rhodes, where we rented a house near the beach. One night, at an unassuming family restaurant, we ate dinner on a terrace by the sea. The only other guests were an Italian family at the table next to us. Our children played and danced together, a lingua franca of skips and hopscotch.

That night I was served a traditional Greek sour pasta called trahana—tiny, pebble-shaped grains made with fermented milk, or yogurt, and semolina. The dish was a loose seafood porridge of trahana, grilled squid, and squid ink, with an iron-sweet flavor that balanced with the sourness of the pasta. We fell in love with this restaurant and struck up a conversation with the waiter, who led us into the kitchen when he found out we were cooks. There we met a young man sitting by himself in the large kitchen of his family's restaurant. He was watching soccer on TV, waiting for wayward travelers like us who might find their way to him.

A charcoal grill was lit outside the back door of the kitchen. Tomatoes rested on grates above the embers. He said his father had built the brick grill himself many years ago. Open on the table was the cookbook *Relae*, from the restaurant in Copenhagen, and in a pantomime I explained that we shared something deep in common.

Back home I worked with chef Sarah Rinkavage on our interpretation of the dish we had eaten that night. Instead of the trahana we used fregola sarda, the toasted, couscous-shaped pasta of Sardinia, into which we folded tiny, sour segments of Meyer lemon to mimic the flavor of the sour milk.

This became one of our most well-known dishes—in part because of its flavors, in part because of the memories, but mostly because of the stained black lips and tongues of the unwitting guests who had no idea what was happening until they looked at one another, smiled, and then burst out laughing with delight.

SERVES 4

Squid Braise

2 tablespoons olive oil

4 cloves garlic, crushed

⅛ teaspoon black peppercorns

Scant 1 cup (7½ fl oz/225 g) red wine

Scant 1 cup (7½ fl oz/225 g) Chicken Stock (page 254)

13 oz (380 g) squid, bodies and tentacles separated, cleaned

Squid Ink Sauce

4 tablespoons squid ink

¾ cup plus 1 tablespoon (7 fl oz/200 g) braising liquid (from above, with the garlic still in it)

2 tablespoons olive oil

To Serve

2 cups (9 oz/250 g) fregola sarda, cooked

2 tablespoons butter

Lemon juice, to taste

2 tablespoons olive oil

12 Meyer lemon segments

½ cup (1 oz/25 g) radicchio, diced

1 x quantity Tonnato Sauce (page 250)

Salt

MAKE THE SQUID BRAISE

Add the olive oil to a shallow pot or rondeaux over low heat. Add the garlic and black peppercorns and toast both lightly in the oil. Next, add the wine and stock and bring to a simmer. Add the squid body and tentacles. Cover the pot with a lid and simmer over medium-low heat until the squid is tender, about 12 minutes. Once cooked, remove the squid from the pot and leave to cool. Reserve the braising liquid.

Slice the tentacles in half, and dice the squid bodies into small squares.

MAKE THE SQUID INK SAUCE

Place the squid ink, braising liquid, and olive oil in a blender and purée until smooth.

TO SERVE

In a small sauce pot over medium-high heat, add the cooked fregola, diced squid body, and a splash of water. When hot, add the squid ink sauce. Let the sauce tighten as it melds with the fregola and squid. Add the butter, allow to emulsify, then season with lemon juice and salt.

Meanwhile, in a small bowl, combine the tentacles, olive oil, Meyer lemon, radicchio, and a pinch of salt.

Spoon a little of the tonnato sauce into the bottom of 4 bowls or a platter. Plate the fregola mix over this, using the back of your spoon to flatten the fregola so you can plate the radicchio-lemon mix on top.

GNOCCHI WITH CRAB AND SPRING VEG

05 18

We love to add seeds to pastas—sesame, coriander, nigella, poppy. Like breadcrumbs, seeds add texture, contrast, and accents of flavor. This is a simple dish of potato gnocchi, crab, asparagus, and peas, emulsified with butter and lemon juice. A primavera, green and bright. But just a teaspoon of poppy seeds turns it into something unexpected; it's a little jest, a *scherzetto*, making a crunchy, nutty delight out of what is otherwise a very typical spring moment from late May.

MAKE THE GNOCCHI

Bring a pot of water to a boil. Add the potatoes and cook until tender. While still hot, transfer to a cutting board, and using tongs or a meat fork, slice the potatoes in half, then scoop the flesh out with a spoon. Discard the skins. Pass the potato flesh through a ricer. Place the riced potatoes on a clean, flour-dusted surface, then spread out to release the steam and cool slightly. You want to work with them very warm, not steaming hot.

Once the steam has released, gather the potato into a single, mountain-shaped pile. Then make a well, a crater in the mountain, into which you can add the rest of the ingredients without them spilling out. Use a fork to mix the flour, egg and yolk, pecorino, and olive oil into the potatoes, a little at a time, until you have a shaggy dough. Using your hands, press the dough into a flat disk, then fold and press it again, upon itself, until the pasta comes together in a ball. You may use additional flour if necessary. Knead gently for 3–5 minutes, adding flour as necessary, until the ball just obtains structural integrity. Test a little piece by pinching off a hunk and attempting to roll it out. If it stays together without tearing, you've accomplished your goal. Don't overwork the dough. And try not to add too much flour.

Let the dough sit for 10 minutes, covered with a dish (tea) towel. Then separate into 4 portions. Dust your clean work surface with flour. Roll each portion out into a long cylinder of ¾-inch (2 cm) diameter. Then, with a small knife, slice the log into 1½-inch (4 cm) segments. Dust them with flour as you go and use a bench scraper to transfer them to a floured sheet tray (rimmed baking tray). Freeze the gnocchi for at least 4 hours.

Bring a large pot of water to a boil. Season the water with salt as you would for pasta. Poach the frozen gnocchi in the pot in batches. As they float to the top, scoop them out with a slotted spoon and put them on an oiled sheet tray. Once cooled, these can sit for up to 3 hours in the fridge, covered, while you prepare the rest of the dish.

MAKE THE SPRING VEGETABLES

Bring a pot of water to a boil and salt generously. Fill another small bowl with a 50/50 mix of ice and water. Cook the asparagus for 1–2 minutes, until al dente—cooked but firm—and immediately plunge into the ice water. In the same boiling water, cook the peas for 30–60 seconds, until cooked but firm, and immediately plunge into the ice water. Remove and dry on a paper towel. Slice the asparagus into inch-long (2.5 cm) bias cuts.

TO SERVE

Warm 4–8 plates or a serving platter. In a large skillet (frying pan) or rondeaux, heat the butter over medium heat until it foams, then add the gnocchi. Sear on both sides, then add the soffritto, peas, asparagus, and preserved lemon slices. Saute for 2–3 minutes, or until hot, then add the crab. Season with salt and lemon juice. Toss with the chopped herbs. Top with leaves of mache, shaved pecorino, and poppy seeds.

SERVES 4-8

Gnocchi

2 russet potatoes (1 lb 3 oz/540 g), washed
2 cups (9 oz/250 g) "00" flour, plus extra for dusting
1 egg + 1 yolk
½ cup (2 oz/50 g) pecorino
2 tablespoons olive oil
½ teaspoon salt, plus extra for cooking
3 grinds black pepper

Spring Vegetables

¾ cup (3¼ oz/90 g) snap peas
¾ cup (3¼ oz/90 g) asparagus

To Serve

3 oz (85 g) butter
1 × quantity Fennel Soffritto (page 194)
12 preserved lemon slices, trimmed of pith
¾ cup (4 oz/120 g) lump crabmeat
1½ tablespoons lemon juice
1 teaspoon chopped tarragon
1 teaspoon chopped mint
1½ teaspoons chopped parsley
1½ tablespoons super-thin-sliced garlic chives
Mache leaves
Pecorino
Poppy seeds
Salt

GEMELLI WITH
SHORT RIB RAGU

SERVES 4-6

Much like the vongole at Lorenzo's (page 180), I've often wanted to serve my grandmother's ragu at Lula. Evelyn cooked a slow-simmered Sunday "sauce" full of short ribs, meatballs, and pork sausage, always enough for both my family and my aunt's family down the street. Like so many Italian-Americans, I have visceral memories of what it was like to walk into my grandmother's narrow galley kitchen with the cauldron gurgling beast-like and crimson red over two back burners, rafts of pork fat and olive oil pooling on the surface. As it simmered over the course of a day, the colors of the tomato caramelized and deepened, staining the oil nearly black. An undercounter radio would play the Dean Martin standards that my grandparents danced to at the Italian-American club on Saturday nights.

The times I've tried to recreate the recipe, despite the way the kitchen begins to smell like hers, the flavors never return. Like a photograph, my recipe for her sauce so close to real, yet is no substitute for the memory. From what was. One winter we tried a different direction with the short rib ragu, incorporating more rosemary, bay leaf, even a little cinnamon. We start the recipe by coating the short ribs in a rub of herbs, tomato paste, and anchovy, which my grandmother would have never thought to do. I love the way anchovy sharpens the woodsy pine of the rosemary, intensifies the browning of the ribs. We topped the dish with ricotta, a dollop which melts into the sauce as you eat. When I was a kid I'd sneak into the kitchen late at night to eat cold bites straight from the plastic container, hunting for morsels of short rib with my fingers. This recipe makes extra for those moments of late-night searching.

2 lb (900 g) short ribs, trimmed
1 teaspoon black pepper
2 cloves garlic, crushed
2 anchovies, finely minced
2 teaspoons minced rosemary,
    plus 2 teaspoons finely chopped,
    to garnish
1 tablespoon tomato paste
¼ cup (2 fl oz/60 g) + 2 tablespoons
    olive oil
1½ oz (45 g) pancetta
½ onion (3¼ oz/110 g), minced
1 carrot (4 oz/120 g), minced
1 stalk celery (1½ oz/45 g), minced
4 cups (2¼ lb/1 kg) canned (tinned)
    whole San Marzano tomatoes, passed
    through a food mill
Scant ¼ cup (1¾ fl oz/50 g) red wine
1 bay leaf
Small pinch ground cinnamon
¼ teaspoon fennel seeds, toasted
    and crushed
Large pinch red chile flakes
4 cups (15 oz/420 g) pasta, cooked
    to al dente
2 tablespoons butter
Lemon juice, to taste
2 teaspoons finely chopped parsley
¼ cup (2½ oz/65 g) Ricotta (page 254)
Parmesan, for grating
Spruce Oil, for drizzling (page 246)
Salt

Preheat the oven to 400°F/200°C. Rub the short ribs with pepper, garlic, anchovies, minced rosemary, tomato paste, 2 tablespoons of olive oil, and 1 tablespoon of salt, and place it on a sheet tray (rimmed baking tray) with the pancetta. Add enough water to cover the meat by a ¼ inch (5 mm). Place the tray in the oven and roast until caramelized, approximately 30 minutes. Do not turn the ribs.

Meanwhile, combine the onion, carrot, celery, and remaining olive oil in a small sauce pot, cooking over very low heat until tender, about 25 minutes. Do not brown. Remove to a blender and purée, then transfer the purée to a large stock pot with the tomatoes and simmer for 45 minutes.

Remove the short ribs and pancetta from the oven and add to the tomato sauce. Using a flat-edged wooden spoon, scrape any caramelized bits from the sheet tray directly into the sauce.

Add the red wine, bay leaf, cinnamon, fennel seeds, and chile flakes, then reduce the heat and simmer until the short ribs are so tender that they fall apart with the simple prod of a fork, about 45 minutes to 1 hour. Remove the meat, shred, then return to the sauce.

Bring a pan of water to the boil and salt generously. Cook the pasta according to package directions until al dente. Transfer the cooked pasta to the pan of short ribs (reserve the pasta water) and continue to simmer for 1 minute, to meld the flavors together. Add the butter, lemon juice, parsley, and a splash of pasta water. Toss to combine and season with salt.

Plate and top with the ricotta in the center. Grate the Parmesan over, then garnish with rosemary and a drizzle of spruce oil.

DUCK AGNOLOTTI

02 18

Agnolotti are self-sealing morsels of stuffed pasta, best with butter-based sauces and meaty fillings. This winter version marries duck confit, one of the most comforting cold weather foods ever, with black trumpet mushrooms from a late harvest in the woods of the Pacific Northwest. When the mushrooms cook down in the pan they resemble the meaty strands of the confit, so we imagined them joined together with a rich, stock-infused sauce. It wouldn't be Lula without a citrusy finish, this time in the form of tiny segments of Meyer lemon that interrupt the meatiness with a bit of zing.

As with the poppy seed on the Gnocchi with Crab and Spring Veg (page 184), we finish this dish with nigella seeds. Nigella are one of the most ancient ingredients of the Mediterranean, but often mistaken, too. I've seen them packaged as black cumin or "onion seeds." Traditionally, nigella are used in baking and savory applications in many recipes spanning India, North Africa, and the Middle East. They have a bitter flavor, a sesame-like crunch, herbaceous scent, and a kind of piquancy that makes the confusing "onion seed" label make sense. Here, they give texture and bitterness to an otherwise rich and silken stuffed pasta.

SERVES 4

Duck Filling

1½ cups (8 oz/225 g) Duck Confit (page 254), picked from bones
3 cloves roasted garlic (from confit)
Scant ¼ cup (1¾ fl oz/50 g) Duck or Chicken Stock (page 254)
2 oz (50 g) Parmesan, grated
1 egg yolk
¼ teaspoon salt
⅓ teaspoon cracked black pepper
2 tablespoons chopped parsley

Agnolotti

1¾ cups (8 oz/225 g) "00" flour
2 eggs + 1 yolk
Coarse semolina, for dusting

Black Trumpet Mushrooms

4 cups (1 lb 5 oz/600 g) black trumpet mushrooms, cleaned
2 tablespoons butter
Lemon juice, to taste
Salt

Meyer Lemon Soffritto

3 tablespoons olive oil
4½ oz (125 g) onion, finely diced
2 cloves garlic, sliced
2 teaspoons grated Meyer lemon zest
⅛ teaspoon salt
⅛ teaspoon chile flakes

MAKE THE DUCK FILLING

In the bowl of a mixer fitted with the paddle attachment, combine all the ingredients. Whip until the meat shreds and emulsifies with the egg and stock. The filling should hold together like a pâté. Add the mix to a pastry (piping) bag and chill.

MAKE THE AGNOLOTTI

To the bowl of a standing mixer fitted with the hook attachment, add the flour, egg, and yolk and mix for 5 minutes. The dough should come together in a ball, but if it seems a little too dry or crumbly you can add a splash of water. Turn the dough out onto a clean surface and knead for 1 minute, until the dough forms an elastic ball. Wrap in plastic wrap (cling film) and let sit for 1 hour or overnight.

Dust a work surface with coarse semolina and set a pasta maker to the widest roller setting. Divide the dough into 4 pieces and flatten each piece to no more than 2 inches (5 cm) wide. Run through the machine, dusting lightly with flour. Repeat this 3 times. Then reduce the settings on the roller by the smallest increment possible and run the piece through the roller repeatedly, each time narrowing the setting until the dough is ¹⁄₁₆ inch (1.5 mm) thick or just translucent. Return the machine to the widest setting and continue with the next piece of dough.

You'll work with 1 sheet of pasta at a time, so keep the other sheets stacked with plenty of coarse semolina between each layer and a layer of plastic wrap over the stack. On the first sheet of pasta, pipe teaspoon-sized morsels of duck filling down the length of the dough, ¾ inches (2 cm) apart. Fold the side closest to you over the duck, extending it at least 1 inch (2.5 cm) past the filling. Then press the dough together to seal. You may need to moisten the pasta for it to stick. Pinch the dough on either side of the filling with your first finger and thumb. This will seal the dough and make the characteristic agnolotti shape. The rolling and pinching should be as tight as possible.

Use a pasta cutter to trim the side of your dough away from you about ½ inch (1 cm) from the agnolotti. Then cut and discard the trim.

Cut between each agnolotto to form individual pillows of pasta. Transfer the angolotti to a semolina-dusted sheet tray (rimmed baking tray) and repeat all steps with the rest of the dough.

MAKE THE BLACK TRUMPET MUSHROOMS

To clean black trumpet mushrooms, fill a large basin or sink with lukewarm water. Tear the mushrooms in half to expose the internal surface of the stem. Soak them in water for 1–2 minutes, agitating them to release stubborn pine needles and dirt. Using your hands, pull the mushrooms from the water. The hope here is that the water will pull the dirt away from the fungi as you lift them up. Drain the water, clean the basin, refill, and repeat as many times as it takes. Sometimes we wash black trumpets 3–4 times.

Heat a large sauté pan or rondeaux. Add the mushrooms to the dry pan, then cook until all their water has released and cooked off. Add the butter, let it foam, then sauté the mushrooms for 2–3 minutes, finishing with lemon juice and salt to taste. Set aside.

MAKE THE MEYER LEMON SOFFRITTO

In a small sauce pot, heat the oil with the onion and garlic to a low simmer. Cook low and slow until very tender, about 25 minutes. Stir through the zest, salt, and chile flakes at the very end.

TO SERVE

Cook the pasta in a large pot of salted boiling water for 3 minutes or until al dente.

In a large saucepan or rondeaux, heat ½ cup (4 oz/120 g) soffritto and mushrooms. Add stock, a splash of pasta water, and the pasta. Cook together to meld the flavors and finish the agnolotti, then add the butter and lemon segments. Toss to emulsify and combine.

Plate in 4 bowls and top with grated Parmesan and nigella seeds.

To Serve

¾ cup + 1 tablespoon (7 fl oz/200 g) Duck or Chicken Stock (page 254)
3 oz (85 g) butter
3 tablespoons Meyer lemon segments
½ cup (2 oz/50 g) grated Parmesan
Nigella seeds, for sprinkling
Salt

Image on page 190

SWEET CORN RISOTTO WITH CAULIFLOWER

I learned to make risotto (and so much else) from *The Zuni Café Cookbook* by Judy Rodgers. It was her technical wisdom, along with my own ear for poetic proverbs about Italian cooking (rice is born in water, dies in wine) that shaped my ideas about cooking risotto. I am unapologetically old school.

I believe in stirring in a single clockwise direction with an heirloom wooden spoon. I believe in keeping a "veil" of stock over the rice to protect the grains. I believe, because ritual brings my attention to what's happening in the pot. It makes me notice how simple, repetitive movements can produce transformative waves. Meditative and clarifying, to me making risotto is almost a form of prayer.

Everyone agrees that you want to cook the rice quickly but evenly, with many more times the volume of stock to rice, which is why the type of stock matters, and why you should stir with care. You don't want to beat or break the hulls with aggressive stirring. A well-prepared risotto is a collection of whole grains of rice, tender and intact. The way the rice becomes glossy and rich and creamy is by coaxing the starch out of the grains and into the surrounding liquid. But if you do that through brute force, you're going to make porridge, not risotto.

Imagine, for a moment, each grain of rice cooking in the pot. The grains at the bottom of the pot are closer to the flame, thus hotter than those at the top. The only way to even out the heat is to stir, maintaining enough liquid so the grains don't overcrowd. If each grain of rice receives the same heat and the same amount of time in that heat, if you use lots of stock and quickly simmer it off, if you stop the process at just the right time, your risotto should come out consistently al dente.

As mentioned, it's said that a good risotto-maker maintains "a veil of stock" above the rice until the last moment, when they "lift the veil" and reveal a beautiful visage of perfectly glossy rice. Knowing when to lift the veil is the hardest part of making risotto and the one step that's most likely to trip you up. So grandma's wooden spoon may just be the talisman you need.

On the virtues of chicken stock: There are a few recipes in this book that would be vegetarian but for the chicken stock we use. Please substitute a vegetable stock if you'd like. However, the chicken stock used in this way gives a lot of foundation and structure.

NB: The truffle butter needs to be made the night before. Alternatively, use regular butter and add a few extra truffle shavings on top.

SERVES 4

Roasted Cauliflower
½ head white cauliflower (4½ oz/ 130 g), trimmed into tiny florets
2 tablespoons extra-virgin olive oil
Salt and freshly ground black pepper

Sweet Corn Purée
½ cup (2¾ oz/70 g) sweet corn kernels

Risotto
1 tablespoon extra-virgin olive oil
4 tablespoons butter
1 leek (2½ oz/65 g), white parts only, washed, sliced in super-thin rounds
¼ teaspoon saffron
⅛ teaspoon fennel seeds, toasted and crushed in a mortar and pestle (not ground)
¼ teaspoon grated orange zest
1 × quantity Chicken Stock (page 254)
½ cup (3½ oz/100 g) arborio rice
3 tablespoons dry white wine
⅕ cup (1¼ oz/30 g) raw sweet corn kernels
2 tablespoons grated Parmesan
1 tablespoon Truffle Butter (page 249)
Lemon juice, to taste
Salt

MAKE THE ROASTED CAULIFLOWER

In a small sauté pan, roast the cauliflower in the oil over medium heat with a pinch of salt and crack of pepper. Keep stirring until tender. Cool and drain on a paper towel-lined tray.

MAKE THE SWEET CORN PURÉE

Add the corn kernels to a blender with ¾ cup (6 fl oz/175 g) water and purée on high for 1 minute. Set aside.

MAKE THE RISOTTO

Heat the oil with 2 tablespoons of butter in a heavy-bottomed pot—the best you have. You want the right-sized pot—too big and the leeks will burn before they cook; too small and the rice will have no surface area against which to toast. When the butter foams, add the leeks, saffron, fennel seeds, and orange zest, and cook over very low heat until tender, 20–30 minutes.

Meanwhile, in another pot, heat the stock to a gentle simmer.

When the leeks are tender, increase the heat to medium-high. Add the rice and an additional 2 tablespoons of butter. Toast the rice in this fat–leek mixture for 2–3 minutes, during which time you'll need to stir constantly, until the rice is fragrant and slightly translucent at the edges. Add the white wine and continue to stir as the wine is reduced. Use your sense of smell to know when the alcohol is fully cooked out of the pot. It should take 2–3 minutes, but the tell is the smell going from burning your nostrils to not. Immediately add enough simmering stock to cover the rice by a ¼ inch (5 mm). Adjust the heat to maintain a firm, steady simmer that comes short of a full boil. Begin to stir. I go in a clockwise direction 3 times, then pass through the center of the rice 2 times. Keep stirring in your own methodical way. Remember, you are stirring, not kneading, the rice.

As the stock cooks off, add more—1 ladleful every few minutes. Don't wait until the rice is exposed and dry. The goal in the first 12–15 minutes of the process is to keep it simmering evenly under this veil of stock, fully submerged. After 10 minutes, taste the rice. After 11 minutes, taste the rice. Then again after 12 minutes. Learn what it's doing.

When the rice is just a little more al dente than you'd be comfortable serving, stop adding stock and use the final minutes to finish the risotto. You'll notice a creaminess has developed, as the starch in the rice is expelled and then assumed by the surrounding liquid. This starchiness is your goal and the reason why a decently made risotto won't need a lot of dairy to finish.

At this point, turn off the heat and add the raw corn kernels. Stir to combine, as the residual heat of the risotto will cook the corn. Next, add the corn purée, Parmesan, and the truffle butter. Season with salt and a few drops of lemon juice, both to taste.

TO SERVE

Divide the risotto between 4 warmed wide bowls or plates. Top each with roasted cauliflower, pine nuts, and preserved lemon, and then shave a ton of truffle over the top with gratuitous gestures.

To Serve

1 tablespoon pine nuts, toasted

1 teaspoon preserved lemon, thinly sliced

1 black winter truffle, for shaving

Image on page 191

FARFALLE WITH GRILLED SQUID

02 15

In 2015, our Pilot Light Chefs foundation was invited to Italy by the Chicago Sister Cities Program to present a lesson to a group of Italian children in Milan. We taught a class on the Chicago hot dog that tied the classic street food of our city to a conversation about immigration and national identity.

We began by telling our Italian audience that the hot dog was actually derived from the German frankfurter. Furthermore, we argued, the hot dog in Chicago had an established and rigorously upheld set of regional rules about exactly what it could be. Our premise was that the Chicago hot dog had as many rules as a DOC wine or an AVPN pizza. For example, we told them, this sausage was never, under any circumstances, to be served with ketchup. There was laughter. But, we insisted, these rules were themselves tied to the identity of the various immigrant populations that came to Chicago and influenced its culture. They were real.

Convincing this group about the history of the hot dog was the easy part of my day. The problem for me was what to serve for lunch. A meal cooked by us visiting chefs was served to the members of the press who had gathered in the elegant dining room of the restaurant. In some loss of sanity, I elected to cook pasta.

What was I thinking? Someone with the last name of Hammel, serving a pasta with squid and sesame seeds to Italians in their own three-star restaurant? I plated seventy-five of these farfalle while twelve puzzled Milanese chefs stared at me as though I was committing a crime.

We grilled the squid over an open fire, and the light char of flame against the oily squid gave the dish an alluring smokiness. I used to toast the fennel seeds for the soffritto in a pot over the wood fire at the same time, and the simple pleasure of smelling those seeds as they cracked open while grilling the squid gave me a quiet peace. I felt as though I could taste the dish before it was made.

MAKE THE FENNEL SOFFRITTO
In a medium sauce pot on low heat, cook the fennel and onions in the oil until very soft, 15-20 minutes. Add the garlic and continue for 5 minutes, melding the flavors together. Add in a small dash of chile flakes.

MAKE THE SQUID
Preheat a gas or charcoal grill to high. In a mixing bowl, toss the squid in the blend oil, salt, and pepper. Grill to tender, approximately 3–5 minutes per side for the bodies, 2–3 minutes for the tentacles. Slice the bodies into bite-sized rings, keeping the tentacles whole unless excessively large, then trim to a single bite size. Set aside.

TO SERVE
Bring a pan of water to the boil and salt generously. Cook the pasta according to package directions until al dente.

Meanwhile, heat the olive oil in a large saucepan or rondeaux and add 3 oz (80 g) soffritto, the grilled squid, and olives. Sauté gently for 2 minutes. Combine the clam juice and vermouth together in a bowl, then add to the pan with the cooked pasta and a ladleful of pasta water. Emulsify in the butter. Toss in the chives and season with salt, pepper, sesame oil, and lemon juice. Plate into 4 separate bowls, or 1 large bowl family-style, and top with more white sesame seeds and a spritz of lemon juice.

SERVES 4

Fennel Soffritto
¼ cup (2 fl oz/ 60 ml) blend oil
3½ oz (115 g) fennel, finely diced
2 oz (50 g) onion, finely diced
2 cloves garlic, sliced
Chile flakes

Squid
1 lb (450 g) squid, bodies and tentacles separated, cleaned
2 tablespoons blend oil
½ tablespoon salt
1 teaspoon black pepper

To Serve
2½ cups (9 oz/250 g) dried farfalle
1 tablespoon olive oil
¼ cup (1¼ oz/30 g) green olives, such as Castelvetrano, pitted and sliced
3 tablespoons clam juice
1 tablespoon vermouth
1½ oz (45 g) butter
3 tablespoons snipped chives
½ teaspoon sesame oil
Lemon juice, to taste
1 teaspoon white sesame seeds, plus extra for sprinkling
Salt and freshly ground black pepper

Sure, Chicago is a meat and potatoes town,
but you don't come to Lula for a big hunk of
protein. We source carefully and use meat and
fish to accompany the seasonal vegetables,
not the other way around.

MEAT

&

FISH

RAW TUNA WITH BLOOD ORANGE AGUACHILE

0218

Cold, bright, juicy winter dishes like this can revive the senses when you're stuck in months of unforgiving Chicago weather. We use blood orange and our pimenton-tomato oil to dress super fresh raw tuna. For a contrastingly feisty herbal flavor we add finely diced celery, while the radish gives both crunch and heat. The result is a so-misinterpreted-it-might-be-heresy version of the Mexican dish of marinated shrimp, chile, and lime.

MAKE THE CELERY MIX

In a small mixing bowl, combine all the ingredients.

MAKE THE BLOOD ORANGE AGUACHILE

In a food processor fitted with the blade, combine all the ingredients with ¼ cup (2 fl oz/60 g) water and purée for 30 seconds. Allow to sit undisturbed for 15 minutes, then pass through a fine-mesh strainer or tamis without pressing or pushing to release liquid. Let the draining happen naturally and slowly. Reserve liquids, discard solids.

TO SERVE

Make sure everything is super cold before starting. In a small stainless-steel bowl, mix the tuna, celery mix, pimenton-tomato oil, salt, lemon juice, olive oil, and chile flakes. Taste for seasoning and adjust the lemon or salt as needed. Plate in a ring mold, using the back of a spoon to gently press the tartare into the mold. Garnish with six "dots" of aioli—we use a squeeze bottle to inject those little dots. Then top with segments of blood orange and a scattering of celery and wood sorrel leaves. Remove the ring mold and pour aguachile around the perimeter of each dish.

SERVES 6

Celery Mix

2½ tablespoons tiny-as-possible celery brunoise

2½ tablespoons tiny-as-possible Spanish black radish brunoise

1 tablespoon minced shallot

1 tablespoon preserved lemon rind, trimmed of pith and finely minced

1 tablespoon minced celery leaves

2 tablespoons olive oil

Blood Orange Aguachile

3 blood oranges, peeled, trimmed of pith, chopped into eighths

1 Fresno pepper, deseeded and trimmed of pith

2 tablespoons lemon juice

½ teaspoon white vinegar

½ shallot (½ oz/15 g)

¼ teaspoon salt

To Serve

12 oz (360 g) sushi grade tuna, diced into ¼-inch (5 mm) cubes

1 tablespoon Pimenton-Tomato Oil (page 246)

½ teaspoon salt, plus extra to taste

1 teaspoon lemon juice, plus extra to taste

1 teaspoon olive oil

pinch red chile flakes

3 teaspoons Preserved Mandarin Aioli (page 248)

¼ cup (2 oz/50 g) blood orange, peeled, trimmed of pith, segmented

Celery and wood sorrel leaves, to garnish

HAMACHI CRUDO WITH BASIL AND ALMOND

0414

The morning of my wedding I found myself in charge of cutting the cured hamachi. We catered the reception for 250 ourselves, not knowing better, not wanting anyone else to cook for us but our own team. I rinsed salt, sugar, lemongrass, cilantro (coriander), and dill from the twelve yellowtail fillets I had cured early in the morning, then sliced like sashimi for service later in the day. There was a chaotic frenzy around me as the cooks loaded the van with the rest of the food and equipment. Then everybody left and I was alone. I cleaned up, then went to dress for the service at the church. My suit hung on the back kitchen door like a disembodied future me. I can say that my heart was pounding. I started to get dressed but stopped. There was a sweet but definitely fishy smell coming from somewhere. I looked at the sink and it was clean. And then I took the obvious path to my own left hand, the one that hadn't held the knife. Yes, it was me.

Leche de tigre is a marinade that gives Peruvian ceviche its characteristic punchy, vibrant, zingy vibe. We were inspired here by some of its common flavors—fish sauce, ginger, lime—in a preparation that briefly marinates raw hamachi in fresh almond milk.

One of our staff members looked over my shoulder, saw this recipe in progress, and commented that no one would serve raw fish at home. This may be one of the simpler recipes in our book and an instance of fanciful magic that anyone can perform. Find a fishmonger you trust and ask for sushi-grade yellowtail. If you can slice a tomato and eat it, you can do this too.

MAKE THE ALMOND MILK MARINADE

Mix the lime, garlic, ginger, cilantro (coriander), and chile together in a bowl. Then blend with the almond milk and salt. Chill in the refrigerator for at least 1 hour.

TO SERVE

Lay each slice of hamachi on a nonreactive tray and season with salt and lime juice.

Divide the slices between 4 chilled, shallow bowls, laying each slice down separately from each other. Spoon the marinade in and around the fish, enough to cover the fish halfway. Add a few drops of basil oil and lemon oil per dish. Garnish with basil leaves and serve.

SERVES 4

Almond Milk Marinade

Juice of 1 lime
1 clove garlic
1 teaspoon grated fresh ginger
3 cilantro (coriander) sprigs, leaves and stems
5 thin, round slices serrano chile, deseeded
1 teaspoon fish sauce
½ cup (4 fl oz/120 g) almond milk
¼ teaspoon salt

To Serve

4¾ oz (140 g) sushi-grade hamachi, sliced as for sashimi
Lime juice, to taste
Few drops Basil Oil (page 246)
Few drops lemon "agrumato" oil
Basil leaves
Salt

SCALLOPS WITH BASIL AND CAULIFLOWER SOTT'OLIO

Sott'olio, or "under oil," is one of those Italian culinary phrases that speaks to me as though it were a poem.

A sott'olio is another preservation technique (like confit) that uses fat to keep out air that would otherwise spoil the food you're trying to save. The simplest explanation is that you submerge heavily marinated, acidic, nearly pickled, height-of-the-season vegetables in lots of oil, creating an anaerobic seal. Then these vegetables can be stored like a preserve. This process made its way from sunny Puglia into many Italian-American homes, including my own. When I was a kid, we bought commercialized sott'olio at the grocery store, where it came in glass jars for our antipasti platters on the holidays.

I am captivated by the idea that you can hold on to something, almost stop time, by covering it in oil.

Once you make a sott'olio, you can serve it with most anything. Here we've sautéed some sweet Maine bay scallops in brown butter with lemon and spooned the warm cauliflower sott'olio over the top. It could have just as easily been a slice of bread.

SERVES 4

Cauliflower
4 cups (32 fl oz/950 g) canola (rapeseed) oil
1 lb 2 oz (500 g) cauliflower, cut into small florets
¾ cups (2¾ oz/70 g) chickpea flour
Salt and freshly ground black pepper

Sott'olio
1 yellow onion (7 oz/200 g), julienned into ¼-inch (5 mm) strips
7 cloves garlic, thinly sliced
6 tablespoons canola (rapeseed) oil
Generous ¾ cup (6½ fl oz/190 g) olive oil, plus extra for storage if needed
½ teaspoon each fennel, cumin, and coriander seeds, toasted, then lightly crushed in a mortar and pestle
¼ cup (2 oz/50 g) golden raisins, soaked in 2 tablespoons dry white wine for 30 minutes, then drained
6 canned (tinned) artichoke hearts (4¾ oz/140g), thinly sliced
½ cup (2¾ oz/70 g) sunflower seeds, toasted
⅓ cup + 1 tablespoon (3½ fl oz/100 g) liquid from Pickled Thai Chili (page 247)
3 tablespoons calamansi vinegar
¼ teaspoon salt

To Serve
8 bay scallops
1 teaspoon canola (rapeseed) oil
1 tablespoon butter
Lemon juice
Purple basil leaves
Maldon sea salt
Salt

MAKE THE CAULIFLOWER

Set up a frying station with a heavy stock pot and a frying thermometer. Heat the oil to 350°F/180°C. Toss the cauliflower florets with the chickpea flour. Fry until golden brown, about 3 minutes, then drain on a paper towel-lined baking tray. Season to taste with salt and pepper. Cool thoroughly at room temperature. Do not refrigerate.

MAKE THE SOTT'OLIO

In a small braiser or sauce pot, cook the onion and garlic with the canola (rapeseed) oil and half the olive oil for 15 minutes at low heat, just enough to soften the vegetables. Add the crushed fennel, cumin, and coriander seeds, and cook for another 20 minutes, until extremely tender. Set aside to cool.

Once cool to the touch, add the raisins, artichokes, sunflower seeds, pickle liquid, vinegar, salt, and the remaining olive oil. Stir to combine, then fold in the cauliflower. Store in a large glass jar. If not submerged, top off with more olive oil.

TO SERVE

On a paper towel-lined tray, lightly season the scallops with salt and pat dry. Heat a stainless-steel or cast iron pan over high heat until nearly smoking (you definitely need some kind of kitchen exhaust/extractor for this; otherwise just poach). Heat the oil and quickly, but cautiously, add the scallops. Sauté for 1–2 minutes, and while this is going on, change the paper towels on your tray. Reduce the heat and add the butter, which will immediately melt, foam, then start to brown. Spoon the browning butter over the scallops for 2 additional minutes, adjusting the heat to prevent the milk solids in the butter from burning, then add a squeeze of lemon juice directly to the pan. Swirl it all together, then use a slotted spoon to remove the scallops and drain them on the towel-lined tray. Reserve the rest of the butter-lemon sauce in a separate container.

To plate, place the scallops in a shallow bowl or coupe plate. Spoon the sott'olio around them. Spoon the lemon-brown butter over that. Sprinkle all with a little Maldon sea salt. Top with basil leaves and serve.

RED SNAPPER WITH BLACK KALE AND SQUASH

02 15

One late snowy night in February, a little girl sat at the Lula counter for dinner with her family. Like her parents, she was dressed for a special night out to celebrate some good fortune that had happened to the adults. They had come from a gala at a hotel downtown, all the way out to Logan Square to "find real food," as the little girl said, clearly quoting one of her parents. They were too exhausted to do much else than have us take care of them. It was a few weeks before Valentine's Day and I was writing a menu. The little girl asked if she could help.

Sure, I said, I'm thinking of ingredients that are red. And they don't have to be actually red, like strawberries, but almost or nearly red, red just when cooked, or red when raw.

How many can you name?

Grape juice. Raspberries. Jello juice.

Jello juice?

Like when cherry jello melts.

Rhubarb, her father muttered. Your mother loves rhubarb.

Beets, I said. Hibiscus, duck, and beets. Would you like to hear the rest of my list? She nodded.

Blood orange, Espelette, persimmon, sumac, rose, I said. Red kuri squash.

Wait, she said. Roses aren't food. And you're making these things up. I don't believe you that all these things are red.

Well, she's got a point. The red kuri squash, also called Hokkaido squash, is actually orange. And persimmon is yellow or maybe amber. But that winter night, as we held the squash and the persimmon together and imagined their colors mixing on a palette, we thought of the crimson-gold-red skin of snapper, with a little frame of black kale below. Red kuri and red snapper. Red things that go together. Grape juice. Strawberries. Red things that suggest love.

SERVES 4

Squash Broth
1 fish carcass (3½ oz/100 g); we used the snapper, no head, bones rinsed
11 oz (300 g) kabocha squash, peeled and diced
3 persimmons, chopped
½ cup (1¼ oz/30 g) dried shiitake mushrooms
5 g dulse seaweed
4 cups (32 fl oz/950 g) Chicken Stock (page 254)
1 teaspoon salt
Apple cider vinegar, to taste

Squash Purée
4 tablespoons butter
10 oz (280 g) kuri squash, peeled and diced
1 teaspoon salt
2¾ oz (75 g) onion, peeled and sliced
2 anchovy fillets (¼ oz/10 g)
1 tablespoon tomato paste
Generous ¾ cup (6¾ fl oz/190 g) Brut cider
1 teaspoon apple cider vinegar
½ tablespoon fish sauce

Persimmon Butter
1 oz (25 g) butter, plus 2¾ oz (75 g) butter, cubed and softened
6 small persimmons, peeled, cored, and chopped
1 tablespoon thinly sliced fresh ginger
1 teaspoon Worcestershire sauce
1 teaspoon apple cider vinegar
¼ teaspoon salt

Black Kale
4 cups (3½ oz/100 g) black lacinato kale
2 tablespoons olive oil
1 clove garlic, sliced
1 Fresno pepper, deseeded and sliced
Lemon juice, to taste
Salt

MAKE THE SQUASH BROTH

In a stainless-steel stock pot, add the fish carcass and cover with cold water. Bring to a simmer, then cook for 20 minutes, skimming any impurities that rise to the top. Add the rest of the ingredients (except the vinegar), keep the heat low, and simmer for 1 hour. Strain through a fine-mesh strainer and season with vinegar.

MAKE THE SQUASH PURÉE

In a medium sauce pot or rondeaux, heat half the butter and, when it foams, add the squash and the salt. Continue to cook over medium-high heat until the squash caramelizes and softens, about 20 minutes. Add the onion, anchovies, and tomato paste. Caramelize for an additional 15 minutes, stirring and adjusting the heat to keep the butter from browning. Deglaze the pan with the cider, reduce for 1 minute, then add ½ cup (4 oz/120 g) water, the apple cider vinegar, and fish sauce. Cook for 5 minutes, then leave to cool. Transfer to a blender and add the remaining butter. Purée on high until smooth and luscious, then pass through a fine-mesh strainer.

MAKE THE PERSIMMON BUTTER

In a small sauce pot, heat 1 oz (25 g) of the butter and add the persimmons and ginger. Caramelize for 5–7 minutes, being careful to not allow the sugars in the persimmons to burn, then add the Worcestershire sauce, vinegar, and 3 tablespoons water. Let cool. Blend in a food processor with the cubed butter, then stir through the salt.

MAKE THE BLACK KALE

Bring a pot of water to a boil and salt generously. Fill a small bowl with a 50/50 mix of ice and water. Cook the kale in the boiling water for 2 minutes until tender, then immediately plunge into the ice water. Remove and dry on a paper towel. Chop the blanched kale as finely as possible.

In a small sauté pan, heat the olive oil, garlic, and Fresno pepper until the garlic starts to brown slightly. Add the kale and cook for 2–3 minutes, until the flavors of the oil marry with the kale. Season with lemon juice and salt.

TO SERVE

Reheat the squash broth and purée, and keep warm while you cook the fish.

Heat a cast iron or stainless-steel heavy sauté pan over high heat until nearly smoking. Turn off the heat. Add the oil and a snapper fillet, skin-side down, immediately return to high heat and cook until the skin is crispy and the flesh medium-rare. Sometimes you'll need to press the fillet against the pan (with the back of a spatula or your brave fingers) to keep the flesh from curling up. Once crispy on one side, add 2 tablespoons of the persimmon butter and baste. Remove from the pan with a fish spatula and rest on a towel-lined tray, skin-side up. Repeat for the other fish fillets.

Add the cooked kale to reheat in the same pan. On a serving plate, first spoon the warmed purée, then place a bed of kale. The purée will help hold the kale in place. Lay the fish over the kale, then top with pumpkin seeds, persimmon slices, and pickled squash. Pour broth around the fish and finish with a drizzle of olive oil.

To Serve

2 tablespoons grapeseed or rice bran oil

4 × 6 oz (175 g) fillets of red snapper

1 teaspoon pumpkin seeds, toasted and roughly chopped

1 persimmon, peeled, cored, and thinly sliced

3 pieces Pickled Butternut Squash (page 247)

Olive oil, for drizzling

Image on page 206

TURBOT WITH SEEDED CRUST AND SALSIFY

"It's this idea of the readymade. It's sampling. I take James Brown, I chop it up, I make a new song." This is the late Virgil Abloh talking in the *New Yorker* about cheat codes, or his "3% rule." These codes describe the relationship between new and old works in his designs in fashion. For Abloh, innovation is achieved by taking forms of classic, even iconic, designs and re-presenting them in a way that's repeated and twisted, undermined and subjugated all at the same time. Changing them just by 3%.

I cooked for Virgil Abloh at the Museum of Contemporary Art (MCA) in Chicago, when a retrospective was shown of his works in 2019. But it happened that we were working on this turbot dish of Sarah's just before Thanksgiving 2021, when we heard the news of Abloh's death. So now I'm thinking of him, of our processes, the cycle of collaborations, our story. On the question of who owns a recipe once it's passed into the replication machine of a restaurant.

Reflecting on it now, so much of our cooking is like this: go back, sample, rephrase, replace, the metonym of ingredients as ideas, or ideas as ingredients. What matters then is the relationship of the chef to the source from which they take. The respect shone, the citations made, the power acknowledged. Well, then, this dish, the Turbot with Seeded Crust and Salsify—does it go back to Bocuse and the rouget with potato slices layered so delicately on the flesh that they mimic actual scales? Or does it go back to one night in 2002 at a "fusion" restaurant in Wicker Park in Chicago, where the bar stools were glowing Lucite orbs and the plates geometric puzzles, where I ate a dish of macadamia-nut-crusted halibut with coconut soubise and thought to myself: *so cool, so smooth, so, like, now*.

NB: "Words get under my skin the same way melodies do. Something catches my attention and I file it subconsciously. It often begins with an archaic or obscure word I have not defined. I just like the sound of it and its elusive meaning gives it a mysterious shine. On the menu of a local cafe is an item called 'salsify.' Before I reach for the dictionary I let my imagination run wild and decide that salsify is a burrowing bronchial root like a rickety old mine that burrows deep into something. It turns out that's mostly correct which encourages me further. All I know is 'salsify mains' sounds good to me."

This is musician Andrew Bird in the *New York Times* talking about his song, "Oh No." Lula was the cafe in this tune. Regardless, it illustrates the point exactly. "Chop it up, make a new song."

SERVES 4

Salsify Purée

1¼ oz (30 g) butter
1 cup (5 oz/150 g) sliced onion
3 cloves garlic
1¾ cups (8¼ oz/235 g) salsify, peeled, sliced, and stored in diluted lemon juice so it doesn't oxidize
Scant ⅔ cup (4¾ fl oz/140 g) dry vermouth
1 cup (8 fl oz/250 g) heavy (double) cream
1 teaspoon salt

Braised Salsify

Scant 1 cup (7½ fl oz/225 g) vermouth
½ cup (4 fl oz/120 g) heavy (double) cream
Leaves and peel of 1 tangerine
4¾ oz (140 g) salsify, peeled and cut on the bias into 2-inch (5 cm) slices
½ teaspoon salt

Tangerine Vinaigrette

¾ cup (4¾ oz/140 g) tangerine supremes (page 142)
2 tablespoons lemon juice
½ cup (4 oz/120 g) olive oil

Seeded Crunch

½ cup (2 oz/50 g) "Party Crunch" (page 248)
2 tablespoons nigella seeds
2 tablespoons flax seeds
2 tablespoons sesame seeds
¼ teaspoon salt, plus extra to taste

MAKE THE SALSIFY PURÉE

In a medium sauce pot, melt the butter, then add the onion, garlic, and salsify. Cook on low heat and sweat, without taking on color, for 10–12 minutes. Once the salsify is semi-tender, add the vermouth and reduce by 60 percent, then add the cream. Cook until the salsify is extremely tender (what we chefs call "blown out"). Add a splash of water if the cream reduces too much before the vegetables are cooked. Blend on high in a blender, pass through a fine-mesh strainer or tamis, and season with salt to taste.

MAKE THE BRAISED SALSIFY

In a small pot, heat the vermouth and reduce by half. Add the cream, tangerine leaves and peel, salsify, and salt, and bring to a simmer, cooking on low heat until just tender, 12–15 minutes. Strain the salsify from the liquid if using right away, or leave in the liquid until using.

MAKE THE TANGERINE VINAIGRETTE

In a nonreactive bowl, stir all the ingredients together.

MAKE THE SEEDED CRUNCH

Combine all the ingredients in a bowl. Check the seasoning and add more salt if needed.

TO SERVE

Heat a cast iron pan until nearly smoking, then turn down the heat and add the oil and turbot fillets, flesh-side down. Immediately return the pan to high heat, then using a fish or offset spatula, gently press the flesh of the fish down to prevent it from curling—just a gentle but firm press—then don't touch the fish again for at least 2–3 minutes. You'll want to scale back the flame a little if the pan seems too hot, or pull the pan off for a moment to reduce the surface temperature of the pan. Just don't move the fish itself until a crust forms and the flesh releases on its own. Sauté the fish until cooked rare, then flip, add the butter, and baste for 1 minute. Transfer to a paper towel-lined tray and spoon the seeded crunch all over the flesh side. Press the seeds into the fish with the back of a spoon.

Warm 4 dinner plates. Reheat the salsify purée and braised salsify if necessary. Spoon the purée onto each plate, then place the braised salsify directly onto the purée. Top with the cooked fillet of fish.

Dress the shaved salsify with the tangerine vinaigrette and supremes of tangerine and plate alongside the fish.

To Serve

2 tablespoons rice bran or grapeseed oil

1 lb 4 oz (570 g) turbot, cut into four 5-oz (150 g) fillets, or substitute a tender white-fleshed flat fish such as fluke

1 tablespoon butter

1 oz (25 g) salsify, peeled, shaved thin, and stored in diluted lemon juice so it doesn't oxidize

1 cup (6 oz/175 g) tangerine supremes (page 142)

Image on page 207

LITTLENECK CLAMS
WITH SORREL ALMOND PESTO

I've been known to say to our cooks that the real test is at the bottom of the bowl. Run a finger through the puddle of sauce left behind and give it a taste. Soak it up with a hunk of bread. If it's delicious, with all the various components of a dish combined, then you know you've done your job.

When we cook, we're looking to build flavor in layers, one step at a time. That is what happens here with the tomatoes, clams, wine, anchovy, and sorrel. We give them time to express themselves first, then meld them into something new. You can't just throw everything in a pot on the stove.

Deep flavors develop sequentially. Each layer needs time to do its thing, to mature. We start this recipe with plump, ripe cherry tomatoes. The fruits burst when the skins rupture in the hot oil. They need to sizzle and splatter and spark, almost like they're about to ignite. Because the fat is the vehicle here, and the path for all this flavor, you need these two to talk with each other—olive oil and tomato. You need them to intensify, reduce, and caramelize, before adding the white wine and clams, because once you do there's no going back.

MAKE THE GREEN BEANS

Bring a pot of water to a boil and season generously with salt. Fill another small bowl with a 50/50 mix of ice and water. Add the green beans to the boiling water and cook until al dente, maybe even a bit too crunchy, since we'll be cooking them again with the clams—about 4 minutes. Immediately plunge the beans into the ice water bath. Once chilled, drain the beans and slice them into thirds, on the bias, to create 1-inch (2.5 cm) segments.

MAKE THE SORREL ALMOND PESTO

Always start with hand-chopped ingredients—this ensures a more even, homogenous texture. Place all the ingredients into a food processor and pulse until a pesto forms.

MAKE THE ANCHOVY SOFFRITTO

Cook all the ingredients together in a medium pot on extremely low heat until tender, about 20 minutes. The soffritto should never brown, the oil should bubble lovingly, and the anchovy should melt away.

TO SERVE

In a small mixing bowl, add the chopped green beans, croutons, and pesto. Toss to coat, then taste and check for seasoning.

In a heavy pot large enough to hold the clams, heat the soffritto and olive oil until very hot. But before the garlic starts to brown, add the cherry tomatoes, crushing them with a potato masher or the back of a fork until they burst. Cook on high for 3 minutes, stirring frequently. The oil will sizzle and crack as the tomatoes release liquid and break down. They shouldn't completely lose form or turn to mush, but rather collapse. Next add the clams, white wine, and chicken stock. Cover and reduce the heat to medium. Cook until the clams open, approximately 3 minutes. Reduce the heat to a simmer and add the butter and green bean-crouton mixture. With a large spoon, toss the clams and beans in the sauce until the butter emulsifies.

Before serving, add lemon juice and additional salt to taste. Plate with an extra drizzle of olive oil and a scattering of sorrel leaves.

SERVES 2

Green Beans

12 green beans (2 oz/50 g), stem ends cleaned
Salt

Sorrel Almond Pesto

1 cup (1¼ oz/35 g) broad leaf sorrel, chopped, plus extra to serve
¼ cup (1½ oz/40 g) Marcona almonds, chopped
1 clove garlic, chopped
1 teaspoon preserved lemon rind, cleaned and chopped
¼ cup (2 fl oz/60 g) olive oil
Salt and freshly ground black pepper, to taste

Anchovy Soffritto

6 cloves garlic, peeled and thinly sliced
2 anchovy fillets, rinsed and chopped
1 Calabrian chile, deseeded and chopped
¼ cup (2 fl oz/60 g) olive oil

To Serve

1 × quantity Sourdough Croutons (page 253)
1½ teaspoons olive oil, plus extra for drizzling
1 cup (6½ oz/185 g) cherry tomatoes
12 littleneck clams (12 oz/350 g)
½ cup (4 fl oz/120 g) dry white wine
½ cup (4 fl oz/120 g) Chicken Stock (page 254)
1 tablespoon butter
Juice of 1 lemon
Salt

CRAB WITH FAVA BEANS AND GREEN GARLIC

Once, to save us from a dreadful February, a chef friend in LA sent a coffin-sized box of green garlic from the Santa Monica Farmers' Market. I will never forget the experience of tearing open that box, how the smell of freshly dug earth and a riot of green spilled out. The box was a portal and I had come back with the monarch of spring.

Many years later, I found myself on vacation in Santa Monica on a Wednesday, market day. I woke in the dark and made a quiet exit from the hotel around 6 a.m. I found my way to Arizona Avenue where, instead of the farm-to-table nirvana I'd expected, I found myself alone with a group of post-party kids hanging out at a street corner. It turned out that markets in California had a much more sensible work-life balance than I did. Even on vacation I was ready to shop produce before dawn.

Speaking of party kids, green garlic is like that angsty teen who's sweet and loving, but growing sharp-tongued and meaner by the day. It's young, premature garlic, picked before it forms a bulb. In the early days of spring, it grows straight up through the ground like a scallion. Harvested young, the root is tender and leek-like, yet still distinctively garlicky, with a mild bite and a less lingeringly bitter taste. The long, slender plants can have red or purple-tinged bottoms and vividly green tops. The entire plant can be used and substituted whenever a recipe calls for spring onion. It's a true harbinger of spring and a lifeline after a long winter.

SERVES 4

Shiitake Soffritto
2¼ oz (60 g) green garlic, whites only, thinly sliced
2¾ (70 g) leeks, brunoise
5 oz (150 g) shiitake, brunoise
½ cup (4 fl oz/120 g) blend oil

Crab
1 shallot, chopped
1 jalapeño, sliced
½ cup (2 oz/50 g) chopped green garlic
4 shiitake mushrooms, sliced
Generous 1½ cups (12¼ fl oz/360 g) heavy (double) cream
1½ cups (6 oz/175 g) lump crab meat, picked and cleaned of shell
Salt and freshly ground black pepper

To Serve
2 cups (11 oz/300 g) fresh fava beans (yielding ½ cup/3 oz/80 g shelled), blanched and cleaned
2 tablespoons olive oil
Juice of ¼ lemon
1 tablespoon chopped parsley
Dill sprigs
⅛ oz (6 g) mojama, shaved
Salt

MAKE THE SHIITAKE SOFFRITTO

In a sauce pot, sweat all the ingredients on low heat until tender and translucent, 15–20 minutes.

MAKE THE CRAB

Combine all the ingredients except the crab, salt, and pepper in a sauce pot. Simmer very gently, until the cream reduces by three-quarters, about 25 minutes. Pass through a fine-mesh strainer or tamis, then allow to cool.

Fold half the cream mixture in with the crab. Season with salt and pepper to taste. The crab salad may be too "tight" or dry. If so, add the rest of the cream mixture as needed.

TO SERVE

Bring a pot of water to a boil and salt generously. Fill another small bowl with a 50/50 mix of ice and water. Cook the favas for 30–45 seconds, or until just tender, then immediately chill in the ice water bath. Remove the inner fava bean from its skin by shucking the outer layer. Dry on paper towels.

Plate the crab at the bottom of each bowl. Fold the fava beans into the shiitake soffritto with 1 tablespoon olive oil, lemon juice, parsley, and salt, to taste, and spoon over the crab. Top with dill, mojama, and the rest of the olive oil.

ROASTED PORK SHOULDER WITH **PRUNE** AND **SHIO KOJI**

0119

Every year we wait for the satsuma mandarins from Penryn Orchard, a tiny fruit farm near Sacramento operated by Jeff and Laurence. Jeff's motto is "Perfect is close enough." Their mandarins, persimmons, plums, and figs are some of the few examples of American fruit that I've felt approach the everyday experiences I had when living in Italy. I hope we humans discover sustainable ways of shipping the best produce from microclimates and microproducers across the country. I imagine a future where chefs won't be limited to the growing seasons in their local area, but can reach out across the globe, without the environmental costs.

This dish has so many border-transgressing ingredients that it's difficult to track the origin to any one place. But it was the mandarins that got us thinking of sweet, salty pork. As with the Carrots, Plums, and Dill (page 166), we use shio koji in a marinade to provide some funk to the caramel of the prune. A rough salsa of peanuts, satsuma, and cilantro (coriander) goes over the top. The BBQ-like crust that forms as the pork slowly roasts became the stuff of legend among our dishwasher team.

In this recipe, we roast the pork in a low conventional oven, using water and basting as a method to control the temperature of the environment, the rate of cooking, and thereby the dryness of the meat. Dryness in a tough piece of meat like a pork shoulder is usually a function of how the protein breaks down during cooking.

All the magic happens within the range of 150–175°F/65–80°C. You need the meat to cook in this range for long enough to convert the collagen to gelatin and render the roast's ample fat, in effect an internal basting process. Fat renders out and coats the meat, giving it a buffer against the dryness of the oven. Tenting the roast in foil gives an additional layer of protection, keeping the moisture in and making sure the meat doesn't dry out before that transformation of collagen takes place. Once you have something succulent and fork tender, a last-minute blast of intense heat in the final minutes of cooking will give you that thick, dark, sweet, sticky crust—soon to be legend in your house, too.

SERVES 6

Confit Shallots
4 shallots (5½ oz/160 g)
1½ cups (12 fl oz/350 g) blend oil

Prune and Shio Koji Marinade
2 cups (11¼ oz/315 g) prunes
½ cup (4 fl oz/120 g) dry sherry
1 arbol chile, deseeded
¼ cup (2 fl oz/60 g) white soy sauce
½ cup (6 oz/180 g) shio koji

Pork Shoulder
2 lb (900 g) pork shoulder
½ oz (15 g) salt

Satsuma Condiment
1¾ oz (45 g) peanuts, roughly chopped
2 teaspoons blend oil
2 guajillo chiles, toasted and deseeded
⅓ cup (2 oz/50 g) prunes, diced
¾ oz (20 g) red onion, thinly sliced, rinsed with cold water
3 oz (85 g) satsuma, peeled and segmented
1 teaspoon fish sauce
2 teaspoons red wine vinegar
Juice of 2 satsumas
¼ teaspoon red yuzu kosho
2 teaspoons soy sauce
1 teaspoon granulated sugar
2 tablespoons olive oil
2 tablespoons mint
¼ cup (⅛ oz/5 g) cilantro (coriander)

MAKE THE CONFIT SHALLOTS

Combine the shallots and oil in a small pot. Simmer on a very low heat, covered, until the shallots are fully tender, 35-45 minutes.

MAKE THE PRUNE AND SHIO KOJI MARINADE

In a sauce pot over medium heat, cook the prunes, sherry, chile, white soy, and 1 cup (8 fl oz/250 g) water for 3–5 minutes to let the prunes soak up some of the liquid. Add the shio koji and confit shallots, transfer to a blender, and blend at high speed until smooth.

MAKE THE PORK SHOULDER

Rub the pork first with the salt, then with the marinade. Chill overnight in an airtight container or vacuum-packed bag. The next day, approximately 4 hours before you want to serve the pork, preheat the oven to 275°F/135°C. Place the pork on a rack in a pan and roast in the oven, basting every 15 minutes. After 1 hour, add a little water to the bottom of the pan, scrape up any crusty drippings, then continue to baste. There should be enough water remaining to cover the bottom of the pan. Cover the pan loosely with foil and return to the oven for approximately 2 additional hours, basting every 30 minutes. After the full 3 hours, test a piece of the pork with a fork. It should be tender. If not, continue to cook for an additional 30 minutes.

Increase the oven temperature to 450°F/230°C. Baste the pork and roast until the outside layer is dark and crisp, but not burnt, 20–30 minutes.

MAKE THE SATSUMA CONDIMENT

Reduce the oven temperature to 350°F/180°C. Toast the peanuts with the blend oil in the oven for 8 minutes, stirring frequently. Leave to cool slightly, then roughly chop along with the guajillo chiles and the prunes. In a mixing bowl, add these ingredients with the onion, satsuma segments, fish sauce, red wine vinegar, satsuma juice, yuzu kosho, soy sauce, sugar, and 5 teaspoons water. Whisk well, then add the olive oil. Fold in the mint and cilantro (coriander) at the last minute.

TO SERVE

Slice the pork and transfer to a serving platter. Drizzle the condiment over the top, then garnish with the satsuma segments, herb leaves, and olive oil.

To Serve
_____

1 satsuma, segmented

Mint and cilantro (coriander) sprigs

1 tablespoon olive oil

_____

Image on page 216

BRAISED PORK BELLY WITH WATERMELON

Using black olives as a salty counterpunch to dishes with prominent sweet notes has been one of our go-to moves at Lula. We dry the olives in the oven until they are like the terra firma version of an anchovy—briny and salty and with that uncanny ability to enhance whatever flavors you'd expect them to overwhelm.

At Lula, our favorite olive to use in these recipes is the oil-cured black Moroccan olive. It's a bit of a misnomer, as the olives are still cured in salt, but then soaked afterwards in olive oil to produce a fruit that is drier, more intense, and blacker in color than a kalamata or niçoise.

The origin of this dish, pairing pork belly with watermelon, has everything to do with the classic combo of prosciutto and cantaloupe that my daughter once thought I'd invented (page 140).

NB: Please pay more attention to the process than the time here. As we've established elsewhere, time is not necessarily a reliable metric for when something is done. Each belly is built with a different ratio of fat to lean meat and each will cook differently. You really need to keep an eye on how it's going, checking the rendering of the fat and the doneness of the lean meat. You're looking for enough fat to render from the fatty side of the belly to make it palatable. Not enough rendering and you get a texture that is goopy and uncooked. Make the roasting process long enough to really pull out most of that fat and leave it tasting like the best bacon ever.

SERVES 4

Pork Belly Rub
2 teaspoons black peppercorns
2 teaspoons coriander seeds
2 teaspoons pink peppercorns
2 teaspoons sumac
½ teaspoon Aleppo pepper
2 teaspoons grated lime zest
2 tablespoons soy sauce
2 tablespoons brown sugar
3 tablespoons salt

Caramelized Honey Glaze
½ cup (6 oz/180 g) honey
½ teaspoon pink peppercorns
½ teaspoon lemon juice
½ teaspoon Aleppo pepper
1 tablespoon sherry vinegar

Roasted Pork Belly
1½ lb (680 g) pork belly

Mint Crema
1 clove garlic, grated
1 cup (8¾ oz/250 g) sour cream
1 cup (1¼ oz/35 g) mint leaves
1 cup (1¼ oz/35 g) cilantro (coriander) leaves
Juice of 1 lime

Black Olive Oil
⅓ cup (1½ oz/40 g) oil-cured Moroccan black olives
Generous ½ cup (4½ fl oz/130 g) blend oil

MAKE THE PORK BELLY RUB

In a frying pan over medium heat, toast the black peppercorns and coriander seeds until just fragrant but not smoking. Leave to cool. Then, in a mortar and pestle or electric spice grinder, crush the black peppercorns, coriander, Aleppo pepper, and pink peppercorns. If using the grinder, do not grind to a fine powder, rather pulse and shake the grinder to produce a coarse grind. Transfer to a mixing bowl and add the remaining ingredients.

MAKE THE CARAMELIZED HONEY GLAZE

Put the honey, pink peppercorns, lemon juice, Aleppo chile, and 1 teaspoon water in a small pan over medium heat. Let this mixture reduce and eventually caramelize without it bubbling up and overflowing. If it threatens to do this, lift the pot off the heat, let the lava subside, and then return to the heat. The color should deepen after 2–3 minutes—this is the sign of caramel. Remove from the heat and let cool for 2 minutes, then stir in the sherry vinegar.

MAKE THE ROASTED PORK BELLY

Score the fat side of the pork belly by cutting parallel, diagonally-oriented slits (approximately ¼-inch/5 mm deep) in the surface of the fat, then rotating the belly 90 degrees and repeating to create a cross-hatch pattern. Scoring promotes the rendering of fat as the belly roasts. Rub the belly with the dry rub mix and refrigerate for 12 hours.

The next day, preheat the oven to 285°F/140°C. Brush any excess rub from the pork belly. Place the belly on a rack in a pan deep enough to hold a decent amount of the fat that will render. Add water to the roasting pan, enough to cover the bottom of the pan without touching the belly. Cover the pan loosely in foil and roast for 2–2½ hours, until the fat has rendered and the lean meat is fork-tender.

Raise the oven temperature to 450°F/230°C and remove the foil. Brush the honey glaze on the belly and roast at the increased temperature for 20–30 minutes to develop a deeply caramelized crust on the belly. Remove the belly and leave to cool for 15 minutes. Then place the belly on a sheet tray (rimmed baking tray) between sheets of parchment paper. On top of this, place another sheet tray weighted down with a heavy object (we use cans of tomatoes). Keep in the refrigerator for at least 6 hours or overnight. The belly will flatten to become a uniform brick of pork. Trim into 5-ounce (150 g) portions.

MAKE THE MINT CREMA

Add the grated garlic to the sour cream. Then, in a blender, purée the mint, cilantro (coriander), 3 tablespoons water, and lime juice until smooth. Fold this mixture into the sour cream. Chill for at least 1 hour.

MAKE THE BLACK OLIVE OIL

Place the olives in a single layer in a dehydrator set to 125°F/52°C and leave for 4–6 hours. Reserve a handful of the dehydrated olives, then put the remainder in a blender with the oil and blend on high until smooth.

TO SERVE

Preheat the oven to 350°F/180°C. Place the pork belly on a sheet tray (rimmed baking tray) and return to the oven, glazing with honey glaze as it reheats for 15–20 minutes. Once hot, slice it into ½-inch (1 cm) thick pieces and arrange the pork and watermelon in alternate slices on a platter or 4 separate plates. Dollop the crema next to the sliced pork/watermelon.

In a mixing bowl, combine the mint, cilantro (coriander), radish, sumac, olive oil, and lemon juice. Spoon this salad next to the pork/watermelon, along with the juices. Drizzle the black olive oil around the plate. Sprinkle the dish with grated black olive, Maldon sea salt, and sumac.

To Serve
_____

5½ oz (160 g) watermelon, sliced ½-inch (1 cm) thick

12 mint leaves

12 cilantro (coriander) sprigs

2 oz (50 g) radish, sliced

¼ teaspoon sumac, plus extra for dusting

2 tablespoons olive oil

1 tablespoon lemon juice

Maldon sea salt

_____

Image on page 217

LAMB MEATBALLS
WITH GNOCCHI

08 18

The seedless Himrod grape from Klüg Farm in Southwest Michigan is the best local fruit available in Chicago. Because the grapes are so sweet, we often pair them with savory dishes like quail, roasted pork, or these tender lamb meatballs, served with Parisienne gnocchi and dill.

This may be one of my all-time favorite dishes from chef Morgan O'Brien. She was a sous at the time, and I remember talking with her about the idea behind this dish—how we wanted the meatballs, gnocchi, and grapes to be the same size, like marbles in a bowl, swirled together in a buttery leek sauce called a soubise. When she presented it to me, it was perfect.

In Escoffier-era classical French cooking, a soubise was a buttery onion purée combined with béchamel, to be served like gravy. Here we use leeks in addition to the yellow onion, deglaze with green verjus, and blend with a small amount of cream in proportion to the allium. The result, while rich, is a lighter, brighter sauce more appropriate for this summertime dish. Green verjus plays off the green Himrod grapes. And the splash of lemon at the end keeps the flavors from getting lazy on your tongue.

Keeping with the classical French theme, we made Parisian gnocchi to match these mini lamb meatballs in soubise. Unlike the potato gnocchi (page 184), these tender morsels of dough are made from a pâte de choux, not potato. Choux pastry is the steam-leavened dough responsible for all manner of French delights, from profiteroles to gougères. Here, in one of its less common savory applications, the dough is cut into bite-sized dumplings (hence the name), simmered in water, then finished in brown butter, much like the preparation of our gnocchi with crab.

SERVES 4

Lamb Meatballs

1¼ oz (30 g) day-old bread, brioche or similar, no crust, diced
¼ cup (2 fl oz/60 g) buttermilk
1 lb (450 g) ground lamb, chilled
1¼ oz (30 g) yellow onion, finely minced
1 teaspoon salt
½ teaspoon smoked paprika
1½ teaspoons ground cumin
⅛ teaspoon baking soda (bicarbonate of soda)
2 tablespoons chopped parsley
¼ cup (¾ oz/20 g) nonfat dried milk powder
2 grinds black pepper
Vegetable oil spray

Soubise

1 oz (25 g) butter
2 tablespoons blend oil
6 oz (175 g) leeks, cleaned and sliced
3¾ oz (110 g) onion, sliced
¼ cup (2 fl oz/60 g) verjus
1 cup (8 fl oz/250 g) heavy (double) cream
2 tablespoons Vegetable Stock (page 255)
½ teaspoon salt
1 tablespoon lemon juice

Parisian Gnocchi

2 oz (50 g) butter
Scant 1 cup (7½ fl oz/225 g) milk
1½ cups (8 oz/225 g) all-purpose (plain) flour, sifted
2 eggs + 1 yolk
½ teaspoon black peppercorns
⅔ cup (2¾ oz/70 g) grated Parmesan
Grated zest of 1 lemon
Salt

MAKE THE LAMB MEATBALLS

Preheat the oven to 400°F/200°C.

In a mixing bowl, combine the dry bread and buttermilk and rest for 10 minutes. Place the ground lamb in a separate bowl with the onion, salt, paprika, cumin, baking soda (bicarbonate of soda), parsley, milk powder, and black pepper. Mix thoroughly with your hands, then add the buttermilk/bread mix. Using your hands or a spatula, mix everything until it becomes a cohesive mass. Refrigerate for at least 30 minutes.

Once cold, portion the meatballs into ⅛ oz (5 g) balls, approximately the same size as a large grape. Line 2 sheet trays (rimmed baking trays) with parchment paper, spray with vegetable oil, add the meatballs, and roast until cooked and golden brown, about 15 minutes.

MAKE THE SOUBISE

Melt the butter and oil together in a medium sauce pot. Add the leeks and onion and cook until soft and translucent, with no color at all, 5–7 minutes. Add the verjus and "deglaze" by reducing by half. Then add the cream and vegetable stock. Cook for an additional 5 minutes, then remove from the heat and add the salt and lemon. Transfer to a blender and purée until the sauce is smooth. Pass through a fine-mesh strainer or tamis.

MAKE THE PARISIAN GNOCCHI

Heat the butter and milk in a small, heavy-bottomed pot. Add the flour and stir with a wooden spoon, keeping the heat on low until the ingredients create a dough. Work it with the spoon, moving it around in the pan as it cooks, 3–5 minutes. Then transfer the dough to the bowl of a stand mixer fitted with the paddle attachment. On the lowest setting, mix the dough and add the eggs and yolk one at a time. Let each egg incorporate into the dough before adding the next.

Add the peppercorns, Parmesan, lemon zest, and 1 teaspoon salt. The resulting dough should be shiny and loose. Transfer the dough to a pastry (piping) bag and chill for at least 1 hour, but preferably 3 hours.

Bring a large pot of water to a boil. Season the water with salt. Trim the end of the pastry bag and expel small, half-ounce (15 g) droplets of dough, roughly the same size as the meatballs, into the pot. Boil for 1 minute after the gnocchi rise to the surface of the boiling water. Remove with a slotted spoon onto a sheet tray (rimmed baking tray) lined with oiled parchment paper.

MAKE THE DILL OIL

Blend the ingredients in a blender on high, then strain through a fine-mesh strainer or tamis.

TO SERVE

Heat a large sauté pan over medium heat and add the oil. Sauté the gnocchi over gentle heat, 2–3 minutes, then add the soubise and 3 tablespoons water. Toss the gnocchi in this sauce, adding water if it tightens too much. The sauce should be loose and yet not runny, what is referred to as "nape" in professional kitchens. If necessary, reheat the meatballs in the oven.

Plate the gnocchi and sauce in 4 shallow bowls. Add the meatballs, setting them in and around the gnocchi. Then add the grapes, similarly set between the meatballs and gnocchi. The idea is to create a situation in which a single bite will get everything at once. Drizzle the dill oil around the plate. Scatter the sunflower seeds and dill over the top.

Dill Oil

½ cup (¼ oz/10 g) dill
1 cup (1¼ oz/30 g) parsley
⅔ cup (5 fl oz/150 g) blend oil

To Serve

1 tablespoon blend oil
3¼ oz (90 g) butter
2¾ oz (75 g) green grapes, whole or halved, depending on size
3 teaspoons toasted sunflower seeds
Dill sprigs

Image on page 222

DUCK BREAST WITH
LEEKS VINAIGRETTE

10 17

The year we opened, I met chef Kelly Courtney as she was planning her first restaurant in Chicago. She used to sit at the bar and watch me poach eggs in the morning. I had no idea she was a protégé of Jeremiah Tower, the ground-breaking chef of Stars in San Francisco, who had been head chef at Chez Panisse in the 1980s, a pivotal time for the landmark restaurant, as it married local Californian ingredients to the pastoral cooking of France and Italy. I had no idea there was such a thing as a culinary history that could bend its arc across nations, time, cultures, in the way I understood literary history to bend. Kelly brought me to my first farmers' market in 1999. Again, I didn't know that markets like the ones I knew in Italy had come to Chicago. It was on a drive to Green City Market that Kelly told me about the books of Alice Waters.

That's how I discovered Chez Panisse and the *Chez Panisse Menu Cookbook*, the *Chez Panisse Café Cookbook*, *Chez Panisse Fruit,* and *Chez Panisse Vegetables*. These weren't bibles; they were more like the diaries of a life I wanted to live. I literally printed out the daily menus that Chez Panisse posted online and studied the ingredients, the seasons of Northern California (what preternatural seasons! Green garlic in October, strawberries in May! And how cold and hard our spring seemed in comparison!), and dishes like lamb à la ficelle and leeks vinaigrette. Through Chez Panisse I was brought to the books of Ruth Reichl, Richard Olney, and Elizabeth David.

Please, be cautious with leeks. Leeks must be cooked tenderly and patiently. An undercooked leek is like a bad kiss. You'll never get over it. I like to use a parchment paper lid to allow steam to release as the leeks braise, preventing a soggy mess while retaining even, constant heat. This is how we coax tenderness from leeks. Once cooked they give up a sweetness that pairs well with the peach and hazelnut. Delicious on its own, yes, but also a lovely accompaniment for a nice slice of roasted duck.

SERVES 4

White Peach Jus
1 tablespoon grapeseed oil
4¾ oz (140 g) leeks, sliced
  and cleaned
9 oz (250 g) onion, sliced
5 cups (40 fl oz/1.2 liters) Duck Stock
  (page 254)
Scant 1 cup (7½ fl oz/225 g) white wine
Scant ⅔ cup (4¾ fl oz/140 g) white
  peach purée
1 teaspoon Dijon mustard
1 tablespoon olive oil

Braised Leeks
7 leeks (6½ oz/185 g), whites only,
  cleaned and trimmed
¼ teaspoon salt
4 cloves garlic
4 thyme sprigs
2 slices lemon
Scant ¼ cup (1¾ fl oz/50 g) white wine

Mustard Vinaigrette
1 oz (25 g) shallot, minced
1 tablespoon minced garlic
1 teaspoon thyme leaves
1 tablespoon distilled white vinegar
1 tablespoon sherry vinegar
1½ teaspoons Dijon mustard
1 teaspoon whole grain mustard
1 teaspoon sugar
4 tablespoons olive oil
1 tablespoon lemon "agrumato" oil

MAKE THE WHITE PEACH JUS

Preheat the oven to 350°F/180°C.

In a medium-sized saucepan, add the grapeseed oil, leeks, and onions and cook over medium-high heat. We're looking for caramelization and tenderness, which will probably take 30 minutes. Once nicely golden brown, deglaze the pan with the white wine. Reduce the jus by half, then add the duck stock. Simmer over gentle but steady heat, reducing while skimming any impurities that rise to the surface. Reduce the liquid down to a single cup (8 fl oz/ 250 g). Strain the sauce through a fine-mesh strainer or tamis directly into a mixing bowl. Whisk in the peach purée, mustard, and olive oil. Transfer to a blender and purée on high until glossy and smooth.

MAKE THE BRAISED LEEKS

In a sauce pot or small rondeaux, add the cleaned leeks and salt with the garlic, thyme, and lemon slices. Cover with the white wine and 1 cup (8 fl oz/250 g) water. Bring to a simmer. Place a parchment paper lid over the leeks and gently braise until fully tender, about 20 minutes. Strain the leeks and leave to cool.

MAKE THE MUSTARD VINAIGRETTE

Place the shallot, garlic, and thyme together on your cutting board and chop them finely, together, until the mix is fully amalgamated. Add this to a mixing bowl with the rest of the ingredients, then whisk until emulsified and creamy.

TO SERVE

To score the duck breasts, thoroughly chill the breasts. You can even place them in the freezer for 10 minutes if necessary. Room temperature or warm duck breast skin will not be easy to cut. Once chilled, place the breasts skin-side up on a cutting board, oriented horizontally. Then use a very sharp knife to carve long, straight, parallel lines every ¼ inch (5 mm), following a diagonal

path across the skin. The blade should cut into the skin no more than ¹⁄₁₆ inch (1.5 mm). Be careful not to cut into the lean flesh itself. These cuts should remain at the surface of the skin. The idea here is that scoring the skin increases surface area, exposing more of the fat to the heat of the pan, which then helps to render it evenly. To create a cross-hatch pattern, rotate the breast 90 degrees and repeat. Season with salt and pepper.

Heat a black steel pan over medium heat, then add the breasts, skin-side down. Turn down the heat to a low setting and render out the fat. Begin to baste the duck once enough fat has accumulated in the pan. Cook to medium-rare, or 130–135°F/54–57°C on a thermometer, then rest the duck breast for 15 minutes in a warm spot.

Meanwhile, heat the butter in a medium sauté pan. Add the braised leeks and gently heat and swirl them around in the foaming, frothy butter.

Reheat the white peach jus in a small pot. Slice the duck breasts and season with Maldon sea salt.

Spoon the jus onto 4 plates, then place the sliced duck in the sauce. Plate the leeks next to the duck breasts, cut-side up, then add slices of white peach in between each leek. Spoon the vinaigrette over the leeks, then garnish the leeks with hazelnuts, Parmesan, and chives.

To Serve

2 duck breasts, skin scored (see note in method)

2 oz (50 g) butter

½ white peach (3 oz/80 g), thinly sliced

1 oz (25 g) hazelnuts, toasted and chopped

4 tablespoons grated Parmesan

2 g snipped chives

Maldon sea salt

Salt and freshly ground black pepper

Image on page 223

SLOW-COOKED
SHORT RIB

11 18

Berries with beef? It's an odd couple that works, especially when you emphasize tartness and tannins with a healthy dose of red wine. While blackberries and blueberries are good common fruits to pair with meat, our favorite is the wild mountain huckleberry sourced from the Pacific Northwest. Our huckleberries come from Rod at Rare Tea Cellars and, combined with red wine, rosemary, a pinch of Aleppo pepper, and rich, reduced beef jus, make a steak sauce with character and complexity.

MAKE THE SHORT RIB RUB

Purée all the ingredients in a blender on high.

MAKE THE SHORT RIBS

Combine the short rib portions and the rub in a vacuum bag and seal tightly. Rest overnight. Cook in a sous vide bath at 134°F/57°C for 28 hours.

MAKE THE RUTABAGA

Season the rutabaga with salt and toss with the orange butter. On a sheet tray (rimmed baking tray), roast the rutabaga at 350°F/180°C until golden and tender, 30–40 minutes.

MAKE THE HUCKLEBERRY SAUCE

Preheat the oven to 350°F/180°C. Place the beef bones on a sheet tray and roast until deeply golden brown, 35–45 minutes. Meanwhile, in a stock pot, combine the butter, onion, chile, rosemary, and orange peels. Over medium-low heat, sweat the aromatics together until the onions are translucent and tender, approximately 15 minutes. Add the huckleberries and bones from the short ribs. Deglaze with the wine and add the soy and stock. Cook until reduced by three-quarters, skimming as needed to remove impurities. Pass through a fine-mesh strainer or tamis. The sauce should be thick enough to coat the back of a spoon.

TO SERVE

In a cast iron skillet (frying pan), heat the blend oil and sear the short rib pieces on all sides, then set aside to rest in a warm place. In a small pot, add the rutabaga pieces, cippolini, Aleppo, and orange butter and warm thoroughly. If needed, reheat the huckleberry sauce.

On 4 plates, spoon the yogurt in a backwards "swoosh." Slice the short rib. Place the beef on the yogurt, then place the rutabaga and onions alongside the sliced meat. Spoon the huckleberry sauce on the plate. It makes a striking contrast with the yogurt.

SERVES 4

Short Rib Rub

1 tablespoon chopped rosemary
Grated zest and juice of 1 orange
¼ teaspoon Aleppo pepper
2 tablespoons tomato paste
½ teaspoon black peppercorns
5 Confit Shallots (page 214), made
  using 1¾ cups (14 fl oz/400 g) oil
¼ cup (2 oz/56 g) blend oil

Short Ribs

2 lb (900 g) bone-in short ribs (remove
  the bones and save for the sauce,
  portioned into 4 pieces)
1 teaspoon salt

Rutabaga

1⅓ lb (600 g) rutabaga, peeled, cut
  with a 2-inch (5 cm) round cutter
1 teaspoon salt
2 oz (50 g) Roasted Orange Butter
(page 249), softened

Huckleberry Sauce

4 short rib bones (11 oz/ 332 g)
1 tablespoon butter
2½ cups (11 oz/ 296 g) onion, peeled
  and sliced
1 arbol chile, deseeded
1 sprig rosemary
4 strips of orange peel
1 cup (7 oz/ 196 g) frozen huckleberries
½ cup (4 fl oz/ 120 ml) red wine
2 tablespoons soy sauce
1 quart (32 fl oz/ 946 ml) beef stock

To Serve

¼ cup (2 fl oz/60 ml) blend oil
Roasted Cippolini Onions, petaled
  out (page 255)
1 teaspoon Aleppo pepper
Roasted Orange Butter (page 249)
2 tablespoons natural yogurt

Back when Lea and I had to do the desserts on our own, it was all panna cotta and figs on a plate. So, for our cookbook, I turned to the pastry chefs who have held the position for the past decade, to share some of their favorite dishes and to show us how it's done.

DESS·DESSERTS·RIS

MISO CORN CAKE WITH SHISO ICE CREAM

08 18

In much the same way we use white miso in our sweet potato soup, chef Amanda Shepard adds it to this corn cake. It's a little moment of savory genius. (Salt in pastry is so under-appreciated.) In this recipe Amanda explores how the umami of the fermented soy and rice plays with a simple set of ingredients. The result is a dessert that's craveable for other reasons than just how sweet it is. The miso seems to bring out the natural "corn" flavor in the cornmeal, which is often lost to the drying and grinding of the mill. It emphasizes savoriness over starch and makes the corn taste almost nutty, which goes so well with the end-of-the-season plums roasted with fresh, bright, summery shiso. The Japanese herb is grown by friends in Indiana. It makes a natural pairing with the plums.

MAKE THE MISO CORN CAKE BATTER

In the bowl of a stand mixer, cream the butter, sugar, vanilla, and white miso on medium speed for 3 minutes, until light and fluffy. Scrape down the bowl, then add the egg. Beat until well combined. Scrape down the bowl again.

In a separate bowl, combine all the dry ingredients. Add one-third of the dry mix to the egg mix and beat on low speed. Then, add one-third of the milk. Repeat this two more times until all the wet and dry ingredients are in the mixing bowl. Before the batter is thoroughly combined, scrape down the bowl one more time. Mix on low speed for a few more seconds, but do not overmix. Store in the fridge for at least 2 hours.

MAKE THE MISO STREUSEL

In the bowl of a stand mixer, cream the butter and the white miso until well combined. Form the butter into a block, wrap in plastic wrap (cling film), and store in the fridge for 2 hours. Cut the chilled miso butter into 1-inch (2.5 cm) cubes and store in the freezer for at least 2 hours.

In a food processor, combine the flour, cornmeal, sugar, and salt. Blend until combined. Add the cold miso butter and blend until the mixture forms a dry crumble. Pour the mixture onto a tray and freeze before storing in a smaller container. (This will keep the streusel from becoming one big mass.)

Preheat the oven to 350°F/180°C. Put only half of the frozen miso streusel on a parchment-lined sheet tray (rimmed baking tray). Bake for 10 minutes, toss the mixture well, then bake for another 4–6 minutes, until golden. Let cool completely.

MAKE THE ROASTED PLUMS

Preheat the oven to 400°F/200°C. Cut the plums into eighths or quarters, depending on whether they're large or small. Place the plums in a roasting pan (tin) so they have plenty of room to roast. Sprinkle with sugar and place the shiso leaves on top. Roast the plums for 6–8 minutes, until cooked and tender but not falling apart. Let cool, then chill in the fridge.

MAKE THE PLUM CARAMEL

In a medium saucepan over high heat, cook the sugar, glucose, and 2½ tablespoons water until the mixture becomes a golden caramel. Turn the heat off, then slowly add the cubed plums, stirring gently with a spoon or spatula. (Be careful! This will cause a reaction in the pot.) Cook over medium heat until the caramel is somewhat thickened, but still thin enough to pour through a fine-mesh sieve. Once you've reached the desired consistency, pass the caramel through the sieve and leave to cool. Store in the fridge.

MAKE THE SHISO ICE CREAM

Fill a large bowl with a 50/50 mix of ice and water. In the ice bath, set a large vessel. Put the shiso leaves in the vessel.

SERVES 6

Miso Corn Cake Batter

4 oz (120 g) unsalted butter
1⅛ cups (8 oz/230 g) granulated sugar
½ teaspoon vanilla extract
2 tablespoons white miso paste
1 egg
1⅛ cups (4½ oz/135 g) all-purpose (plain) flour
½ cup (2½ oz/65 g) cornmeal (polenta) (we use Anson Mills)
1 tablespoon baking powder
¼ teaspoon salt
Scant ½ cup (3¾ fl oz/115 g) whole milk

Miso Streusel

4 oz (120 g) butter
1 tablespoon white miso paste
⅔ cup (3 oz/80 g) all-purpose (plain) flour
½ cup (2 oz/50 g) cornmeal (polenta)
½ cup (3¼ oz/90 g) sugar
1 teaspoon salt

Roasted Plums

4–5 medium plums (8½ oz/240 g)
Granulated sugar, for sprinkling
8–10 shiso leaves

Plum Caramel

⅝ cup (4¼ oz/125 g) sugar
1 tablespoon liquid glucose or corn syrup
3–4 medium plums (6 oz/175 g), flesh cut into small cubes

In a large pot over medium heat, combine the milk, cream, and vanilla bean (pod). In a separate bowl, combine half the sugar, the glucose powder, milk powder, and stabilizer. Once the milk reaches 122°F/55°C, slowly start to whisk in the powder mixture. Continue cooking, whisking constantly, until the mixture reaches 158–167°F/70–75°C.

Then, in another bowl, whisk the remaining sugar into the egg yolks. Working quickly, pour one-third of the hot milk into the eggs and whisk immediately, then pour this mixture back into the pot. Stir with a spatula until the mixture reaches 185°F/85°C. Turn off the heat, stir for 1 minute, then pour into the shiso vessel. Let cool completely, then pass through a fine-mesh sieve. Store in the fridge overnight, then churn in an ice cream machine according to the manufacturer's instructions. Once the ice cream is done churning, drizzle and lightly fold the plum caramel into the ice cream base before freezing.

TO SERVE

Preheat the oven to 375°F/190°C. Place six 4-inch (10 cm) ring molds on a parchment-lined sheet tray (rimmed baking tray), then spray with vegetable oil spray. Scoop ¼ cup (60 g) of batter into each mold. Flatten the batter to fill the mold. On top of the batter, place 4 small slices of roasted plum, making sure they don't touch the ring mold. Sprinkle 1–2 tablespoons of the uncooked, frozen miso streusel on top of each cake. Bake for 12 minutes, then rotate the pan and bake 4 more minutes. The cakes should be golden brown on the edges. As soon as you remove them from the oven, carefully pull off the ring molds. Leave to cool slightly and serve sprinkled with the cooked miso streusel, and with the ice cream and roasted plums alongside.

Shiso Ice Cream

12–15 shiso leaves

2 cups + 2 tablespoons (17½ fl oz/ 525 g) whole milk

Generous ¾ cup (6¼ fl oz/185 g) heavy (double) cream

¼ vanilla bean (pod)

¾ cup (5 oz/150 g) sugar

⅓ cup (1½ oz/45 g) glucose powder

⅓ cup (2 oz/50 g) nonfat dried milk powder

2 teaspoons ice cream stabilizer

5 egg yolks

To Serve

Vegetable oil spray

Image on page 232

SWEET POTATO PIE WITH CARDAMOM MARSHMALLOWS

Pastry chef Kelly Helgesen has an ability to reimagine canonical desserts in a subtle, yet completely transformative way. Kelly put her spin on ice cream cake (corn, blueberry), pavlova (vanilla bean, peach), and classic American holiday dessert with this sweet potato pie. The cardamom marshmallows turn this slice into something luxe and elegant. Chef Helgesen shapes the marshmallows into mini cylinders, like the ones in a packaged hot chocolate, and then toasts them with a blowtorch just before serving. The result is like a meringue top on a pumpkin pie—a mashup of two of my favorite holiday desserts.

SERVES 6–8

Gingersnap Crust

5 oz (150 g) butter, softened, plus 2 oz (50 g) butter, melted

1 cup (7 oz/200 g) granulated sugar

1 teaspoon salt

2 teaspoons baking soda (bicarbonate of soda)

1 large egg

⅓ cup (3 oz/100 g) blackstrap molasses

2⅔ cup (11½ oz/320 g) all-purpose (plain) flour

2 teaspoons ground ginger

1 teaspoon ground cinnamon

Sweet Potato Filling

3 medium sweet potatoes (2 lb/900 g)

1⅓ cups (10 oz/275 g) dark brown sugar

1 teaspoon salt

1 teaspoon ground cinnamon

½ teaspoon ground ginger

¼ teaspoon ground cloves

1 cup (8 fl oz/250 g) heavy (double) cream

3 large eggs

1 teaspoon vanilla paste or extract

½ teaspoon apple cider vinegar

MAKE THE GINGERSNAP CRUST

Preheat the oven to 350°F/180°C. In the bowl of a stand mixer fitted with the paddle attachment, combine the room-temperature butter, sugar, salt, and baking soda (bicarbonate of soda). Mix on medium speed for 2 minutes, then scrape the sides and bottom of the bowl. Add the egg and mix on medium speed until just combined. Scrape the bowl, then add the molasses and mix on low speed. Finally, add the flour and spices and mix on low speed, scraping the bowl again to ensure the dough is completely combined. Then put the dough on a sheet of parchment paper, top with another sheet, and gently roll the dough to an even thickness all the way to the edges of the paper. Bake for 18–20 minutes, when the edges will be browned and the center will be set. Allow to cool completely, then break up the mix and blend in a food processor to create fine crumbs.

Put 14 oz (400 g) cookie crumbs in a bowl (this will be about half the crumbs—the remainder will keep in the fridge for 7 days), pour over the warm melted butter, and toss to coat evenly. The crumbs should loosely stick together when pressed in your hand. Press the crumbs evenly into the bottom and up the sides of a 9-inch (23 cm) pie plate (dish). Bake at 350°F/180°C for 12 minutes. The crust will smell very fragrant and slightly toasty.

MAKE THE SWEET POTATO FILLING

A silky smooth, roasted sweet potato purée is the key to a velvety sweet potato pie filling. Preheat the oven to 350°F/180°C. Scrub each sweet potato, then wrap each one individually in foil. Put the wrapped sweet potatoes on a sheet tray (rimmed baking tray) and bake until soft, about 1 hour, flipping halfway through. Allow to cool, then remove the peel and mash the sweet potatoes in an ovenproof dish. Return to the oven for about 40 minutes, stirring every 10 minutes to cook out excess liquid and concentrate the sweet potato filling. Allow to cool enough to handle, then press the sweet potatoes through a fine-mesh sieve and cool completely. This will yield more than enough for 1 pie.

Reheat the oven to 350°F/180°C. In the bowl of a stand mixer fitted with the paddle attachment, combine the sweet potato purée, brown sugar, salt, and spices on low speed until combined. In a separate bowl, whisk together the remaining ingredients, then mix into the sweet potato mixture on low speed. Scrape the sides and bottom of the bowl to ensure the filling is combined, then pour into the baked gingersnap cookie crust and bake for 20 minutes, then reduce the heat to 325°F/160°C and continue baking for 20–25 minutes, until the very center is just slightly glossy and barely set. It will puff up and crack if overbaked. Cool to room temperature.

MAKE THE CARDAMOM MARSHMALLOWS

Combine the cardamom pods and ½ cup (3½ oz/100 g) granulated sugar in a small pot with 3½ fl oz (100 g) water, then bring to a boil to dissolve the sugar. Remove from the heat, cover with plastic wrap (cling film), and allow to steep. Once completely cool, strain out the cardamom pods and chill the syrup in a shallow dish big enough to fit the gelatin sheets.

Bloom the gelatin in the cold cardamom syrup until soft, about 15 minutes. Line 2 sheet trays (rimmed baking trays) with silpat mats. Combine 3¾ fl oz (110 g) water, the glucose, and remaining sugar in a small pot and cook on high.

Meanwhile, put the egg whites in the bowl of a stand mixer fitted with the whisk attachment. Once the sugar syrup reaches 244°F/118°C, start whipping the whites on medium speed. Continue cooking the syrup until it reaches 258°F/126°C, then turn off the heat and slowly stream the hot sugar syrup into the egg whites. Then, immediately pour the bloomed gelatin and liquid into a hot pot; the residual heat from the pot will melt the gelatin. Slowly pour the gelatin liquid into the egg whites and whip on high speed until very thick and slightly warm.

Transfer the marshmallow fluff into a piping bag fitted with a plain tip and pipe straight lines down the trays, leaving about ½ inch (1 cm) between each rope. Allow to cool at room temperature for 2 hours. Dust with a mixture of equal parts powdered (icing) sugar and cornstarch (cornflour), release from the silpat mats, and roll the marshmallows to ensure all sides are coated with the powdered sugar mixture. With scissors, cut each marshmallow rope into ½-inch (1 cm) pieces. Again, toss the cut marshmallows in the powdered sugar mixture to prevent them from sticking, then dust off excess

Pile the marshmallows on top of the cooled pie, then toast with a kitchen blowtorch or put under the broiler (grill) for 2–3 minutes.

Cardamom Marshmallows
---

5 green cardamom pods, toasted and crushed
2 cups (14 oz/400 g) granulated sugar
6 gelatin sheets
3¾ oz (115 g) glucose
3 oz (75 g) egg whites, at room temperature
Powdered (icing) sugar and cornstarch (cornflour), for dusting

---

Image on page 233

MATCHA PISTACHIO FINANCIER

A financier is an almond flour and egg white cake traditionally made in a rectangular shape. Legend has it that a French baker working near the Bourse, the Wall Street of Paris, named this dish for his customers. Or that the shape resembled a gold bar. Regardless, pastry chef Kim Janusz came up with her own version. She replaces almond flour with pistachio and created a crunchy coconut topping to emphasize the crisp edges of the bake. The soft, almost creamy interior and crisp edges remind me of the pleasures of the outside edge of a brownie. The flavors remind me of pistachio gelato, like when you take that first bite of the edge of the cone. It's a perfect little morsel.

SERVES 4

Pistachio Paste

¼ cup (2 fl oz/60 g) olive oil
1 cup (3¾ oz/ 115 g) pistachio flour
⅓ cup (1½ oz/40 g) powdered (icing) sugar
¼ teaspoon salt

Coconut Crunch

1 cup (2½ oz/65 g) unsweetened coconut chips
2 tablespoons 2:1 simple syrup (see Candied Hazelnuts, page 238)
3½ teaspoons turbinado sugar
¼ teaspoon salt

Matcha Pistachio Financier

1½ teaspoons matcha powder
1½ cups (6½ oz/185 g) powdered (icing) sugar
⅓ cup (1¼ oz/45 g) all-purpose (plain) flour
⅓ cup (1¼ oz/45 g) pistachio flour
½ teaspoon salt
4 egg whites
3¾ oz (115 g) butter
Vegetable oil spray

MAKE THE PISTACHIO PASTE
Combine all the ingredients in a blender and blend until smooth.

MAKE THE COCONUT CRUNCH
Preheat the oven to 325°F/160°C. Combine all the ingredients in a bowl and mix until thoroughly coated. Spread in a single layer on a tray covered with a silpat mat and toast for 8 minutes. Stir and return to the oven for another 6–8 minutes, until golden and fragrant. Cool completely.

MAKE THE MATCHA PISTACHIO FINANCIER
Preheat the oven to 350°F/180°C.

Place the matcha powder, powdered (icing) sugar, flours, and salt in the bowl of a stand mixer fitted with the whisk attachment. Mix on low until combined. Add the egg whites all at once and return to low speed, then stop and scrape down the sides of the bowl and mix again until the batter is smooth.

Meanwhile, melt the butter in a saucepan over high heat. Once the butter is completely melted and starts foaming, begin whisking. Cook the butter, whisking continuously, until dark brown and it smells nutty.

With the mixer on the lowest speed, carefully stream the hot butter into the batter—make sure you add the browned bits at the bottom of the pan! Once all the butter is incorporated, scrape the mixer bowl down once more.

Generously spray your desired molds (I use mini Bundt pans/tins, but cupcake pans/tins will also work) with vegetable oil spray and fill each one a bit more than halfway. Bake until risen and starting to brown and a toothpick inserted comes out clean. Let sit and cool for a few minutes, then unmold while still warm.

Drizzle pistachio paste on top of each financier, then use that paste as a "glue" to adhere your coconut crunch topping.

TOASTED BAY LEAF AND CHOCOLATE CRÈME BRÛLÉE

12 21

Once I knew a chef who boiled fifty bay leaves in water so that he could taste the flavor of the herb. Because we can all agree that it is a mystery. We buy our bay leaves fresh and then freeze them for use in stews, sauces, stocks, and, yes, this chocolate crème brûlée. The herb gives a medicinal note to aroma, like eucalyptus or pine, but as a flavor it reads more round and floral. In this brûlée it works to balance the intensity of the dark chocolate.

MAKE THE BRÛLÉE BASE

Place the cream in a pot. Turn the largest burner on the stove up to full blast. Using tongs, toast the bay leaves one at a time over the open flame until they pop and start to turn black in spots, then immediately place them into the cold cream to stop the cooking. Bring the cream and bay leaves to a boil, then turn off the heat. Steep for 30 minutes at room temperature. When the 30 minutes are almost up, melt the milk and dark chocolate together in a sauce pot. Strain the bay leaf cream through a fine-mesh sieve and place into a clean pot to heat. Combine the cream and chocolate in a separate sauce pot when both are hot.

Preheat the oven to 325°F/160°C.

In a separate bowl, beat the egg, yolks, and sugar together. Temper the eggs by adding a small amount of the warm chocolate cream into the egg mixture, then combine all the egg mixture with the remaining chocolate cream and stir in the salt. Pour into 8 oz (225 g) ramekins and place the ramekins in a baking dish. Fill the dish with boiling water, to come halfway up the sides of the ramekins. Bake for 30–40 minutes, or until the centers are barely set. Remove the ramekins from the baking dish and leave to cool. Refrigerate for several hours and up to a couple days.

MAKE THE CANDIED KUMQUATS

In a pot, cover the kumquats with cold water and bring to a boil. Drain. Repeat once more with fresh cold water.

Take the blanched kumquats and pierce each one a few times with a small knife.

Bring the sugar and 1 cup (8 fl oz/250 g) water to a boil and add the kumquats. Cook in the syrup on low heat for 15 minutes, then let sit overnight.

The next day, bring the kumquats and syrup back to a boil and cook for another 10 minutes. Leave to cool.

MAKE THE CANDIED HAZELNUTS

For a simple syrup, heat the sugar with ¼ cup (2 fl oz/60 g) water in a small pan until the sugar melts. This will make more than you need (save the extra for the Matcha Pistachio Financier on page 236).

Preheat the oven to 350°F/180°C. Chop the hazelnuts into halves or quarters—don't chop them into dust. Combine the nuts with the sugar syrup, turbinado sugar, and salt until well coated. Spread in a single layer on a tray covered with a silpat mat and toast for 8 minutes. Stir and return to the oven for another 8 minutes, or until they're a deep caramel color. Let cool and break into bite-sized pieces.

TO SERVE

Top each brûlée base with sugar in a thin layer. Use a kitchen blowtorch to caramelize the sugar, or place the ramekins under a broiler (grill) close to the heat source and cook until the sugar melts and browns. Let sit until cool to the touch.

Combine the cream and crème fraîche in a bowl and whip until soft peaks form.

Top the bases with a dollop of whipped crème fraîche and broken hazelnut candy. Squeeze the seeds out of a few kumquats and tear the flesh into pieces. Garnish with kumquat pieces and anise hyssop.

SERVES 6

Chocolate Crème Brûlée Base
2¾ cups (23 fl oz/680 g) heavy (double) cream
12 fresh bay leaves (don't use dried)
4¾ oz (140 g) good-quality milk chocolate
3 oz (80g) good-quality dark chocolate
1 egg + 4 egg yolks
½ cup (3½ oz/100 g) granulated sugar
½ teaspoon salt

Candied Kumquats
12 kumquats
1½ cups (11 oz/300 g) sugar

Candied Hazelnuts
½ cup (3½ oz/100 g) sugar
1 cup (4½ oz/125 g) hazelnuts
2 tablespoons + 1½ teaspoons turbinado sugar
½ teaspoon salt

To Serve
6 tablespoons sugar
½ cup (4 fl oz/120 g) heavy (double) cream
2 tablespoons crème fraîche
1 anise hyssop sprig

The debut cookbook from executive chef Jason Hammel, showcasing the all-day seasonal food and arty vibe of his iconic Chicago restaurant

The story of twenty years of cooking, love, friendship, and community told through food. This stunning book takes the reader behind the scenes of Lula Cafe, from its creation and connections with local farms and suppliers, to the 90 classic dishes and seasonal treats that have secured its position as one of Chicago's most-loved eateries.

Beautiful food photography and an innovative, bold design make this book a real feast for the senses.

Jason Hammel is known for his creative cuisine and has been a mentor to a generation of chefs. He is also executive chef of Marisol at Chicago's Museum of Contemporary Art.

PHAIDON

100

YEARS OF
CREATIVITY

TURMERIC
TANGERINE **TEACAKE**

Before she became the pastry chef at Lula, I used to follow chef Emily Spurlin from afar, jealous of the many unusually haunting flavor combinations she created for her pastries and composed desserts. Once she and I finally worked together, this turmeric teacake was one of her first creations. We were in a flush of citrus from California, particularly tangerines and satsuma mandarins. Emily paired these with turmeric, for the color, but also for the way the spice bounced against the baking spices, olive oil, and tangy yogurt in the cake. The importance of freshness in dried turmeric spice can't be overlooked. Fresh, high-quality turmeric sings bright, flowering, zesty notes that are a natural match for winter tangerine.

SERVES 4

Citrus Glaze
⅓ cup (2½ fl oz/75 g) orange
  or tangerine juice
1 tablespoon + 1 teaspoon lemon juice
1 oz (25 g) granulated sugar
1 tablespoon honey
¼ oz (10 g) fresh ginger, grated

Turmeric Icing
Scant ½ cup (2 oz/50 g) powdered
  (icing) sugar
½ teaspoon ground turmeric
2 teaspoons orange or tangerine juice

Tangerine Teacakes
1 satsuma (or other tangerine)
Generous ¾ cup (3½ oz/100 g)
  all-purpose (plain) flour
1⅛ teaspoons baking powder
¼ teaspoon salt
1 teaspoon ground ginger
1 teaspoon ground turmeric
½ teaspoon ground cinnamon
½ teaspoon ground cardamom
Pinch ground black pepper (optional)
1 teaspoon grated orange or
  tangerine zest
½ cup (3¾ oz/115 g) granulated sugar
1 egg
¼ cup (2 fl oz/60 g) olive oil
Generous ⅓ cup (3½ fl oz/100 g)
  natural yogurt
½ teaspoon vanilla extract

MAKE THE CITRUS GLAZE

Add all the ingredients to a small saucepan and bring to a boil, then reduce the heat. Simmer until the mixture thickens and becomes syrupy, about 5–10 minutes.

MAKE THE TURMERIC ICING

Whisk all the ingredients until smooth. The consistency should be relatively thick but have enough movement to very slowly drip down the sides of the cake. Add more powdered (icing) sugar if too runny and more juice if too thick.

MAKE THE TANGERINE TEACAKES

Preheat the oven to 350°F/180°C and grease 4 small loaf pans (tins) or muffin pans (tins). Prepare the tangerine by removing the peel and as much pith as possible. Divide into segments and slice them crosswise to make small triangles about ¼ inch (5 mm) thick. Set aside.

In a large bowl, whisk the flour, baking powder, salt, and spices together and set aside. In another bowl, add the orange or tangerine zest to the granulated sugar, and rub together with your fingers until the zest is evenly distributed into the sugar. Add the egg and whisk until combined. Slowly add the olive oil, whisking constantly to emulsify, then add the yogurt and vanilla extract and mix until homogenous. Add the wet mixture to the dry mixture and fold with a rubber spatula just until combined and no lumps remain.

Portion ⅓ cup (75 g) into each tin and smooth the top of the batter. Add 8–9 pieces of tangerine segment over the top.

Bake for 15–20 minutes, until the cakes are just starting to get some color (you don't want them too dark to preserve the color) and a toothpick comes out clean.

Once the cakes come out of the oven, brush them generously with the citrus glaze, then leave to cool. Once completely cooled, dot the top of the cakes with 3 small blobs of turmeric icing.

To make a full-sized version, double the cake recipe, top with wheels of citrus, and bake in a greased and parchment-lined 8-inch (20 cm) cake pan (tin) for 30–45 minutes until cooked through. The shelf life of the cake is 2 days at room temperature and up to 5 days in the refrigerator.

CARROT CAKE

09 99

In the early days of Lula we bought desserts from a local bakery, including a nut-free carrot cake that everyone grew to love. Eventually, skilled pastry chefs were hired to make their own creations. But the first rule of order was to come up with a version of the fan favorite, the classic carrot cake.

Because everybody loved it. Simple, tender, uncomplicated. The carrot was soft and smooth, more like cashmere than the scruffy, itchy wool of a "healthy" carrot cake. There were no nuts or raisins, or coconut, nothing to get in the way. It had no pretense toward being good for you in any way. It was just sweet joy.

In the late 2000s, pastry chef Melissa Trimmer tested many versions until she landed on the recipe that we use today. Over the years I lost track of Melissa until one day while on vacation at Dollywood in Pigeon Forge, Tennessee, she messaged me—she had seen me at the park but couldn't say hi, as she was caring for a toddler who had eaten one too many cinnamon breads. It reminded her of those days tasting carrot cake recipes and she asked if it was still on the menu. Yes, I said, though since Melissa's time we've made many changes to the classic. This version was created by pastry chef Kim Janusz in 2021, though as always, the original recipe for the cake itself remained the same.

MAKE THE CARROT CAKE

Preheat the oven to 350°F/180°C. Line a sheet tray (rimmed baking tray) with parchment paper and spray with the vegetable oil.

Place the carrots in a food processor and process until very fine. In a separate bowl, combine the flour, spices, baking soda (bicarbonate of soda), and salt. In the bowl of a stand mixer fitted with the paddle attachment, combine the eggs, oil, sugar, and vanilla extract until light and pale. Add the dry ingredients to the mixer and mix until thoroughly combined, scraping down the bowl as necessary. Add the carrots and mix just until the carrots are evenly incorporated. Pour the batter onto the prepared tray and bake for 20–25 minutes.

MAKE THE CREAM CHEESE MOUSSE

In the bowl of a stand mixer fitted with the paddle attachment, mix the cream cheese and butter. These should be at the same consistency when combined, otherwise your frosting (icing) will have lumps. If needed, you can microwave them in short 10-second bursts to soften. Add the sugar, vanilla, and salt and mix until combined, scraping down the sides of the bowl.

Remove from the stand mixer bowl into a medium bowl and wash the mixer bowl.

Place the cream in the clean mixer bowl and whip to stiff peaks. Fold the whipped cream into the cream cheese mixture with a spatula. Do not overmix.

TO SERVE

Punch out 3 circles of cake using a 6-inch (15 cm) cake ring. Place the circles in the freezer for 30 minutes so they are easier to handle. Clean the cake ring, line with acetate, and set on a plate or cake stand.

Place the first layer of cake in the bottom of the ring, brush lightly with carrot syrup, then top with half the cream cheese mousse, spreading evenly to the sides. Place another layer of cake on top of the mousse. Brush with carrot syrup, then spread with 2–3 tablespoons of raspberry jam. You want just enough jam to make the layers stick together. Top with the final layer of cake and press lightly to make the layers adhere to each other, then brush with carrot syrup. Spread the remaining cream cheese mousse evenly to the sides, then chill for at least 4 hours, or overnight.

Garnish with fresh mint or basil leaves and edible flowers.

MAKES 1 × 6-INCH (15 CM) CAKE

Carrot Cake
Vegetable oil spray
1 lb 2 oz/500g carrots, peeled and cut into 1-inch (2.5 cm) chunks (reserve the peels)
Scant 2 cups (8 oz/225g) all-purpose (plain) flour
1 tablespoon cinnamon
2 teaspoons ground ginger
1½ teaspoons baking soda (bicarbonate of soda)
½ teaspoon salt
3 eggs
Scant 1 cup (8 fl oz/240g) blend oil
1½ cups (10½ oz/300 g) granulated sugar
1 teaspoon vanilla extract

Cream Cheese Mousse
8 oz (225 g) cream cheese, softened
3 oz (75 g) butter, softened
Scant ⅔ cup (3 oz/75 g) powdered (icing) sugar
1 teaspoon vanilla extract
Pinch salt
⅓ cup + 1 tablespoon (3½ fl oz/ 100 g) cream

To Serve
1 × quantity Carrot Syrup (page 246)
2–3 tablespoons Raspberry Jam (page 252)
Fresh mint or basil leaves
Edible flowers

Many of these building blocks are recognizable condiments, like gremolata and harissa, though our versions often jump to the side of tradition. If you have the space, keeping these condiments on hand will create an orchestral pantry of flavors at the ready. It will make a quick dinner less a thing of panic and more creative, fun, and delicious. Feel free to use them however you like. Whether you're making a simple plate of grilled veggies or late-night pasta, these will come in handy when you need a little savory note, zingy finish, or delightful, surprising crunch.

BUILDING BLOCKS

OILS AND AROMATICS

Store all oils and aromatics in an airtight container in the refrigerator. Use within 7 days.

ROASTED GARLIC

3 heads garlic, top sliced to expose cloves
2½ cups (18 fl oz/550 g) vegetable oil, plus extra as needed

Preheat the oven to 300°F/150°C. In a small baking dish or loaf pan (tin), add the garlic and the oil. If the oil doesn't cover the garlic all the way, add more to submerge it. Cover the dish with foil and cook the garlic until golden, tender, and lightly roasted, about 1 hour. Leave to cool, then store the garlic in the oil. When ready to use, squeeze the roasted garlic purée out of the cloves.

BASIL OIL

¾ cup (1½ oz/40 g) basil leaves
3 tablespoons canola (rapeseed) oil
3 tablespoons olive oil

Fill a bowl with a 50/50 mix of ice and water. Add the basil to a pan of boiling water and blanch for 45 seconds. Then immediately shock the basil in the ice water. Squeeze out excess water, then blend the basil on high with the oils.

NASTURTIUM OIL

2 cups (1½ oz/45 g) nasturtium leaves
½ teaspoon capers
1 clove garlic
½ cup (4 fl oz/120 g) blend oil

Blend all ingredients on high until smooth, then pass through a fine-mesh strainer.

PIMENTON-TOMATO OIL

1 tablespoon pimenton (Spanish paprika)
2 cups (11½ oz/325 g) cherry tomatoes
1 cup (8 fl oz/250 g) olive oil

In a small saucepan, heat the pimenton, tomatoes, and oil. Bring to a light simmer, then turn the heat to low and cook for 1 hour very gently. Strain through a fine-mesh strainer.

CHAMOMILE OIL

⅓ cup (2½ fl oz/75 g) grapeseed oil
2 tablespoons chamomile flowers

Heat the oil and chamomile in a small saucepan set over medium heat. Keep the temperature between 140–180°F/60-80°C for at least 40 minutes and up to 1 hour. Allow to cool, then strain.

PINE/SPRUCE OIL

1½ cups (1¼ oz/35 g) parsley
1 cup (3 oz/80 g) spruce tips
1 cup (8 fl oz/250 g) grapeseed oil

Fill a bowl with a 50/50 mix of ice and water. Bring a small pan of water to a boil. Add the parsley to the pan and blanch for 45 seconds. Then immediately shock the parsley in the ice water. Squeeze out excess water. Steep the spruce tips in the grapeseed oil for 1 hour. Blend all together on high, then strain through a piece of cheese cloth.

CARROT SYRUP

Reserved carrot peelings
½ cup (3½ oz/100 g) sugar
1 cinnamon stick

Place the reserved carrot peels in a heatproof bowl. Bring the sugar, cinnamon stick, and 3½ fl oz (100 g) water to a boil in a pan and pour over the peels. Let cool, then strain.

QUICK PICKLES

Store all pickles in a jar in the refrigerator and use within 30 days.

PICKLED BUTTERNUT SQUASH

1 cup (8 fl oz/250 g) apple cider vinegar
¼ cup (2 fl oz/60 g) mirin
1 teaspoon salt
½ cup (4 fl oz/120 g) water
1 arbol chile
2 pieces dulse
2 cups (4½ oz/135 g) butternut squash, peeled, then sliced thin on a mandoline

Place all the ingredients (except the squash) in a small stainless-steel or nonreactive saucepan and bring to a boil. Place the squash in a glass jar. Pour the brine over and let sit for at least 1 day before using.

PICKLED CARROTS

1 cup (8 fl oz/250 g) distilled white vinegar
½ cup (4 fl oz/120 g) sherry vinegar
1 cup (8 fl oz/250 g) water
4 tablespoons granulated sugar
1 teaspoon coriander seeds
1 arbol chile
1 bay leaf
8 baby carrots (11½ oz/325 g)

In a stainless-steel or nonreactive saucepan, bring all the ingredients (except the carrots) to a boil. Place the baby carrots in a glass jar. Pour the brine over and let sit for at least 1 day before using.

PICKLED THAI CHILE

1¼ cups (10 fl/300 g) white vinegar
1 cup (8 fl oz/250 g) water
2 tablespoons granulated sugar
¼ teaspoon salt
1 cup (2½ oz/65 g) Thai chiles

In a stainless-steel or nonreactive saucepan, bring all the ingredients (except the chiles) to a boil. Place the chiles in a glass jar. Pour the brine over and let sit for at least 1 day before using.

PICKLED GOLDEN RAISINS

1 cup (8 fl oz/250 g) distilled white vinegar
½ cup (4 fl oz/120 g) water
½ cup (3½ oz/100 g) granulated sugar
1 teaspoon salt
1 cup (5 oz/150 g) golden raisins

Bring the vinegar, water, sugar, and salt to a boil. Place the raisins in a glass jar. Pour the brine over and let sit for at least 1 day before using.

FRIED GRAINS AND SPICE MIXES

Store all grains and mixes in an airtight container in a cool, dark place, and use within 30 days.

PUFFED RICE

¾ cup (3½ oz/100 g) cooked rice
Canola (rapeseed) oil, for frying
Salt, paprika, and ground nori, for dusting

Dehydrate the rice using a dehydrator if you have one, or lay it out on a tray overnight. Bring a small pot of canola (rapeseed) oil to 400°F/200°C. Drop the rice into the fryer in batches. It will float to the top and puff up. At that point, remove it with a strainer onto a paper towel-lined tray. Repeat with the rest of the rice. Season the puffed rice with a dusting of salt, paprika, and ground nori.

FRIED CHICKPEAS

4 cups (32 fl oz/946 g) canola (rapeseed) oil
1 × 14 oz (400 g) can chickpeas, drained and rinsed
1 tablespoon Tagine Spice Mix (page 248)
1 teaspoon salt

Heat the oil to 350°F/180°C in a large pot—enough to contain more than 2 times the volume of the oil and chickpeas. The oil will bubble up, so be careful. Add the chickpeas to the oil and fry until crispy. Remove with a strainer onto a paper towel-lined tray, then toss with the tagine spice mix and salt.

"PARTY CRUNCH"

1 cup (5 oz/150 g) roasted sunflower seeds, chopped
1 cup (2¼ oz/60 g) fried shallots, chopped
½ cup (3½ oz/100 g) fried dry amaranth
2 teaspoons black lime powder

Combine everything together.

AROMATIC SPICE MIX

1 tablespoon coriander seeds
4 whole cloves
½ teaspoon black peppercorns
1 whole star anise
¼ teaspoon ground turmeric
1 teaspoon cumin seeds
1 teaspoon fennel seeds
⅛ teaspoon ground mace
½ teaspoon yellow mustard seeds
¼ teaspoon ground cinnamon

Combine all the ingredients in a spice grinder or mortar and pestle. Grind to a powder.

VADOUVAN SPICE MIX

1 teaspoon ground turmeric
2 tablespoons yellow mustard seeds
1 tablespoon cumin seeds
2 tablespoons coriander seeds
1 tablespoon fenugreek seeds
¼ teaspoon Aleppo pepper
5 cardamom pods
Very small pinch ground nutmeg
½ teaspoon ground cloves
¼ teaspoon cayenne
1 teaspoon salt, plus extra to taste
3 tablespoons nutritional yeast
2 cups (7½ oz/220 g) fried shallots
1 tablespoon granulated onion
1 tablespoon granulated garlic

1 tablespoon dried oregano
¼ cup (¼ oz/10 g) dried parsley

Mix all the dried spices together in a spice grinder or mortar and pestle and roughly crush. Place in a bowl and add the salt, nutritional yeast, shallots, onion, garlic, oregano, and parsley. Season to taste.

TAGINE SPICE MIX

1 tablespoon cumin seeds
½ tablespoon brown mustard seeds
1 tablespoon fenugreek seeds
12 whole cloves
2 tablespoons coriander seeds
1 tablespoon plus ½ teaspoon black peppercorns
6 tablespoons ground turmeric
1 teaspoon ground nutmeg

Toast all the whole spices separately, then grind in a spice grinder or mortar and pestle. Mix in the other powdered spices.

AIOLIS AND BUTTERS

Store all aiolis and butters in the refrigerator and use within 7 days.

PRESERVED MANDARIN AIOLI

1 egg + 2 egg yolks
1 tablespoon lemon juice
1 tablespoon honey vinegar
1 tablespoon distilled white vinegar
½ oz (15 g) preserved mandarin, trimmed of pith and seeds, minced super-fine
1 cup (8 fl oz/250 g) blend oil

In a food processor, combine the egg, yolks, lemon juice, vinegars, and mandarin and purée for 30 seconds. With the processor running at high speed, slowly drizzle in the oil to create a thick emulsion.

ROASTED GARLIC AIOLI

2 egg yolks
8 cloves Roasted Garlic (page 246)

3 tablespoons lemon juice
⅛ teaspoon salt
1 cup (8 fl oz/250 g) blend oil

In a high-speed blender, add the egg yolks, garlic, lemon juice, salt, and 1 tablespoon water. Blend on high, then slowly stream in the oil to create a thick emulsion. Season.

DILL AIOLI

1½ cups (2¼ oz/60 g) dill, chopped
2 cloves garlic
2 tablespoons lemon vinegar
2 egg yolks
¼ teaspoon salt
1 cup (8 fl oz/250 g) grapeseed oil

In a food processor or blender, purée the dill, garlic, vinegar, egg yolks, salt, and ¼ cup (2 fl oz/60 g) water. Then, with the machine running, stream in the oil.

SWEET POTATO BUTTER

11½ oz (320 g) sweet potatoes, peeled
1 tablespoon oil from Roasted Garlic (page 246) or blend oil
¼ teaspoon salt
1 tablespoon apple cider vinegar
¼ teaspoon xanthan gum
¼ cup (2 fl oz/60 g) blend oil

Preheat the oven to 350°F/180°C. Wrap the potatoes and garlic oil in foil and roast for 45–60 minutes until blown out. Purée the cooked sweet potato with the salt and apple cider vinegar in a blender. Add the xanthan gum and blend again. With the blender still running, stream in the blend oil to emulsify until silky smooth.

ROASTED ORANGE BUTTER

1 orange (9½ oz/280 g), halved
¼ teaspoon Aleppo pepper
1 tablespoon chopped rosemary leaves
8 oz (225 g) butter, diced and softened
¼ teaspoon salt

Preheat the oven to 275°F/135°C. On a sheet tray (rimmed baking tray) with a roasting rack, roast the orange for 25–30 minutes. Slice off the rind. Let the orange cool, then purée the flesh in a food processor with the rest of the ingredients. Set aside and chill.

TRUFFLE BUTTER

2 oz (50 g) butter, softened
8 g black truffle, grated
⅛ teaspoon salt
Grated lemon zest

Place the butter in a mixing bowl. Fold in the truffle, salt, and lemon zest to taste. Chill overnight before using.

SAUCES AND (MORE) VINAIGRETTES

Store all sauces and vinaigrettes in the refrigerator and use within 7 days.

SIMPLE VINAIGRETTE

1 tablespoon honey vinegar
1 tablespoon white balsamic vinegar
2 tablespoons olive oil

In a nonreactive bowl, whisk all the ingredients together.

HONEY VINAIGRETTE

2 tablespoons minced shallot
¼ teaspoon cracked black peppercorns
½ teaspoon seeded, thinly sliced Thai chile
2 tablespoons honey vinegar
1 tablespoon white vinegar
2 tablespoons sherry vinegar
¼ cup (2 fl oz/60 g) olive oil

In a nonreactive bowl, whisk all the ingredients together.

YUZU KOSHO VINAIGRETTE

½ teaspoon green yuzu kosho
4 thyme sprigs, leaves picked
1 teaspoon honey
2 cloves garlic, grated
Juice of 2 lemons
Small pinch chile flakes
¼ cup (2 fl oz/60 g) olive oil

In a nonreactive bowl, whisk all the
ingredients together.

ARTICHOKE VINAIGRETTE

⅓ cup (1¼ oz/35 g) golden raisins
¼ cup (1¼ oz/35 g) sunflower seeds
2 tablespoons white wine
1½ cups (5 oz/150 g) jarred artichoke
   hearts, thinly sliced
2 tablespoons lemon juice
1½ teaspoons honey
⅛ teaspoon salt
¼ cup (2 fl oz/60 g) lemon "agrumato" oil

In a small saucepan over medium heat,
simmer the raisins, sunflower seeds, and
wine for 2–3 minutes to cook off the alcohol
and "bloom" the raisins. Then transfer
to a nonreactive bowl and whisk in the
remaining ingredients.

FISH SAUCE AND LIME VINAIGRETTE

1 shallot (1¼ oz/30 g), finely minced
Grated zest and juice of 2 limes
2 teaspoons honey
1 teaspoon fish sauce
1 teaspoon minced serrano pepper
2 tablespoons canola (rapeseed) oil
2 tablespoons olive oil

In a nonreactive bowl, mix the shallots with
the lime juice and zest. Rest for 5 minutes,
then whisk in the remaining ingredients.

CAPER LEMON DRESSING

2 teaspoons Dijon mustard
½ cup (¼ oz/10 g) parsley leaves

¼ teaspoon minced garlic
¼ teaspoon ground black pepper
2 tablespoons diced red onion
1 tablespoon capers, plus 1½ teaspoons brine
1 tablespoon + ½ teaspoon lemon juice
Grated zest of 1 lemon
½ cup + 2 teaspoons (4½ fl oz/130 g)
   blend oil

Combine all the ingredients with 1½
teaspoons water in a high-speed blender
and purée until smooth.

SPICY PEANUT SAUCE

4 tablespoons blend oil
11 oz (300 g) onion, finely diced
2½ teaspoons ground coriander
2 tablespoons + 1½ teaspoons sambal
1 tablespoon + 2 teaspoons grated fresh
   ginger
1 tablespoon plus 1 teaspoon minced garlic
1¼ cups (10 fl oz/300 g) Indonesian medium
   sweet soy sauce (we use ABC)
1 cup (9 oz/250 g) chunky peanut butter
3 tablespoons lime juice

In a medium sauce pot, combine the blend
oil, onion, coriander, and sambal. "Sweat,"
meaning cook over low heat, until the onions
soften and meld, approximately
15–20 minutes. Add the ginger and garlic and
cook for an additional 10 minutes, further
softening the aromatic vegetables. Add the
soy and reduce over low heat for 40 minutes.
Remove from the heat and stir in the peanut
butter and lime juice.

TONNATO SAUCE

1 egg yolk
¼ cup (4¾ oz/140 g) high-quality oil-packed
   tuna
¼ cup (1¾ oz/45 g) canned (tinned) artichoke
   hearts
2 salt-packed anchovies, rinsed
1 teaspoon capers
2½ tablespoons lemon juice
1 clove garlic
¼ cup (2 fl oz/60 g) olive oil
½ cup (4 fl oz/120 g) canola (rapeseed) oil

Add all ingredients, except the oils, to a blender with 2 tablespoons water. Mix the oils in a separate bowl. Blend everything on high and then stream the oils in, slowly and cautiously, until a thick aioli forms.

DILL GREMOLATA

½ cup (½ oz/15 g) dill
1 tablespoon grated fresh horseradish
1 tablespoon preserved lemon
1 clove garlic
¼ cup (⅛ oz/6 g) parsley leaves
¼ cup (⅛ oz/6 g) celery leaves
¼ cup (2 fl oz/60 g) olive oil

Put all the ingredients except the olive oil into a mound on your cutting board. With a sharp knife, start chopping everything down. Then start drizzling the olive oil little by little onto the cutting board, while alternating the drizzling and chopping until you get down to a fine herb and oil paste.

CARROT TOP GREMOLATA

1 cup (2½ oz/65 g) carrot tops
1¼ cups (1 oz/25 g) cilantro (coriander)
Grated zest and juice of 1 lemon
1 clove garlic
1 cup (8 fl oz/250 g) olive oil
¼ teaspoon salt

Chop the carrot tops, cilantro (coriander), lemon zest, and garlic together on a cutting board until finely minced. Add the olive oil and continue chopping directly on the board until the gremolata has a pesto-like consistency. Transfer to a container and stir in the salt and lemon juice.

GREEN HARISSA

½ teaspoon fennel seeds
1 teaspoon cumin seeds
½ teaspoon caraway seeds
1 teaspoon coriander seeds
2 medium (3¼ oz/90 g) jalapeño peppers
2 medium (5 oz/150 g) Anaheim peppers
2 scallions, ends trimmed
3 tomatillos (4¼ oz/125 g)
1 cup (¾ oz/20 g) parsley leaves, chopped
1 cup (¾ oz/20 g) cilantro (coriander) leaves, chopped
1 teaspoon salt
½ cup (4 fl oz/120 g) olive oil

Toast all the spices separately. Keep separate and allow to cool before grinding then mixing. Set aside.

Prepare to roast the vegetables directly over an open gas flame. At Lula, we use a perforated hotel pan, but you can also hold things with a pair of tongs over the flame. Place the peppers directly in the gas flame until charred, but not completely. You want a little color to show through. Allow to cool uncovered (this allows them to keep their bright color and prevents overcooking). Char the scallions; as with the peppers, you're looking for a nice mix of char and bright color. Char the tomatillos similarly and quickly, to keep them semi-firm. Once cool, peel the skins of the peppers and remove the seeds with a knife. Chop the peppers along with the tomatillos until very smooth, the texture of pesto. Empty the mixture into a medium mixing bowl. Chop the scallions separately and add to the mixing bowl.

Add all the chopped parsley and cilantro (coriander), 2 teaspoons of the ground spice mix, and salt to the mixing bowl and stir. Once combined, stir in the olive oil. The oil will not emulsify.

GOLDEN TOMATO AND SHALLOT JAM

1¼ lb (550 g) sungold cherry tomatoes
1 small red shallot (1½ oz/45 g), minced
2 tablespoons white balsamic vinegar
Juice of 1 lemon

Preheat the oven to 250°F/120°C. Line a sheet tray (rimmed baking tray) with parchment paper. Prick each tomato with the tip of a paring knife, to allow excess moisture to release as they cook. Bake until the tomatoes shrivel slightly, raisin-like, though you do not want to dry them out entirely. Depending on the humidity and the fan in your oven, this process takes 3–4 hours. Set aside and leave to cool. Mix the shallots with the vinegar and lemon juice. Roughly chop the tomatoes, approximately into eighths. Mix the tomatoes into the shallot mixture.

RASPBERRY JAM

2½ cups (10½ oz/300 g) raspberries, fresh or frozen
⅝ cup (4 oz/120 g) sugar
2 tablespoons glucose or light corn syrup
2 teaspoons pectin
Lemon juice, to taste

Place the raspberries, half the sugar, and the glucose or corn syrup in a pot and bring to a boil. Cook for a few minutes, until the raspberries have released their liquid and are starting to break down.

Combine the pectin with the remaining sugar in a small bowl, then add to the boiling raspberries, whisking constantly. Boil until thickened, then remove from the pan. Season with a squeeze of lemon juice. Place a sheet of plastic wrap (cling film) directly on the surface of the cooling jam to avoid a skin forming. Cool at room temperature or in an ice bath before using.

MARIGOLD HONEY

2 cups (1 lb 8 oz/680 g) honey
½ cup marigold flowers

Mix the honey and marigold flowers in a pan and heat gently to 140°F/60°C to infuse.

BAKING

Use all fresh breads and doughs immediately.

CORNMEAL TART DOUGH

1¼ cups (5 oz/150 g) all-purpose (plain) flour, chilled, plus extra for dusting
3 oz (85 g) butter, diced and chilled
¼ cup (1¼ oz/35 g) coarse blue cornmeal
¼ teaspoon salt
5 tablespoons iced water

In a food processor, add the flour, butter, blue cornmeal, and salt. Pulse until the butter crumbles into the flour, then remove the lid and add the water in an evenly distributed stream over the dough. Pulse a few more times to incorporate the water. Turn out onto a lightly floured surface and knead by hand 4 times. Wrap and chill for 2 hours.

OLIVE OIL CRACKERS

½ teaspoon instant yeast
¼ cup + 2 tablespoons (3 fl oz/90 g) warm water (110°F/45°C)
½ cup + 1 tablespoon (3½ oz/100 g) semolina
1 tablespoon rye flour, plus extra for dusting
⅛ teaspoon salt
Maldon sea salt, to taste

In a mixing bowl, combine the yeast and warm water together, allowing the yeast to bloom, approximately 5 minutes. In a separate mixing bowl, combine the semolina, rye flour, and salt together. Fit a stand mixer with a dough hook and add both the water-yeast mixture and the flour mixture. Knead for 4–5 minutes. Lay the dough out on a lightly floured work surface, then knead for 3 minutes, until it develops into a well-defined ball. Return the dough to the mixing bowl, brush with olive oil, and cover. Allow to rise for 1 hour at room temperature. Once it has risen, separate into 2 portions. Place into separate containers and refrigerate overnight.

Preheat the oven to 400°F/200°C. Temper the dough by allowing it to rest at room temperature for 5 minutes. Next, set to rolling your crackers as thin as possible. At Lula we use a pasta machine. It is possible to do it by hand, but the machine certainly works more efficiently. Line 2 half-sized sheet trays (rimmed baking trays) with parchment paper. Brush the parchment with olive oil. Dust your work surface and the pasta machine lightly with flour. Roll the dough out to the thinnest setting and gently lay each piece of dough on the sheet trays. Brush the dough with olive oil and sprinkle with Maldon sea salt. Bake in the oven for 3 minutes, rotate the pan, and bake for another 2–3 minutes.

BRIOCHE

For the brioche dough:
2 cups (9½ oz/275 g) all-purpose (plain) flour
¼ cup (1¼ oz/30 g) whole-wheat flour
¼ cup (2 oz/50 g) granulated sugar
1 teaspoon salt
½ teaspoon active dried yeast
½ cup plus 1 tablespoon (4½ oz/130 g) active sourdough starter
¼ cup plus 2 tablespoons (3 fl oz/90 g) whole milk
2 eggs, plus extra for the egg wash
2½ oz (85 g) butter, softened

Combine the flours, sugar, salt, and yeast in the bowl of a stand mixer. In a separate bowl, combine the milk and eggs, then add to the dry ingredients with the sourdough starter. Mix on low speed until combined. Add the butter 1 tablespoon at a time. Mix on medium speed for 10 minutes, until the butter is fully incorporated. Leave for 2 hours in a warm place, then refrigerate overnight.

You can cook the brioche now, or add the cardamom filling (below). Preheat the oven to 350°F/180°C. Roll the dough into a cylinder, about 9 inches (23 cm) long. Transfer to a greased 9 × 5-inch (23 × 12.5 cm) loaf pan (tin). Proof until risen above the top of the pan, 2 hours. Egg wash the top and bake for 45 minutes, or until golden and cooked through.

For the cardamom filling:
¼ cup (2 oz/50 g) sugar
1 teaspoon ground cardamom
1 tablespoon ground cinnamon
2 tablespoons all-purpose (plain) flour

Whisk together the ingredients. Roll the brioche dough into an 18 × 12-inch (46 × 30 cm) rectangle. Spread the cardamom filling evenly over the top. Roll the dough into a cylinder. Fold the cylinder in half and twist the ends in opposite directions to create the swirl. Proof and cook as above.

SOURDOUGH CROUTONS

¼ cup (2 fl oz/60 g) olive oil
½ sourdough boule (4 oz/120 g), crust removed and not particularly fresh, torn into chunks
Salt

Heat the oil in a large sauté pan until fragrant, then add the chunks of bread and a little salt. You'll need 2 hands and some skill to "toss" the bread over the heat frequently until a golden crust forms on all sides of the croutons. If you find this hard, lower the flame and use tongs to turn the bread as it toasts on every side. The benefit to tossing it in the pan is that you can easily adjust the distance of the pan's bottom to the heat, which increases your control over the toast. Sometimes bread can brown unpredictably and rapidly, hence the caution here. You want something toasty on the outside and still soft in the center. An additional splash of olive oil may be needed for particularly spongey or dried out sourdough. Do not walk away from this or answer the phone or anything else. When golden brown, immediately cool in a single layer on a tray or rack. This is like toasting marshmallows over a fire.

DAIRY AND MEAT

Store all dairy and meat products in the refrigerator and use within 7 days.

WHIPPED GOAT CHEESE

½ cup (3¾ oz/115 g) goat cheese
¼ cup (2 fl oz/60 g) whole milk
1 tablespoon thinly sliced chives
Grated zest of 1 lemon, plus ½ teaspoon lemon juice
½ cup (4 fl oz/120 g) heavy (double) cream
Salt and freshly ground black pepper

In a medium bowl, whisk together the goat cheese and milk until combined. Add the chives, lemon zest and juice, and salt and black pepper to taste. In a separate bowl or stand mixer, whip the cream to stiff peaks. Fold the whipped cream into the goat cheese mixture using a rubber spatula and taste to adjust for seasoning. Keep chilled.

RICOTTA

16 cups (3.8 liters) milk
½ cup (4 fl oz/120 g) lemon juice, plus extra to taste
¼ cup (2 fl oz/60 g) heavy (double) cream
¼ cup (2 oz/50 g) crème fraîche
Salt and freshly ground black pepper

In a stainless-steel or nonreactive pot, add the milk and 1 tablespoon salt. Heat on medium-high, stirring infrequently until the milk hits 180°F/80°C (and not just in one spot; it needs to be thoroughly 180°F/80°C). Turn off the heat. Add the lemon juice, then stir once. Let sit for 10 minutes. The milk will break into curds and whey; do not disturb this age-old process. Line a strainer with cheese cloth. Using a ladle, carefully strain the mixture through the cloth. Allow time for the cheese to drain. In a stainless-steel or nonreactive mixing bowl, fold the cheese into the cream, and crème fraîche, with lemon juice, salt and pepper to taste.

DUCK CONFIT

3 lb 6 oz (1½ kg) duck legs and necks
   (2 necks and 4 legs)
2 tablespoons salt
2 teaspoons cracked black pepper
2 teaspoons fennel seeds
3 cups (1 lb 3 oz/570 g) duck fat
1 head garlic
1 shallot
10 thyme sprigs

Rub the duck legs and necks with the salt, pepper, and fennel. Let sit overnight, refrigerated.

Preheat the oven to 275°F/135°C. In a heavy braiser or Dutch oven, melt the duck fat. Place the duck legs and necks in the fat with the garlic, shallot, and thyme. The duck should be fully submerged. Use additional duck fat (or olive oil if necessary) to ensure they are completely under the surface of

the fat. Cover all with foil or a tight fitted lid. Cook in the oven for 2–2½ hours. At intervals, check the temperature of the confit. You want a slow, steady simmer in the fat, not a hearty boil.

Beginning at 2 hours, check the meat for doneness. The meat is ready when it has released its grip on the bones—not necessarily "falling off the bone" but for sure resigned to release. Tender is a step before mush.

This will make more than you need. Duck confit is great on sandwiches and in omelets or soup. It can be stored in the fat for long periods of time if refrigerated. Traditionally, a confit was a technique meant for preservation, not just flavor. Reserve the garlic for use in other recipes (page 188).

STOCKS

Store all stocks in the freezer for up to 3 months.

CHICKEN STOCK

2½ lb (1.2 kg) chicken bones
1 onion
2 carrots
2 leek tops
1 head garlic
3 stalks celery
5 parsley stems

In a stock pot, place the chicken bones and 16 cups (3.8 liters) cold water and bring to a simmer over low heat. Maintain a gentle heat to keep the stock simmering. Skim off any impurities that float to the surface. Simmer for 3 hours, then add the remaining ingredients. Simmer for 1 more hour and then strain, discarding all bones and vegetables. Leave to cool.

DUCK STOCK

Bones of 1 whole duck (approximately
   2¾ lb/1.3 kg)
2 cups (3¼ oz/90 g) green leek tops,
   washed and chopped

10 cloves garlic

2 onions, peeled and sliced

Preheat the oven to 375°F/190°C. Roast the duck bones on a sheet tray (rimmed baking tray) for 1 hour. Drain away any excess fat and save for another use (crispy potatoes, for example). Add the bones and 5 cups (1.2 liters) water to a large stock pot and bring to a gentle simmer. Skim off the detritus as it rises to the top. After 3 hours, add the vegetables and continue to cook for 1 more hour. Strain, discarding all bones and vegetables, then leave to cool.

VEGETABLE STOCK

2 medium onions, unpeeled, halved through root

1 tablespoon blend oil

1 medium carrot, unpeeled, chopped

1 celery stalk, chopped

1 head garlic, halved

1 leek top

½ head fennel, chopped

1 bay leaf

½ cup (¾ oz/20 g) dried mushrooms

2 parsley sprigs

1 thyme sprig

1 tablespoon black pepper

Two 4 × 4-inch (10 × 10 cm) pieces kombu

Preheat the oven to 350°F/180°C. Toss the onions in the oil, then place on a baking sheet in the oven for 30 minutes, or until slightly caramelized around the edges. In a stockpot, place the onions, carrot, celery, garlic, leek top, fennel, bay leaf, and dried mushrooms with 16 cups (3.8 liters) cold filtered water. Bring to a boil, then reduce the heat and simmer for 1 hour. Add the parsley, thyme, black pepper, and kombu. Remove from the heat and allow to steep, 30 minutes. Strain and leave to cool.

VEGETABLES

Store all vegetables in an airtight container in the refrigerator and use within 7 days.

ROASTED BEETS

3 rosemary sprigs

6 thyme sprigs

7 cloves garlic

2 tablespoons olive oil

1½ teaspoons salt

1 lb (450 g) red baby or smallish beets (beetroot), scrubbed clear and root ends trimmed

Preheat the oven to 375°F/190°C. Roughly chop the herbs (stem and all) with the garlic on the same cutting board, then mix with olive oil and salt. Toss the beets (beetroot) in a mixing bowl with the herb-salt mixture and wrap individually in foil. Roast until fork-tender, 1–1½ hours, depending on the size of the beets. Peel and cut into wedges.

ROASTED CIPPOLINI ONIONS

16 cippolini onions (8 oz/225 g)

2 tablespoons blend oil

3 thyme sprigs, leaves picked

¼ teaspoon salt

Preheat the oven to 375°F/190°C. Cut the onions in half (keep the skin on) and toss with the oil, thyme, and salt. Place on a sheet tray (rimmed baking tray), cut-side down, and roast until tender. When cool, separate into individual petals.

ROASTED PEPPERS

6 red bell peppers

2 tablespoons blend oil

Preheat the broiler (grill) to medium. Toss the peppers with the oil on a sheet tray (rimmed baking tray) to coat and arrange cut-side down. Broil, rotating the baking sheet halfway through, until the skin is blackened, 12–14 minutes. Preheat the oven to 200°F/95°C and continue to roast the peppers until very soft but not mushy, about 1 hour. Let cool slightly, then scrape off and discard the skins. Cut the peppers lengthwise into ½-inch (1 cm) wide strips.

ART AT LULA

A restaurant is not on every artist's list of dream venues. But Lula is special. There is something affirming about seeing serious, thoughtful, artistically ambitious work surrounded by real life—bouncing off people's conversations, altering the way people experience a lived space, changing in feel, but holding its own whether sunlight is streaming in the windows at breakfast, or candles are flickering in the shadows at last call.

For the first show I organized at Lula, co-curated with Marianne Fairbanks, we decided to draw on the remarkable community that surrounded the place. We began by inquiring among staff, patrons, and friends about what sorts of objects they collected and whether they might be willing to let us hang some of them on the walls. The results were remarkable.

There was a collection of beautiful antique wooden dress hangers, a grouping of fragments of intricate black lace, a collection of toy cars, and many other wonderful, unique, surprising objects. But the star of the show was contributed by a young server who lent us a huge collection of pressed butterfly wings in tiny cellophane envelopes which had belonged to her grandmother. We hung these lightly on pins in a giant cluster on one wall and they were a revelation. They would shimmer in the light when the front door opened, letting in the slightest breeze. They transformed the space.

Over the dozen-plus years that followed, Marianne and I exhibited work by artists as far afield as Finland, France, Italy, and South Korea, as well as plenty of work from Logan Square and around Chicago, the greater Midwest, and across the US. Marianne and I moved in overlapping but distinct circles of creative community and had different tastes and interests, which expanded the variety of work we could bring to the space and lent a sense of the unexpected to the changing of each show, even for us.

We didn't begin documenting the work until the sixth or seventh year, so many of the shows are all but lost to memory now. But many stand out. One that comes vividly to mind was a show of brilliant, traditional ceremonial Haitian voodoo flags, rendered in sparkling sequins. There was an exhibition of massive, beautifully atmospheric photographs depicting a lost interplanetary colony on the edges of the solar system by Todd Baxter. Claire Ashley installed a group of colorful, oddly shaped abstract inflatables. Another favorite was a collection of giant marker drawings, at once childlike and highly accomplished, depicting stills from *Star Wars* by Katara Mallory.

Lula is a unique space in which to show art. The bar, after the first expansion, was built out of humidors left over from the cigar store that had previously occupied the space. It thus doubled as a set of glass-topped display cases, allowing us to pair small, intimate works along with the larger pieces that went on the dining room's walls. The display cases allowed us to showcase the remarkable book art and sketchbooks of several brilliant local cartoonists and designers, including Jeffrey Brown, Sonnenzimmer, and, memorably, Laura Park's exquisitely inked and water-colored, jewel-like writing and drawing work that is still largely unpublished to this day, and almost unseen outside of the confines of Lula Cafe.

In fact, some of the best shows at Lula were by artists who showed only rarely or never again afterward. Others were by established artists who valued the unique stage and wide audience the walls provided. And Lula has also provided a springboard to gallery representation and attention in other circles.

Sometime in the late 2000s, a president of the School of the Art Institute reportedly said in an interview that Lula was the best place in the city to see new art. We were never able to confirm the quote, so who knows. But on behalf of the many brilliant artists who have shown here over the years Marianne and I were curating, and of the many more that have followed under current curator, Melina Ausikaitis, we'll take it.

Memories by Anders Nilsen, curator 2001–18

OUR COLLABORATORS

OUR CHEFS

Over the course of a year, I revised and edited menu items from 1999 to 2022. Working with former chef Sarah Rinkavage, we cooked the dishes exactly as they were on the menu on a certain date, though sometimes edited for simplicity or ease. I want to say clearly that I didn't write all these recipes by myself in some kind of aesthetic trance. Over the twenty-plus years at Lula many chefs have composed dishes alongside me. Each week I'd ask the team to bring two or three ideas to the table and from there we would "edit" them into life. Then the chefs would take on certain preparations and do the real hard work of making an idea into a recipe. In some cases, ideas would fall immediately into place on the plate. In others, chefs would test things multiple times and then we'd taste, revise, retaste, and revise them into something uniquely, undeniably ours. Often the final result was indistinguishable from what was scribbled in our notebooks.

All the chefs who contributed savory recipes for this book—Andrew Holladay, Sarah Rinkavage, Lauren Freeburg, and Morgan O'Brien—started with me on the line as cooks. I've always collaborated best with chefs who've worked their way up, because they've grown organically into a creative role, seen it from the inside. They understand the pantry, the products, our vision, my quirky palate (no avocado, please).

You may notice that most of these recipes come from the last ten years. We were too busy to write things down in the beginning. Also, I lost a bunch of notebooks in a flood.

OUR FARMERS

I could write endlessly about my relationship to the farms and farmers who grow our vegetables, raise animals, and harvest grains. I submit that cooking with the seasons is the best way to get to know the people who grow your food. And until you know them, until you've seen how hard they work and to what lengths they go to prove the worth of responsible stewardship of our land, until you've experienced their reaction when you acknowledge the beauty and grace of their work, you won't be able to feed your soul. I believe this. My connection to farms gives me peace and community and a sense that not all hope is lost.

Our farmers have become close friends. I've made this clear in many places in this book. I'd love to take you on a tour of these Midwestern lands, but instead I ask that you continue to search out small producers in your own communities. As the organic and local food movement is co-opted into larger corporate interests, as even the most tiresome fast-food chain promotes "responsible" relationships to agriculture, it's more apparent to me that true meaning and the potential for change happens in the smallest, most intimate ways. So the farmers' markets matter. The neighborhoods as well. The windowsill gardens, too.

I lost my favorite farm in the pandemic. I still grieve over this. My hope now is that we will continue to make new connections, as we have recently with Froggy Meadow; to build relationships in which real conversations happen, not just small talk. I don't want to make it easy; I want to make it deep. To know the answer to this question: Over all the options one has in life, why did you choose this difficult work?

INDEX

RECINE NOTES

Butter should always be unsalted, unless otherwise specified.

All **herbs** are fresh, unless otherwise specified.

Eggs are medium (UK small) unless otherwise specified.

Individual **vegetables** and **fruits**, such as onions and apples, are assumed to be medium, unless otherwise specified.

All **milk** is whole (3% fat), homogenized, and lightly pasteurized, unless otherwise specified.

All **salt** is fine sea salt, unless otherwise specified.

All **sugar** is granulated, unless otherwise specified.

Exercise a high level of **caution** when following recipes involving any potentially hazardous activity, including the use of high temperatures, open flames and when deep-frying. In particular, when deep-frying add food carefully to avoid splashing, wear long sleeves and never leave the pan unattended.

Cooking times are for guidance only. If using a fan (convection) oven, follow the manufacturer's instructions concerning the oven temperatures.

All herbs, shoots, flowers, and leaves should be picked fresh from a clean source. Do exercise caution when **foraging** for ingredients, which should only be eaten if an expert has deemed them safe to eat. In particular, do not gather wild mushrooms yourself before seeking the advice of an expert who has confirmed their suitability for human consumption. As some species of mushrooms have been known to cause allergic reaction and illness, do take extra care when cooking and eating mushrooms and do seek immediate medical help if you experience a reaction after preparing or eating them.

Exercise caution when making **fermented products**, ensuring all equipment is spotlessly clean, and seek expert advice if in any doubt.

When no **quantity** is specified, for example of oils, salts, and herbs used for finishing dishes, quantities are discretionary and flexible

All spoon and cup **measurements** are level, unless otherwise stated. 1 teaspoon = 5 ml; 1 tablespoon = 15 ml. Australian standard tablespoons are 20 ml, so Australian readers are advised to use 3 teaspoons in place of 1 tablespoon when measuring small quantities.

Both metric and imperial measurements are used in this book. Follow one set of measurements throughout, not a mixture, as they are not interchangeable.

ACKNOWLEDGMENTS

After twenty-three years there is a deep well of thanks.

First, to the staff of Lula, current and past. I want to list your names here but there are just so many who matter deeply to me. To all who worked those crazy brunches, the patio summer nights, in the dish pit during crossover, in the basement prepping for a wedding. I thank all of you.

I want to shout out the pandemic era crew, who will forever be close to my heart. Everyone who was here that day of the closure, to the small crew who saw us through the shut down and then our return, who filled all those ramekins and packed all those bags, thank you.

I want to give grace to our leadership today for bringing hope for the future and a path forward. For giving me the space to write this book and contributing so much to what Lula has become. Thank you to Andrew Piras, Leizl Basilio, Natalie Sternberg, Rachel Kalom, Kyle Lacasse, Morgan O'Brien, Ryland Chambliss, Nay Hyun, Lauren Freeburg, Kristian Madere, Kim Janusz, Matthew Clark, Matt Kohl, Anna Heerwagen, Emilio Enriquez, and in particular to my longtime consigliere Andrew Holladay.

Without the tenacity and good graces of commissioning editor Emily Takoudes, I doubt the book would ever have come to life. Thank you for appreciating the humor and allowing me to bring these stories to life, for giving me the space to finish. And to the designer Melanie Mues and the team at Phaidon, especially project editor Rachel Malig, thank you for bringing this project into such a bright, vibrant life.

Sarah Rinkavage tested and retested the recipes and then prepped the entire photo shoot herself. Working with her again on this project has been a blessing. She is always a light. Photographer Carolina Rodríguez captured and styled every plate herself (with assistance from Grace Coudal) with wit and style and a vivid eye, certainly making it prettier than I had dreamed (thanks to Elise Bergman for the rec!). Emily Spurlin brought desserts and my spirits to life. Kevin Quinn did the baking and Classics testing, despite having a brand new bee-bo at home. And Nina Slesinger helped me think through my ideas and gave me critical initial feedback on the stories and reminiscences in this book, both through astute line edits and deeper conversations on style, and her assistance made the early drafts assume a final form.

Thank you to my friends—Josh, Matthias, Paul, Yoshi, Anders, Andy, especially—who held on during the most trying moments of the pandemic. To our team at Pilot Light Chefs who understand the power of speaking through food. To everyone at Marisol at the MCA. To all my colleagues in the industry (and especially at HUA and the IRC) who came together over Zoom and text to find a path toward a better future, especially the Chicago culinary community who has always treated us with respect. And to all my chef friends, from our early morning GCM complaint sessions (hey now, Mindy) to long talks on the phone in the alley, we're in this together.

We are indebted to our curator Melina Ausikaitis and to all those who have contributed to the space through their art, craft, and design, particularly Nitewerk for the iconic Red and Blue.

To Jade, Colleen, Dennis, John, Katie, Polly, Miriam, the Daniels, Tai, Angelo, and the many other managers whose contributions are forever. To all the chefs and sous chefs over the years, shout out to Hunter, Duncan, JV, Yoni, Kelly, Amanda, Melissa, JT, Jane, Kate, Melven, Carolyn, Bunny, the Erics, Nicole.

And the farmers! To Jon from Butternut (who once drove two hours to bring veggies for a photo shoot) and Jeremy from Froggy Meadow. I want to remember Green Acres fondly for everything they did for us over the years. Marc from what I'll always call "Pro in Mo" helped procure random ingredients on a moment's notice. And shout-outs to Tracey at Three Sisters, Abby at Klüg, Pete at Seedling, Mike at Werp, Marty at Spence, as well as the folks at Penryn, Avron, Herban, Timberfeast, Gunthorp, Jen Rosenthal, Frillman Farms, Greg at Publican Quality Bread.

Now that I have the chance, I want to say that I love and am grateful for my mother, Jacqueline, whose connection to family, appreciation for the beauty in language, and ambitious drive I share, my stepfather, Jim, smartest man in any room, and my sisters, Danièle and Alexandra, despite her dislike of turbot (or any fish, actually). And to my aunt Lois, thank you for being such a kind, caring soul.

This book is dedicated with forever love and endless faith to my wife and co-founder, Amalea. She is the spirit of Lula. She supported the making of this book in innumerable ways, with patience and understanding, with kindness and faith in me, in us, plus, as always, a great deal of helpful feedback.

Lastly I want my children, Ismene and Cass, to know that I am grateful for them as well. For what they did. Yes, you made Lula, too. Restaurants, as you know, take a great degree of sacrifice in one's daily life. Being a restaurant family... well, it's *a lot*. I know you've missed me sometimes. And I've missed you. I still feel like you are little enough to sit up on the pass. Little enough to hold. *Vi voglio bene.* Putting those words in an actual printed book for you right now so they stay with you forever.

Phaidon Press Limited
2 Cooperage Yard
Stratford
London E15 2QR

Phaidon Press Inc.
65 Bleecker Street
New York NY 10012

phaidon.com

First published 2023
Reprinted 2023
© 2023 Phaidon Press Limited

ISBN 978 1 83866 753 5

A CIP catalogue record for this book
is available from the British Library
and the Library of Congress.

Senior Commissioning Editor: Emily Takoudes
Project Editor: Rachel Malig
Production Controller: Zuzana Cimalova
Photography: Carolina Rodríguez
Design: Melanie Mues, Mues Design, London

Printed in China

The publisher would like to thank Evelyn
Battaglia, Vanessa Bird, Danielle Centoni,
Julia Hasting, Joao Mota, and Ellie Smith
for their work on the book.

ABOUT THE AUTHOR

Jason Hammel is the executive chef and
co-owner of Lula Cafe, a Chicago community
institution since 1999, known for its
creative, seasonal cuisine and artistic ethos.
He is also the consulting chef at Marisol in
the Museum of Contemporary Art, Chicago,
and a co-founder of Pilot Light, a not-for-
profit organization dedicated to bringing
food education to classrooms across the
United States.

Chef Hammel was born in New Haven,
Connecticut and graduated from Brown
University, following which he lived and
traveled in Italy before moving to Illinois
to complete his master's in English at Illinois
State University. He has received numerous
awards, presented at conferences, and
published articles on cooking and culture.
He is known as an advocate for sustainability
in the industry. *The Lula Cafe Cookbook* is his
first book.